Radio *Shack*®
TRS-80
GRAPHICS

For the Model I and Model III

DAVID A KATER
SUSAN J THOMAS

TRS-80
GRAPHICS
GRAPHICS
GRAPHICS
GRAPHICS
TRS-80
TRS-80
GRAPHICS
GRAPHICS
GRAPHICS
TRS-80
TRS-80
GRAPHICS
GRAPHICS
GRAPHICS
TRS-80
TRS-80
TRS-80
GRAPHICS
For the Models I & III

TRS-80 GRAPHICS

For the Model I and Model III

David A. Kater

Susan J. Thomas

Radio Shack
a Division of Tandy Corp.
Ft. Worth, Texas 76102

TRS-80 and Micro Movie are registered trademarks of the Tandy Corporation. Level III BASIC is a registered trademark of Microsoft, Inc.

The authors of the programs provided with this book have carefully reviewed them to insure their performance in accordance with the specifications described in the book. Neither the authors nor BYTE Publications, Inc., however, makes any warranties concerning the programs and assumes no responsibility or liability of any kind for errors in the programs or for the consequences of any such errors. The programs are the sole property of the authors and have been registered with the United States Copyright Office.

Library of Congress Cataloging in Publication Data

Kater, David A.
    TRS-80 graphics for the Model I and Model III.

    Includes index.
    1. TRS-80 (Computer)—Programming.
2. Computer graphics. I. Thomas, Susan J. II. Title. III. Title: T.R.S.-80 graphics for the Model I and Model III.
QA76.8.T18K37   001.55'3   81-21671
ISBN 0-07-033303-3   AACR2

Edited by Bruce Roberts.

Cover and Book Design
by Ellen Klempner

Cover illustration generated
on computer by Glenn Entis

Production Editing by Tom McMillan.

Illustrations by Jack Wittry.

Typesetting and Production by
LeWay Composing Service,
Fort Worth, Texas.

Printed and Bound by
Kingsport Press,
Kingsport, Tennessee.

To:
Richard L. Kater
whose aspirations
and dreams
inspired this book.

About the Authors

David A. Kater is a former college math instructor who was sidetracked from that career by his growing addiction to computers. In 1978, he cofounded the Computer Institute of San Diego and began a consulting business. His work with computers grew to the point that in 1980 he resigned from full-time teaching to devote all his energies to writing and consulting in the computer field.

Susan J. Thomas was a Finance student at San Diego State University when she first became interested in microcomputers. Her work on **TRS-80 Graphics** furthered this interest and led her to include in her studies a Computer Science major.

ACKNOWLEDGEMENTS

There are many whose encouragement and support made it possible to continue a labor of love that was over a year in the writing. We thank you all. We are especially indebted to many who reviewed portions of the early manuscript and whose comments and suggestions were immensely helpful:

Professor James W. Allen, Grossmont College Computer Science and computer entrepreneur, San Diego, CA.

Professor John Donald, San Diego State University Math Science, San Diego, CA.

Thomas Kasper, hardware hacker par excellence, San Diego, CA.

Richard L. Kater, Engineer, Lockheed California Co., father, and all around good guy, Woodland Hills, CA.

Colonel Ed Laidlaw, machine language zany, Chula Vista, CA.

Dr. David A. Lien, renowned author and publisher, Compusoft, Inc., San Diego, CA.

Professor David Lunsford, Grossmont College Mathematics and Computers, El Cajon, CA.

Special thanks go to David A. Thomas and Mike Hunter, whose persistent typing fingers found and corrected many a program error, and to David F. Thomas for his generous support.

Finally, thanks to the microcomputing community. We are proud to be a part of this fledgling industry in which enthusiasm and innovation continue to run rampant.

TRS-80 GRAPHICS

For the Model I and Model III

Contents

Basic Tools ———— PART I ————

Applications   PART II

Other Vistas ────── PART III ──────────

15: Turbo-Charged Graphics

Appendices ────── PART IV ──────────

Appendix A

Appendix B

Appendix C

Appendix D

Appendix E

Appendix F

Preface

1 Goals and Assumptions of this Book

TRS-80 Graphics for the Model I and Model III was created to explain how to control graphics on the TRS-80 in simple, everyday language. We hope that by working through examples with us, and by seeing graphic techniques spring to life on your own video display, you will be inspired to take the plunge and to incorporate graphics into your own programs. We also hope that you will find the reading easy and the content informative, challenging, and entertaining.

We have assumed that you are familiar with the mechanisms of the TRS-80, and that you have dabbled in BASIC just enough to know that you want to learn more. The first few chapters of the book review each of the statements and functions — the basic tools — we use throughout the book. If you are a serious programmer, these chapters will serve as a quick pitstop on your way to the fast lane.

You can benefit from this book even if you are still standing knee-deep in packing foam from your new TRS-80, wondering what the difference between PRINT and INPUT is. Just set a nice, leisurely pace, and do a lot of experimenting on your own. Your computer will be happy to tell you what it will and will not accept.

2 How to Use this Book

Every book ought to have a "How To Use This Book" section, even though no one may read it. The section should include useful information such as:

- which sections of the book can be skipped without loss of continuity (for those in a hurry or with specific interests)
- how the reader can derive the most benefit from the book
- what special quirks we authors use — notational conventions for example.

Organization of the Book

Part 1 (Chapters 1 - 7) is a tutorial on general programming techniques and emphasizes those used to generate or support graphics. Chapter 1 defines graphics, gives sample applications, and then covers editing and topics related to using this book with a computer. Those familiar with the TRS-80 may need only to scan through Chapter 1. For the rest of us, the editing section is a must. Chapters 2 through 5 are the heart of the book. In these chapters, we develop most of the techniques used throughout the book. Read Chapters 2 through 5 sequentially. Advanced readers can breeze through Chapters 2 and 3, then slow down for a closer look in Chapters 4 and 5. Chapters 6 and 7 contain some advanced techniques and observations that can be bypassed without loss of continuity if you so choose.

Part 2 (Chapters 8 − 14) explores the use of the techniques covered in Part 1 in a variety of applications. These applications chapters are, for the most part, independent of each other and can be covered in any order. Explore the subjects that interest you most. Feel free to go a little ape over the various applications!

Part 3 (Chapter 15) looks at some of the hardware and software additions that can be used to enhance your graphic creations. This final chapter is independent of the rest of the book, and may be studied at any time.

Finally, there are also appendices in which you will find several useful summaries and tables.

How Do I Use Thee? Let Me Count The Ways

This book is *not* a standard text! You will learn from it only by doing, watching, and pondering. Like a good aged wine, the text should be savored. Let your patient little computer teach you, step by step. By typing and running our carefully chosen programming examples, you can see the results of every technique presented. Then, ponder, ponder, and ponder some more. Review the program to make sure you understand what makes it tick. The comments included after program RUNs will often help in this review with a line-by-line analysis of the program. So, if you are puzzled by a particular program, keep reading. Help may be just a few lines away.

You will get the most out of this book by typing in the examples, and then studying them until they reveal all of their secrets to you. After you have made all the recommended modifications to a particular program, go back and experiment with changes of your own. Save your creations on disk or tape for later use.

Notational Conventions Used in This Book

This symbol, usually to be found at the end of important computer programs, is a reminder to you to SAVE the program. You can store it either on cassette or on disk, depending on your system. This way, you'll be able to call up the program later.

As you can see by our title, this book covers graphics for both the Model I and the Model III. But (there's always a ''but''), there *will* be differences between the two. In the margin you will sometimes see one of these little critters. (Look familiar?) This is our way of indicating a special note for one of the machines.

In TRS-80 Graphics, anything you type into the computer will appear in DOT-MATRIX TYPEFACE LIKE THIS. The computer messages and output will also be in dot matrix. This includes all statements, functions, listings, variables, commands, and maybe even the kitchen sink. Exceptions: line numbers within the text portion and certain other oddities.

```
40 CLS: PRINT@ P, A; : GOTO 30
```

To save your eyes (and ours), we've liberally interspersed spaces within the program listings. But to save your typing fingers and the amount of memory you will need (not *you* — your computer!), you may omit all those spaces except, of course, those inside quotation marks. For example, the line above could be typed in merely as:

```
40 CLS:PRINT@P,A;:GOTO30
```

Optional Program Cassette/Diskette

For your convenience, an optional cassette or diskette is available with recordings of several of the larger programs. We hope that this will both minimize the amount of typing you do, and, more importantly, eliminate any problems that might slow your progress. The programs are labeled in the book with an asterisk (*) as shown below:

```
10 REM - ASTERISK INDICATES PROGRAM AVAILABLE
20 REM - ON CASSETTE OR DISKETTE
```

See the last page of the book for purchase information.

Scope And Limitations

Languages And Operating Systems

"Does anyone speak COBOL here? How about PASCAL?"

"Sorry. You took a wrong turn somewhere. Try down the hall, second door on the left."

The TRS-80 was born speaking BASIC, and so BASIC is the language we shall use. Except for a few instances in Chapters 6 and 7 all the examples in this book are written in BASIC.

But, which BASIC are we talking about? Disk, Level II, Model III? For the most part, it doesn't matter. The differences will surface only occasionally throughout the book. Where necessary, you will be given specific instructions for your computer. Model III BASIC has a few extra features that will not work on the Model I; these will be treated as we proceed.

Hardware Requirements

The minimal system necessary is a TRS-80 with Level II or Model III BASIC. You could limp along with Level I, but it is not recommended. For all the examples, 16 K (16,384 characters) of available random-access memory (RAM) is adequate. Most of the programs will run on TRS-80 work-alike systems, but watch out for different PEEK and POKE locations. If you have a disk system, remember that Disk BASIC occupies about 12 K, so you should have at least 32 K of RAM. You will also need some kind of storage medium. Storing programs on disk, cassette, or stringy floppy can save you plenty of retyping if your system suddenly freezes up or if a curious passerby accidently knocks out the plug.

BASIC TOOLS

Introduction

A First Look at Graphics

By Way of Webster

Nearly every dictionary offers several definitions for the word ''graphic.'' The meaning most closely related to the central theme of this book is:

GRAPHIC — of or relating to the pictorial arts.

Pictures. That's what this book is all about. Pictures that describe, inspire, and stimulate. Pictures that will enhance your computer programs. Pictures that can be used for serious applications or for pure delight and entertainment.

Every art form is defined and limited by the medium it uses. Pictures painted on a canvas do not have the same effect as those done on egg shells, walls, or bodies. Oils, pastels, and watercolors give very different results. For each work of art, the artist chooses the materials that will best express the ideas in mind. We particularly appreciate those artists whose creations transcend the norm for a given medium.

So it is with our graphic creations. We will limit our canvas to the video screen, our brush to the BASIC language, and our paint to the TRS-80 character set. Our challenge is to develop new and inspiring images using this well-defined set of tools.

The ultimate goal of this book is to expose you to a variety of techniques so that you will be able to create and manipulate your own graphic images. Along the way, we will pause to investigate other aspects of the BASIC language such as string storage and keyboard input. An understanding of these subjects will enable you to better use the graphic capability of the TRS-80.

The Canvas and Paint

We have at our disposal the full range of keyboard characters and a screen that supports 1,024 character positions. For drawing purposes, we have access to tiny rectangular pixels, or graphic blocks. These pixels measure about 1/16 inch wide by 1/8 inch high. With 6,144 of them on the screen, we are afforded a fair degree of flexibility in our displays.

Can we situate individual dots anywhere we want? No, the graphic blocks are the smallest unit we have access to without addition to or modification of the existing hardware. In fact, this turns out to be something of a blessing. Each graphic block is made of 12 dots; this adds up to 73,728 dots on the screen. Do you have an idea of the enormous programming effort it would require to individually control all those dots (not to mention a tremendous drain of memory.)? BASIC would have to be redesigned, and we would lose several of the features the TRS-80 now enjoys. Furthermore, the speed needed to create and animate large figures dot-by-dot would force us to

abandon BASIC and use machine language. With graphic blocks, we have both a powerful BASIC and the ability to easily create the graphics for a wide range of applications.

2 Sample Graphic Applications

Graphics can be used in a broad array of computer program applications. Here are some examples.

a)

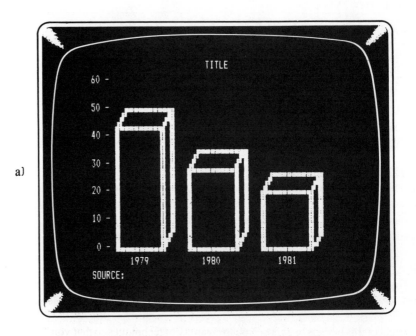

b)

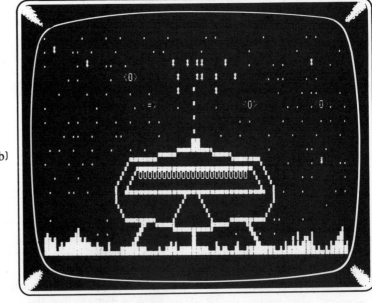

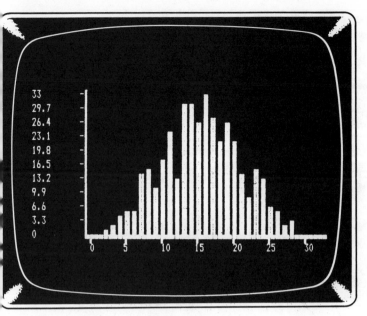

c)

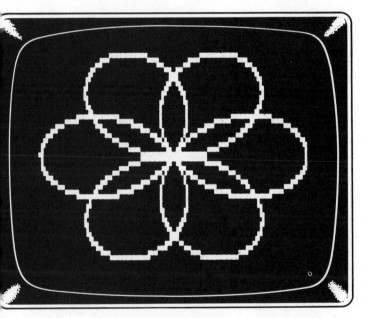

d)

e)

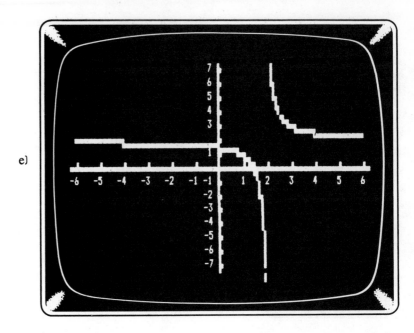

Figure 1.1 Examples of graphic applications: a) business, b) games, c) statistics, d) design, e) mathematics.

3 Using This Book With A Computer

Typos

By typing and running BASIC programs yourself, you can actually see graphic techniques demonstrated on the TRS-80 screen and thus fully explore the ideas in this book. Although this approach gives tremendous ''hands-on'' experience, it does require a lot of typing and editing. Tiny typing errors can make a useless mess out of the most carefully conceived programs. To eliminate any possible frustration, type carefully and then double-check your typing in every program before you run it. Keep a special lookout for semicolons at the end of PRINT lines. We have made every effort to keep the programs error-free. Take your time and enjoy.

Working With BASIC

A short review of some of the features of BASIC may help before we jump in with both feet. (Those familiar with BASIC may want to skim over this section.) Turn on the computer and bring up BASIC.

Here is a sample program:

```
NEW
10 CLS: P=320: Q=640
20 PRINT@P, "SAMPLE PROGRAM"
40 PRINT@Q, "PRESS <BREAK> TO STOP"
50 GOTO 50
```

Let's enter this program, taking advantage of the AUTO function in TRS-80 BASIC. Type

```
NEW (ENTER)
AUTO (ENTER)
```

From this point on, the computer will generate line numbers for you. Type in each line followed by the (ENTER) key. Feel free to use ? as an abbreviation for PRINT. Notice that line 30 is missing. Just press (ENTER) to bypass that line. When you get to line 60, press (BREAK) to stop the automatic line numbering. Now type RUN. Press (BREAK) to stop the program, then type LIST.

The AUTO function will be a big time-saver as your fingers travel over the keys and through this book. Another example of the AUTO function is AUTO 100,5. This generates line numbers starting at 100 in increments of 5.

TRS-80 BASIC also features an ''immediate mode.'' Most BASIC statements can be typed in without line numbers, and they will execute immediately. Try PRINT P,Q. As you can see, P and Q retain their values even after the program stops. They will change back to zero, however, if the program is modified in any way. As another example of the immediate mode, type CLS: P=340: Q=657: GOTO 20 and you are right back in the program again. Press the (BREAK) key to stop.

Editing

Because you will frequently need to modify program lines, it is important that you have a good working knowledge of the editing features of Radio Shack BASIC. If you are not familiar with these features, you should carefully study Chapter 9 of the BASIC Reference Manual before you continue in this book. It will be well worth your time, even if you intend to write BASIC programs only occasionally. Work through the examples in the manual, then practice editing with the sample programs presented here.

Here is a list of the special function keys:

EDIT	—	Enter edit mode
A	—	Cancel any changes and restart
n C	—	Change n characters
n D	—	Delete n characters
E	—	Save changes and exit edit mode
H	—	Hack and insert
I	—	Insert
n K c	—	Search and kill
L	—	List the line
Q	—	Cancel changes and exit edit mode
n S c	—	Search for nth occurrence of c
X	—	Extend the line
n (◄)	—	Backspace n spaces
n (SPACEBAR)	—	Display the next n characters
(SHIFT) (◄)	—	Escape insert mode
(ENTER)	—	Exit edit mode

Note that several of the keys in the list are preceded by an 'n'; some are followed by a 'c'. 'c' represents any single character. 'n' represents an optional number. For example, in using 'n S c,' 4SD would mean search for the fourth occurrence of the character D; and.SD would mean search for the first occurrence of the character D. (The number 'n' is assumed to be one if it is omitted.)

EXAMPLE 1

Type in the following one line program. Don't forget to press the (ENTER) key after the line.

```
NEW
10 PRINT "A="A : GOSUB 90: PRINT: GOTO 10
```

Let's change it to

```
10 PRINT "A="; TAB(8)A : GOSUB 90:   GOTO 10
```

Try the following editing sequence. Remember, don't press (ENTER) while you are editing.

You type	Screen shows	What happened
EDIT 10 (ENTER)	10 _	Enter edit mode
2D	10 !PR!	Oops! Hit D when we should have hit S
A	10 _	Cancel the change
2SA	10 PRINT "A="_	Search for second A
I	10 PRINT "A="_	Enter insert mode
; TAB(8)	10 PRINT "A="; TAB(8)_	Insert data
(SHIFT) (⬆)	10 PRINT "A="; TAB(8)_	Exit insert mode
SP	10 PRINT "A=";TAB(8)A :GOSUB 90: _	Search for a P
6D	10 ... GOSUB 90:!PRINT:!_	Delete 6 characters
L	10 ... GOSUB 90:!PRINT:! GOTO 10 10 _	List rest of line
L	10 PRINT "A="; TAB(8)A : GOSUB 90: GOTO 10 10 _	List again to check
(ENTER)	>_	Exit edit mode

Now type L I ST. Your line should appear as

```
10 PRINT "A="; TAB(8)A : GOSUB 90:   GOTO 10
```

EXAMPLE 2

Type in the following BASIC program. Use the AUTO function if you choose. Press
(ENTER) after each line.

```
NEW
10 FOR I=1 TO 127
20 SET(I,20)
30 SET(I,25)
40 NEXT I
```

Let's assume that we want to modify the program to

```
10 FOR I=1 TO 10
20 SET(I,40):SET(6,I)
40 NEXT I
```

One approach would be as follows (press (ENTER) only when shown below):

You type	Screen shows	What happened
EDIT 10 (ENTER)	10 _	Enter edit mode for line 10
S2	10 FOR I=1 TO 1_	Search for the 2
H0	10 FOR I=1 TO 10_	Hack and insert 0
(ENTER)	10 FOR I=1 TO 10 >_	Exit edit mode
30 (ENTER)		Delete line 30
EDIT 20 (ENTER)	20 _	Enter edit mode for line 20
S2	20 SET(I,_	Search for the 2
C4	20 SET(I,4_	Change it to a 4
X	20 SET(I,40)_	Go to the end of the line and insert
:SET(6,I)	20 SET(I,40):SET(6,I)_	Enter the rest of the line
(ENTER)	20 SET(I,40):SET(6,I) >_	Exit edit mode

Now type LIST to check your work. It looks like a lot of effort the first time through,
but once you have used these techniques a few times, you'll wonder how you
managed without them.

You are now cleared for take off.

Basic Graphics on the TRS-80

The TRS-80 Video Display

The Screen

Our fun will now continue with a look at the video display of the TRS-80. The screen consists of 16 rows and 64 columns, or a total of 1024 positions. The first row is numbered from 0 to 63. Row two is numbered from 64 to 127. The numbers continue in sequence to the last row, which is numbered from 960 to 1023. See figure 2.1.

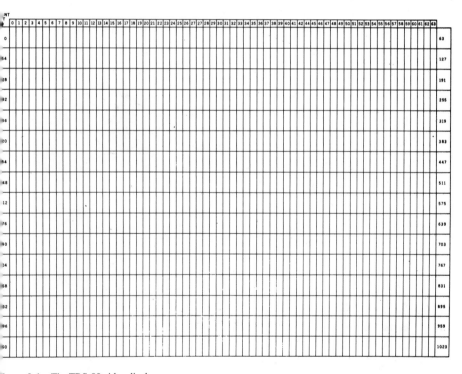

Figure 2.1   The TRS-80 video display.

If all 1024 print locations are used for printing characters, what about spaces between lines? Well, the people at Tandy cleverly included some blank space within the characters. Each keyboard symbol is located in the upper two-thirds of the character; the lower third is blank to allow for space between lines.

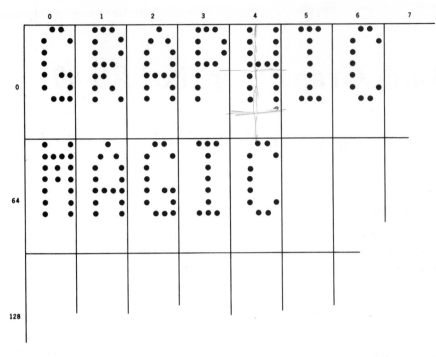

Figure 2.2   Dot matrix characters.

The Cast of Characters

Let's take a closer look at a typical character. Somewhere deep within the electronic maze of the TRS-80 is the character generator, a section of memory that remembers the exact dot pattern that comprises each symbol displayed on the video screen. As an example, figure 2.3 shows how the letter A is stored in the Model I. The Model III character generator is quite different.

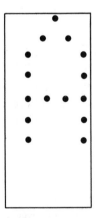

Figure 2.3   Dot configuration for Model I character 'A.'

Notice that all the blank space around the actual symbol A is a part of the character. When A is printed, the entire print position is replaced by the new character. There is no way to combine two characters in the same position with the TRS-80.

Print Coordinate System

Printing Strings

One programming technique that is fundamental to graphic applications is the use of strings in PRINT statements. A string is a collection of any printable keyboard characters and is enclosed in quotes. Several strings, separated by commas or semicolons, can be included in one PRINT statement. Crank up your TRS-80 and load BASIC so we can take it for a whirl. In immediate mode, type

```
LET A$="THIS IS MY TRS-80"
PRINT A$, "FROM "; "TANDY"
```

The string "THIS IS MY TRS-80" is stored in the string variable A$, then printed in the second line. The string "FROM " is printed at the next available tab stop since it follows a comma. Tab stops are located in columns 0, 16, 32, and 48. The string "TANDY" is printed directly after "FROM " since the two are separated by a semicolon.

Each string variable can contain up to 255 characters. Of course, with only 64 characters per line on the screen, a string of 255 characters long would cover nearly four full lines.

Type

```
NEW
5 CLEAR 1000
10 PRINT STRING$(255,"1");
RUN
```

The STRING$ function repeats a single character up to 255 times. Unfortunately, that is one short of four full lines. To fill four full lines, edit line 10 to

```
10 PRINT STRING$(255,"1"); "1";
```

To fill the entire screen, we simply need to print a few more strings. Add

```
20 PRINT STRING$(255,"2"); "2";
30 PRINT STRING$(255,"3"); "3";
40 PRINT STRING$(255,"4"); "4";
50 GOTO 50
RUN
```

Before you start patting yourself on the back, count the rows of 1s. What happened to the fourth row? Well, every time something is printed in position 1023 (bottom right-hand corner), the screen has a bad habit of scrolling (everything is shifted up one line, leaving the bottom line blank). Press (BREAK) to stop the program and to display the ready prompt. Change line 40 to

```
40 PRINT STRING$(255,"4");
```

and RUN it again. This time, no scrolling. All four rows of 1s stay on the screen, but we lost the last 4. How can we add that 4 without losing the top line? We'll have to use some old-fashioned trickery on this one. Press (BREAK) to stop the program, and enter

```
45 POKE 16383, 52
RUN
```

That did the trick, but how does it work? Printing at screen position 1023 causes the entire screen to scroll, but poking something there eliminates the scroll. 52 is the TRS-80's code for the printed 4, and 16383 is the POKE statement's way of referring to position 1023. (We will investigate PEEK and POKE instructions thoroughly in Chapter 5.)

Don't forget to press **BREAK** to stop the program.

TAB

Using the TAB function, we can print a character or string of characters anywhere on a line. The format for the TAB function is PRINT TAB(EXPRESSION). The expression must equal a number from 0 to 255 or an error occurs. The TAB function counts from the beginning of the current line to the position specified by the value of the expression. Type, in immediate mode

```
PRINT "012345"; TAB(10) "COLUMN TEN"
```

The string "COLUMN TEN" is printed in the column numbered 10. It does not skip 10 spaces after "012345". Type

```
NEW
10 FOR I=0 TO 5
20 PRINT TAB(I) "*"
30 NEXT I
RUN
```

Add a semicolon to the end of line 20:

```
20 PRINT TAB(I) "*";
```

and RUN it again. The trailing semicolon keeps the cursor on the same line. We will use trailing semicolons throughout this book, so stay on the alert for them. Note that no punctuation is necessary after the TAB.

What will happen if the value of the expression in a TAB function exceeds 63? That depends on the particular computer you have. Type

```
NEW
10 FOR I=0 TO 255
20 PRINT "1" TAB(I) "2"
30 NEXT I
RUN
```

The Model I with the old ROM chip won't tab past 63. It treats TAB(80) as if it were TAB(80-64). The Model III and the Model I with the new ROM chip will tab up to 127. This new chip treats TAB(80) as TAB(80), but treats TAB(200) as if it were TAB(200-128).

TAB has several interesting features. For instance, it has its own built-in integer function. That is, TAB(6.8) works just like TAB(6); it simply drops the decimal fraction. You can also use several TABs in a single PRINT st____ ___ry

PRINT TAB(20) "20" TAB(30) "30"

PRESTO! Now try

PRINT TAB(20) "20" TAB(10) "10"

What happened? The TAB function simply refused to backspace. If the program calls for a TAB to a position that the cursor has already passed, the computer will ignore the TAB and continue printing from the current cursor position.

Using TAB With Other Functions

We can do a lot of graphics by combining the TAB function with other built-in functions. Enter

```
NEW
10  I=0
20  I=I+.25
30  X=2*SIN(I)
40  PRINT TAB(24 + 12*X) "WARREN INTERFACE"
50  GOTO 20
RUN
```

Use the (BREAK) key to stop. Lines 10, 20, and 50 create a loop that increases the value of I by .25 during each pass. Line 30 stores a value in X that could range from -2 to $+2$. The expression $24 + 12*X$ in line 40 will range from $24 - 24 = 0$ to $24 + 24 = 48$. The string "WARREN INTERFACE" is printed at the calculated TAB location. The SIN function determines the shape of the curve.

You might want to use your name in place of Warren's. Go ahead and use the handy editing features of your TRS-80 to make the change. (You might as well learn them now. See Chapter 9 of your BASIC Reference Manual.) If your name happens to be Martha Monitor, the edit sequence is as follows (don't press (ENTER) unless directed):

```
EDIT 40 (ENTER)
SWHMARTHA MONITOR" (ENTER)
```

Let's change a line or two while our creative juices are flowing. Change line 30 to

```
30  X=SIN(I)+COS(2*I)
```

The edit sequence is

```
EDIT 30 (ENTER)
22DX+COS(2*I) (ENTER)
```

Add line 45:

```
45  PRINT TAB(18-15*X) "ROBBIN SHIFTLOCK"
```

Now RUN the program, using (BREAK) to stop. The image is not very symmetrical because the two names cross. We can fix that by changing lines 40 and 45 to

```
40  PRINT TAB(18 +9*X) "M";
45  PRINT TAB(45-9*X) "R"
```

(Note the trailing-semicolon in line 40.)

And RUN. Much better. We could even imitate the ever-popular biorhythm by the following (don't use lines 30, 50, 70, or 90 if your typing fingers are sore):

```
NEW
10  I=0
20  I=I+.2
30  PRINT "*";
40  PRINT TAB(11+10*SIN(I)) "P";
50  PRINT TAB(21)"*";
60  PRINT TAB(31+10*SIN(1.3*I)) "E";
70  PRINT TAB(41) "*";
80  PRINT TAB(52+10*SIN(1.1*I)) "M";
90  PRINT TAB(62) "*"
100 GOTO 20
RUN
```

We can also combine the TAB with RND and certain string functions. Type and RUN

```
NEW
10 FOR I=0 TO RND(6)
20 PRINT TAB(10*I+RND(10))STRING$(RND(3), "*");
30 NEXT I
40 PRINT
50 GOTO 10
RUN
```

The RND function in line 10 chooses a random integer from 1 to 6. Line 20 prints groups of up to three asterisks at various TAB positions across a single line. The number of groups printed is determined in line 10. Line 40 moves the cursor down to the next line, and line 50 starts the process again.

For a crazy display using the CHR$ function, change line 20 to

```
20 PRINT TAB(10*I+RND(10)) STRING$(RND(3),
CHR$(RND(191)));
RUN
```

The CHR$ function replaces the asterisks with a random American Standard Code fo
Information Interchange (ASCII) character. Some of these characters are control codes that do strange things to the video display. (We will cover all the codes in detail in Chapter 4.)

More Uses Of TAB

The uses of the TAB function do not stop with games and art. The example below illustrates a business application. The program graphically determines break-even points on projected costs and revenue.

```
NEW
10 PRINT "REVENUE"; TAB(9) "COST"
20 FOR X=0 TO 12
30 C = INT(.3*(X-5) [2+3)
```

```
40 R = INT(15*X*EXP(-X/3))
50 PRINT " "; R; TAB(9)C;
60 K = 22.5 + R
70 L = 22.5 + C
80 IF C<R THEN 110
90 PRINT TAB(K) "R"; TAB(L) "C"
100 GOTO 120
110 PRINT TAB(L) "C"; TAB(K) "R"
120 NEXT X
RUN
```

(In line 30, [means exponentiate.)

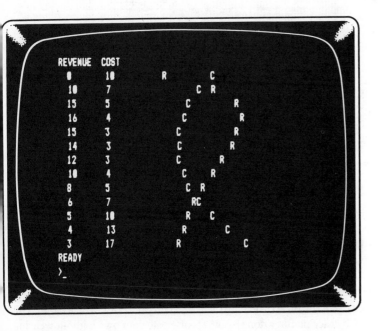

Figure 2.4   Cost/revenue breakeven points.

The cost and revenue are calculated by the functions in lines 30 and 40. The C and R will be printed in an order determined by line 80. This line and the two PRINT statements at 90 and 110 solve the crossover problem we experienced earlier with Warren Interface and Robbin Shiftlock.

PRINT@ Statement

Suppose you want to lay out a title page for a short report but you still don't have the slightest idea of how to go about it. Let's print out the sample display shown in figure 2.5.

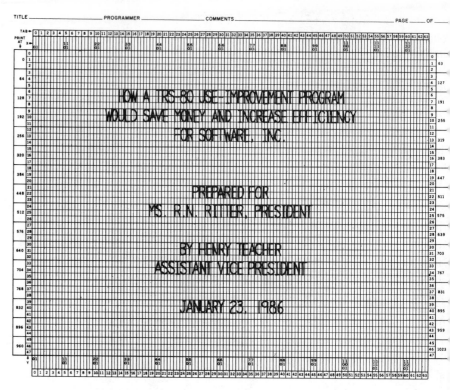

Figure 2.5   Title page layout.

We strongly recommend that you carefully lay out graphic displays on a video display worksheet before writing any program. Laying out a display by first using pencil and eraser could save you hours of using trial and error later to touch up poor displays on the screen. You may find it desirable to make a copy of the video display worksheet on a sheet of acetate similar to those used with overhead projectors. Try your local copy center. You can write on acetate with overhead pens and erase with a cloth. This way, you can easily trace pictures done by others or create your own without wearing out your eraser. See Chapter 11 for programming hints on how to center each line without having to count spaces. You will find a worksheet at the back of the BASIC manual, and copies are available from Radio Shack at a nominal charge.

The entire title page could be created using one PRINT statement per line and a few TABs as needed. But the real power of presenting graphic screen displays of any kind comes from the ability to print information directly to any of the 1024 positions on the screen. The PRINT@ statement (read *print at*) gives us this capability. The format of the PRINT@ statement is PRINT@ position, item list. The position must be an algebraic expression equal to an integer from 0 to 1023. Remember, each position on the video screen is assigned a number from 0 to 1023.

The item list may include variables, constants, and expressions. Here are two examples:

```
PRINT@ 400, X$(20), RND(5-Z)
PRINT@ 64*(L-1), "HERE WE ARE AT LINE"; L
```

To calculate a particular PRINT@ location, use the video display worksheet (figure 2.5). Add the PRINT@ number at the beginning of the desired row to the column number at the top of the sheet. For example, the first line to be printed in figure 2.5 is n the third row, which starts at position 128. The first character of that line is in column number 14. Thus, the required PRINT@ location is 128 + 14 = 142. So we use

```
NEW
5 CLS
10 PRINT@ 142, "HOW A TRS-80 USE-IMPROVEMENT PROGRAM"
```

The rest should be easy now.

```
20 PRINT@ 204, "WOULD SAVE MONEY AND INCREASE
   EFFICIENCY"
30 PRINT@ 279, "FOR SOFTWARE, INC."
40 PRINT@ 474, "PREPARED FOR"
50 PRINT@ 531, "MS. R.N. RITTER, PRESIDENT"
60 PRINT@ 664, "BY HENRY TEACHER"
70 PRINT@ 724, "ASSISTANT VICE PRESIDENT"
80 PRINT@ 856, "JANUARY 23,1986"
90 GOTO 90
RUN
```

If you don't want to wear out your calculator working with PRINT@ locations, you can refer to Appendix A.

Playing with PRINT@

Let's take a closer look at the PRINT@ statement. Enter

```
NEW
10 CLS
20 S$="*"
60 PRINT@ 480, S$;
RUN
```

Don't laugh at the funny line numbering! We will get to the missing lines soon enough. This program will print an asterisk somewhere near the middle of the screen. To print *s all over the screen, we can place the PRINT@ statement in a loop and randomly change the position of the asterisk. Add these lines:

```
30 FOR I=1 TO 300
40 R=RND(1023)
90 NEXT I
```

and change line 60 to PRINT@ R, S$; and RUN. Not bad if you like your *s in bunches. To simulate one * moving at random around the screen, we need to erase each * after it is printed. Add

```
80 PRINT@ R, " ";
```

and RUN the program. Why, you can hardly see those little critters! We need to add a time delay before erasing each *. So change line 30 to

```
30 FOR I=1 TO 30
```

and add

```
70 FOR J=1 TO 100 : NEXT J
```

Note that the colon allows us to have two statements on the same line. At this point, type L I S T to make sure your listing looks like this:

```
10 CLS
20 S$="*"
30 FOR I=1 TO 30
40 R=RND(1023)
60 PRINT@ R, S$;
70 FOR J=1 TO 100 : NEXT J
80 PRINT@ R, " ";
90 NEXT I
```

RUN the program. Yes, that's much better. Line 70 creates the time delay, and changing line 30 saves us from waiting forever for the program to finish.

Trouble In River City

Now change line 20 to

```
20 S$="THIS IS MY TRS-80"
RUN
```

Running this version of the program illustrates several problems that any would-be creator of screen animation must face. Notice that only T, the first letter of the string S$, is erased. We can erase the entire string by changing line 80 to

```
80 PRINT@ R, STRING$(LEN(S$), " ");
```

This line will print one blank for every character in the string S$. Another problem is that any string printed near the end of a line will appear on two separate lines. Not only does this look bad, but it also causes an automatic screen scroll when it occurs in the bottom line. The scrolling of the screen causes the print line to move up one row so that it is no longer in position R. Line 80 then has no effect. RUN the program several times until you see a line that is not erased. The correction for this is fairly simple: By screening the values of R, we can print only those strings that have starting and ending positions on the same line. Add

```
50 IF INT(R/64) <> INT((R+LEN(S$)+1)/64) THEN 40
RUN
```

Line 50 guarantees that the starting position, R, and the ending position, R+LEN(S$), of each string printed will be on the same line. The +1 protects print position 1023.

Your final listing should look like this:

```
10 CLS
20 S$="THIS IS MY TRS-80"
30 FOR I=1 TO 30
40 R=RND(1023)
```

```
Ø  IF  INT(R/64)  <>  INT((R+LEN(S$)+1)/64)  THEN  40
Ø  PRINT@  R,  S$;
Ø  FOR  J=1  TO  100  :  NEXT  J
Ø  PRINT@  R,  STRING$(LEN(S$)," ");
Ø  NEXT  I
```

he PRINT@ statement is an extremely powerful tool in generating graphics. By no
eans have we exhausted its potential in these few examples.

Plot Coordinates

ew Numbering Scheme

ow that you are expert at printing characters to any of the 1024 print positions on the
creen, let's consider a finer partitioning of the screen. Each of the screen locations
an be divided into six rectangular graphic blocks. These blocks are arranged in three
ows and two columns as shown in figure 2.6.

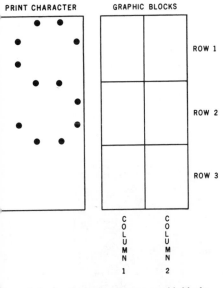

igure 2.6   A print character versus graphic blocks.

his gives us 6 times 1024, or 6144 locations for our plotting purposes. We can create
ome exciting pictures using these blocks.

o light up an arbitrary graphic block on the screen, you have to ignore the old
umbering scheme of 0 through 1023, and think of the screen as 16 times 3 or 48
ows, and 64 times 2, or 128 columns of graphic blocks. The 48 rows are numbered 0
hrough 47 and the 128 columns are numbered 0 through 127 as shown in figure 2.7.

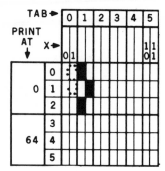

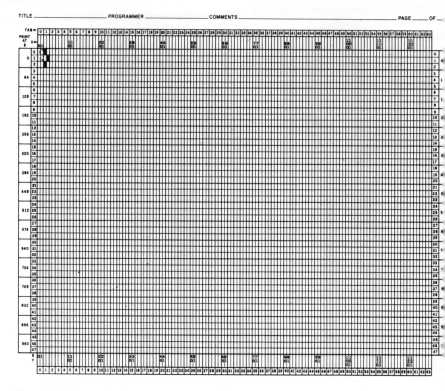

Figure 2.7   New numbering scheme.

Each block is located by both its horizontal distance (0 − 127) and its vertical distance (0 − 47) from the upper-left corner. To locate the block at (40,20), start at (0,0) and move 40 to the right and 20 down.

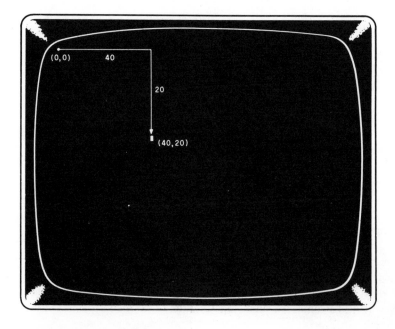

Figure 2.8   The block at (40,20).

member, the first number is the horizontal component, the second number, the
rtical.

ET and RESET

ou can control individual graphic blocks with the SET and RESET statements. The
ET statement lights up a graphic block, and the RESET statement erases it. The
rmat for these statements is

```
ET(X,Y)
ESET(X,Y)
```

ere X is the horizontal component and Y the vertical.

e new numbering scheme may seem strange at first, but it is much easier to use in
aphing functions than the PRINT@ scheme. Using immediate mode (i.e., no line
mbers), type in

```
EW
ET(40,20)
ESET(40,20)
```

e SET statement lights block (40,20); the RESET statement erases that same
ock. (It works now, but watch out when the screen starts to scroll!) To light up the
ur corners of the screen, type

```
S
ET(0,47)
ET(127,47)
ET(127,0)
ET(0,0)
```

hat happened to the R in READY (print position 0)? SET(0,0) lit up a graphic
ock in the upper left-hand corner of print position 0, right on top of the R. What do
u think would happen if we SET a rectangle in the "dead space" of print position 0
low the R? Can we use rectangles for underlining purposes? See figure 2.9.

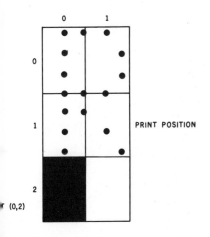

gure 2.9 Underlining?

Try

```
CLS
SET(0,2)
```

No luck? This exercise points out a subtle but important fact of TRS-80 graphics. Lighting up a single graphic block affects the entire print position in which it is located. When you type SET (0 , 2), the TRS-80 displays in print position 0 a character that looks like figure 2.10:

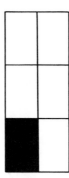

Figure 2.10   A graphic character.

This character replaces the R that was there before it. Remember, only one character per print position on the screen. For your reference, the 64 graphic characters are listed in Appendix B.

Testing, Testing

Let's look at one last example as a review. How does the computer interpret a SET (4 , 3) instruction? As shown in figure 2.11, the computer acts on the instruction as a request to print a graphic character in print position 66.

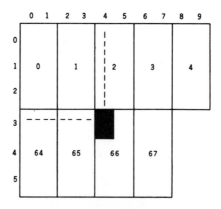

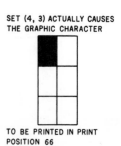

SET (4, 3) ACTUALLY CAUSES
THE GRAPHIC CHARACTER

TO BE PRINTED IN PRINT
POSITION 66

Figure 2.11   A SET(4,3) instruction.

he SET/RESET numbering scheme is only for the convenience of us humans. ortunately, as long as we are careful not to overlap characters, we can think of the creen as having two completely separate numbering systems—one for graphic locks, and one for characters.

Io Arguments, Please

he SET and RESET statements both require two arguments, X and Y. The word argument'' is used quite a bit in mathematics in reference to functions. It simply eans the values on which a function acts. For example, in the equation = SIN(X), the argument of the SIN function is X. The function bases its alculations on the value of X.

efore we can use any function to its fullest capacity, we must have a clear nderstanding of what kind of information it can digest. We found out earlier, for xample, that the TAB function can handle any expression having a value between 0 id 255, but no values outside this range are allowed. The X and Y arguments for the ET and RESET functions have their limitations as well. The first argument (we will se X to be consistent with standard algebraic notation) must be between 0 and 127. he second argument, Y, has to be between 0 and 47. If you use values outside these nges, you are asking for an 'ILLEGAL FUNCTION CALL' '?FC ERROR' in nondisk BASIC). Try it if you like. Type, in immediate mode,

ET(-10,5)

he arguments of the SET and RESET functions can include variables and xpressions as well as numbers. If this were *not* so, drawing a single horizontal line of ctangles across the screen would require that some lucky soul type in a whopping 28 SET statements:

```
0  SET(0,20)
0  SET(1,20)
0  SET(2,20)
  -  -  -  -  -  -  -
270  SET(126,20)
280  SET(127,20)
```

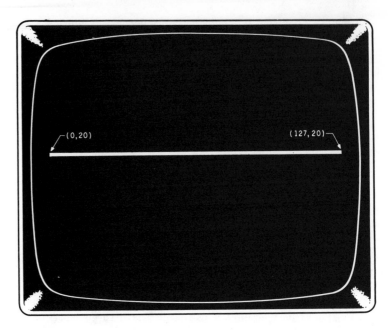

Figure 2.12   Our first horizontal line.

Not for me, thank you! It's much easier to use the variable X in the first argument and
a simple FOR/NEXT loop to do the same thing

```
NEW
5 CLS
10 FOR X=0 TO 127
20 SET(X,20)
30 NEXT X
RUN
```

The arguments can also be replaced by functions. Type

```
NEW
10 CLS
20 SET( RND(128)-1 , RND(48)-1 )
30 GOTO 20
RUN
```

The first random number function in line 20 generates a number from 1 to 128. One i
then subtracted to give us a number in the range from 0 to 127—exactly the right
range for the horizontal argument of the SET statement. A number between 0 and 47
is generated for the vertical argument, and the point is thus plotted. Line 30 sends
control back to the SET statement, where another point is created. If you wait long
enough, the entire screen will fill up with rectangles. Press (**BREAK**) when you are
ready to move on.

The SET and RESET functions have a built-in integer function that ignores decimal
fractions. For instance, SET(3.9,2) gives you the same result as SET(3,2).
To see how this works, type in and RUN the following:

```
NEW
10 CLS
20 FOR X=0 TO 127
30 SET(X,.1*X)
40 NEXT X
50 GOTO 50
RUN
```

The first ten values of the vertical component (0.1, 0.2, ..., 0.9) are truncated to 0, the next ten values are truncated to 1, and so on. So, we get horizontal bars in rows 0,1,...,12. Give the computer and yourself a (BREAK).

POINT

Another statement that uses the same numbering scheme as the SET and RESET statements is POINT(X,Y). The X and Y arguments have the same limitations and use as those of SET and RESET. The POINT(X,Y) statement tests whether the graphics block at location (X,Y) is lit or not. If (X,Y) is lit, POINT is equal to 1. If (X,Y) is not lit, POINT is equal to 0. At first glance, these two numbers seem a bit arbitrary, but they do have a very special meaning in Radio Shack BASIC. The IF statement interprets any expression with a value of 0 as false, and any other value as true. Therefore, the -1 works in an IF statement as a true and the 0 works as a false. To convince yourself of this, type

```
NEW
10 INPUT X
20 IF X PRINT "TRUE" : GOTO 10
30 PRINT "FALSE"
40 GOTO 10
RUN
```

Enter several different values for X, and use (BREAK) to stop. Zero should be the only false value. To see how the POINT statement can be used, type

```
NEW
10 CLS
20 PRINT@ 460, CHR$(RND(64)+127);
30 IF POINT(24,21) THEN 60
40 PRINT@ 470, "UPPER LEFT BLOCK IS NOT LIT"
50 GOTO 70
60 PRINT@ 470, "UPPER LEFT BLOCK IS LIT    "
70 INPUT "PRESS <ENTER> TO CONTINUE"; A$
80 GOTO 10
RUN
```

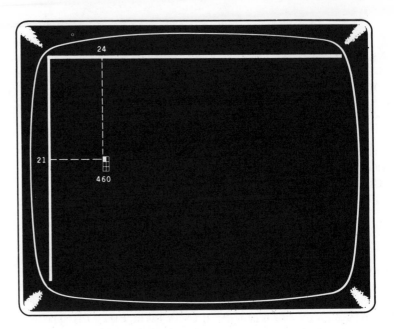

Figure 2.13   Probing with the P O I N T function.

A random graphic character is printed at location 460, and the P O I N T statement is used to test the upper left-hand corner of that position. If it is lit, the P O I N T function is true and the I F statement sends us to line 60. If it is not lit, control falls through to line 40. The process will be repeated until you press (BREAK).

Don't despair. This statement does have other, more exciting uses. P O I N T can be used to test the collision moment of two moving objects in arcade games, for example. Also, it can be used to reverse any portion of a graphics display to black on white. You will see these applications in later chapters.

Programming Techniques With SET and RESET

Looping

This chapter will cover some general programming techniques as·well as the SET and RESET statements.

IF, GOTO

Your TRS-80 is just about the best thing that has happened to repetitive procedures. Many graphic applications require some kind of repetition. Even drawing a straight line across the screen is done by systematically lighting up a series of graphic blocks, one by one. The repetition is accomplished in a computer program by executing the same instructions repeatedly in a loop. There are several ways loops can be created in a program. One option is to branch back to a previously executed instruction with an IF statement. From BASIC, type

```
NEW
10 CLS
20 INPUT A$
30 PRINT A$
40 IF A$<>"STOP" THEN 20
RUN
```

When you see the ?, type in a short string of characters and press the (ENTER) key. If the string of characters you type does not equal STOP, control passes to line 20. The IF statement will continue to loop back to line 20 until you type STOP (ENTER).

Another option is to create your loop with a GOTO statement. Just be careful in your use of GOTOs. They are easy to use, but they often lead to trouble in the form of hard-to-read programs or infinite loops. Change line 40 in the above program to

```
40 GOTO 30
LIST
```

and RUN. Good grief! What have we done? Don't panic—simply press the (PANIC), that is, the (BREAK) key. Whew! Disaster averted. Pressing the (BREAK) key causes the program to stop running, while leaving the program still in memory. Now type LIST to verify that the program is alive and well. In fact, it is so alive and well that you can have it continue execution by typing CONT or CONTINUE. Press (BREAK) again. Two other ways of stopping an infinite loop are to hit the reset button and to turn off the power. Both of these options may cause you to lose your program from memory so they should be used only as a last resort.

FOR/NEXT Loops

If you know in advance exactly how many times you want your loop to repeat, use a FOR/NEXT loop. The FOR statement allows you to control the number of times the loop will repeat; the NEXT statement is used as the last instruction in the loop. The NEXT statement sends the program back to the FOR statement where the decision is made to either continue the loop or not. To see this in action, type

```
NEW
10 CLS
20 FOR I=1 TO 10
30 PRINT TAB(I) I
40 NEXT I
```

and RUN.

All the logic for the loop is handled by the FOR and NEXT statements. The FOR statement causes the variable I to start at 1 and to increase by ones until it reaches 10. The NEXT statement causes an automatic jump back to the FOR statement. Line 30 i executed ten times as the value of the variable I changes from 1 to 10.

Setting The Stage

To further illustrate the use of FOR/NEXT loops and infinite loops, let's draw a border around the edge of the screen using graphics blocks.

Figure 3.1   A screen border.

This is easily done using four FOR/NEXT loops, one for each line. Change lines 20 and 30 to

```
20 FOR I=0 TO 127
30 SET(I,0)
```

and RUN. This loop draws a straight line across the top of the screen. As the variable I varies from 0 to 127, the SET statement in line 30 lights up locations (0,0), (1,0), (2,0), ..., (127,0). (Remember, the first number in a SET statement selects the horizontal position and the second number selects the vertical position of the graphic block.)

But what about the READY prompt that ruined our nice display? The little rascal appears every time a BASIC program finishes execution—quite a nuisance when we are trying to create a work of art. An easy way to neutralize the prompt is to fool the computer into thinking that it has not finished simply by giving it more work to do. Add

```
999 GOTO 999
RUN
```

This line keeps the computer running in circles at line 999 while we sit back and admire our creation. To stop the program, press the (BREAK) key. Infinite loops do come in handy after all.

Type LIST to verify that your program looks like this:

```
10 CLS
20 FOR I=0 TO 127
30 SET(I,0)
40 NEXT I
999 GOTO 999
```

Now enter

```
50 FOR I=0 TO 127
60 SET(I,47)
70 NEXT I
```

and RUN. This will draw the top and bottom lines of the screen border. To finish the border, press (BREAK) and add

```
80 FOR I=0 TO 47
90 SET(0,I)                    (Left side)
100 NEXT I
110 FOR I=0 TO 47
120 SET(127,I)                 (Right side)
130 NEXT I
```

RUN it just to be sure everything is typed in correctly. When you are ready to regain control of your computer, press the (BREAK) key.

A Different Approach

On your way to becoming a graphics whiz, you will notice that there are usually several ways of getting identical results on the screen. As your programming expertise increases, you will strive to create faster and more concise programs. Let's see if we can condense this last program a bit, just for practice.

First of all, notice that the variable I goes from 0 to 127 in both of the first two loops. Our first improvement will be to combine them into one loop where we will plot two points for each value of I. Type DELETE 50-70 and add

```
35 SET(I,47)
```

RUN this version of the program. Presto! The top and bottom rows are now drawn at the same time. The same improvement can be made with the second pair of loops. Delete lines 110 through 130, then add

```
95 SET(127,I)
```

and RUN. Your new listing should look like this:

```
10 CLS
20 FOR I=0 TO 127
30 SET(I,0)
35 SET(I,47)
40 NEXT I
80 FOR I=0 TO 47
90 SET(0,I)
95 SET(127,I)
100 NEXT I
999 GOTO 999
```

Is this the ultimate in drawing a screen border? Well, not quite. First, we can use multiple statement lines to compress the coding a bit. For example, lines 30 and 35 can be combined. Change line 30 to

```
30 SET(I,0) : SET(I,47)
```

The same thing can be done with lines 90 and 95. Change line 90 to

```
90 SET(0,I) : SET(127,I)
```

and delete lines 35 and 95.

Second, we can actually draw the entire screen border with one FOR/NEXT loop in which I varies from 0 to 127. During the first part of the loop while I is in the range of 0 to 47, we will use all four SET statements. But once I passes 47, we will use only the first two SET statements since the screen is wider than it is tall. This selective use of I can be achieved with an IF statement separating the two pairs of SET statements. Change line 40 to

```
40 IF I>47 THEN 100
```

and delete line 80 to get

```
10 CLS
20 FOR I=0 TO 127
30 SET(I,0) : SET(I,47)
40 IF I>47 THEN 100
90 SET(0,I) : SET(127,I)
100 NEXT I
999 GOTO 999
```

Go ahead and RUN it to see how the lines are drawn. There may be better ways to draw a screen border, but this version is certainly a lot cleaner than the original 13-line monstrosity!

Random Patterns

Infinite loops can be used to create never-ending graphic patterns. In order to continually vary the pattern, we can use the built-in random number function, RND. Type

```
NEW
10 PRINT RND(6);
20 GOTO 10
```

and RUN. Press the (BREAK) key when you've had enough. The RND function acts on the argument 6 and generates a random integer from 1 to 6. The random number function will act on any positive integer in the same manner. Note that if the argument is zero, it gives a random decimal from 0 to 1, but we won't be needing that as often. We can use the RND function in graphics to choose the horizontal and vertical coordinates in a SET statement. Type

```
NEW
10 CLS
20 H=RND(20)
30 K=RND(10)
60 SET(H,K)
100 GOTO 20
RUN
```

Random numbers are chosen in lines 20 and 30 and stored in the variables H and K. Then line 60 lights up a rectangle at location (H,K). Line 100 causes the process to repeat. The arguments in lines 20 and 30 determine the size of the rectangle created by this program.

Although it may not be obvious on the screen, the first row and column of the screen are not being used since the RND function starts at 1. The point (0,0) is the base from which the points in the rectangle are plotted. Then, each point is plotted by moving H units to the right and K units down from (0,0).

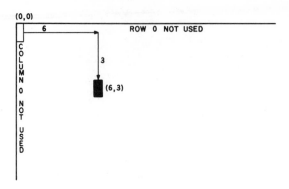

Figure 3.2   Positioning a dot.

Notice that we could create duplicate copies of the rectangle by placing the SET statement in a loop. Change line 60 to

```
60 SET(X+H,K)
```

and add

```
40 FOR X=0 TO 100 STEP 25
90 NEXT X
RUN
```

Let it run until you see the pattern. Line 40 sets up the points (0,0), (25,0), (50,0), (75,0), and (100,0) as the base points from which five rectangles are created. On every pass through the loop, a point is plotted in each rectangle; this point is in the same relative position in each rectangle.

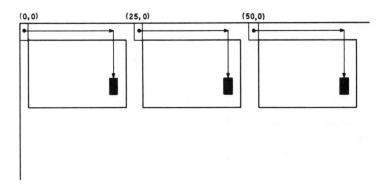

Figure 3.3   Cloning.

We could cover the entire screen with duplicates of our original rectangle by adding a loop for the vertical direction. Change line 60 to

```
60 SET(X+H,Y+K)
```

add

```
 FOR Y=0 TO 36 STEP 12
 NEXT Y
JN
```

he 60 causes each rectangle to be drawn by starting from a base point of (X,Y) and
n moving horizontally H units and vertically K units.

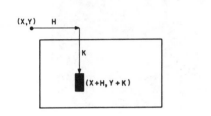

ure 3.4   A typical rectangle.

entually, the rectangles will become solidly filled in. To keep the display in a state
constant change, every time we light a rectangle, we will erase the one to its right
typing

```
 RESET(X+H+1,Y+K)
JN
```

it run a while to verify that the rectangles don't fill in. Your final listing should be
follows:

```
 CLS
 H=RND(20)
 K=RND(10)
 FOR X=0 TO 100 STEP 25
 FOR Y=0 TO 36 STEP 12
 SET(X+H,Y+K)
 RESET(X+H+1,Y+K)
 NEXT Y
 NEXT X
0 GOTO 20
```

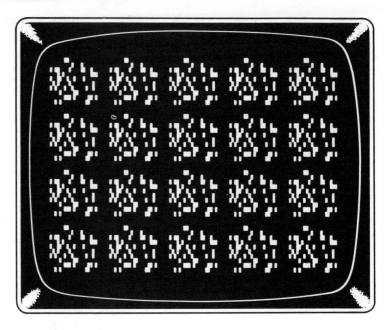

Figure 3.5   Random rectangles.

READ/DATA

Now for a little fun. Let's exercise our creative talents by drawing our first picture.
We'll use another looping technique that features the READ and DATA statements to
control the placement of points on the screen. The picture we are going to produce is
shown in figure 3.6. Be advised again that it is best to start the design on a video
display worksheet.

Figure 3.6   Design of the dragon.

Once the "masterpiece" is on paper, we have to then develop a strategy for reproducing it on the screen in the most painless fashion. The approach will vary, of course, with the kind of picture you attempt to produce. Figure 3.6 can readily be drawn using a collection of horizontal lines of varying lengths. Only three numbers are needed to position a horizontal line segment on the TRS-80 screen: its starting and its ending column numbers and its vertical position. For example, to draw a line from X = 5 to X = 10 in row Y = 20, we could use the following program:

```
NEW
10 CLS
20 READ X1, X2, Y
30 FOR X=X1 TO X2 : SET(X,Y) : NEXT X
50 DATA 5, 10, 20
```

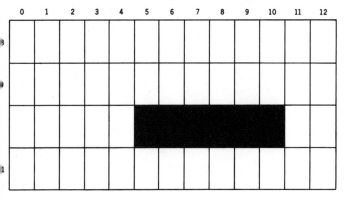

Figure 3.7   Drawing with DATA 5,10,20.

Enter and RUN this program. Line 20 reads the numbers 5, 10, and 20 into the variables X1, X2, and Y. Line 30 is a complete loop that draws the line. Using this approach, we can scatter horizontal lines anywhere on the screen. Now add

```
40 GOTO 20
60 DATA 50,125,42,80,80,30,22,61,16
```

and RUN. Don't worry about the OUT OF DATA error yet. Notice the single dot generated by 80,80,30. You can add your own numbers, but be careful not to go backwards (e.g., 40,20,20). See Chapter 8 for ways to do that.

Clean Exit

Well, we could paint just about any picture possible using our beloved rectangles and this little routine if we supplied enough data, but there has to be a smoother way to exit the program. OUT OF DATA IN LINE 20 just doesn't do the trick. So, we are forced either to count lines or to use ON ERROR GOTO. Make these changes:

```
10 CLS: ON ERROR GOTO 90
90 GOTO 90
```

The program listing should be the following:

```
10 CLS: ON ERROR GOTO 90
20 READ X1, X2, Y
30 FOR X=X1 TO X2 : SET(X,Y) : NEXT X
40 GOTO 20
50 DATA 5, 10, 20
60 DATA 50,125,42,80,80,30,22,61,16
90 GOTO 90
```

RUN it. An error occurs in line 20 when there is no more data to read. The error trap set in line 10 directs the computer to line 90. Line 90 causes the computer to get stuck in an infinite loop—we could either sit back and admire the display or hit the (BREAK) key. Another way to make a clean getaway is to count the number of lines to be drawn, but counting tends to be difficult and a bother if your data is constantly changing. We will opt for the ON ERROR GOTO approach.

Now for the acid test. Below are the data lines needed to draw the top part of figure 3.6. Delete

```
50
60
```

and enter

```
1010 DATA 63,66,2
1020 DATA 60,65,3
1030 DATA 56,67,4
1040 DATA 55,55,5,57,62,5,64,70,5
1050 DATA 23,31,6,55,55,6,58,61,6,64,69,6
1060 DATA 21,32,7,47,67,7,84,85,7
1070 DATA 16,33,8,46,69,8,83,91,8
1080 DATA 10,34,9,60,71,9,81,101,9
RUN
```

Looks good so far, but don't go away. We are going to improve the program in the next section.

2 Subroutines

Computer programs have a nasty habit of growing in unexpected ways and then becoming very unmanageable. Who cares about a few extra lines and repetitious coding in a program? You do! Whenever a procedure is to be repeated several times, it should be written once and set aside as a *subroutine*, a very useful tool that we will now explore.

Subroutines can help us to cut down significantly on the amount of data required to draw the dragon. Notice in figure 3.6 (in the preceding section) that most of the rows in the picture require several horizontal lines. Row 6, for example, uses four line segments:

```
23,31,6    55,55,6    58,61,6    64,69,6
```

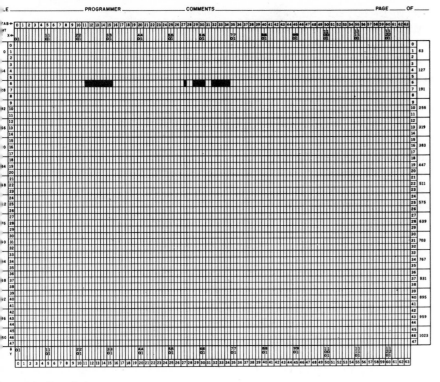

Figure 3.8   Row six data.

the 6 must be repeated for each segment even though it is used for all four of them.
This redundancy can be eliminated if we instruct the computer to print all line
segments in the same row unless instructed differently. An IF statement and a short
subroutine will do the trick. Change line 20 to

```
20 READ X1 : IF X1<0 GOSUB 100 : GOTO 20 ELSE READ X2
```

and add

```
  Y=2
100 REM
110 Y=Y+1: RETURN
LIST
```

Don't RUN it yet. Your listing through line 110 should look like this:

```
  Y=2
10 CLS: ON ERROR GOTO 90
20 READ X1 : IF X1<0 GOSUB 100 : GOTO 20 ELSE READ X2
30 FOR X=X1 TO X2 : SET(X,Y) : NEXT X
40 GOTO 20
50 GOTO 90
100 REM
110 Y=Y+1: RETURN
```

This routine will allow us to delete all the row numbers in the data and to replace them
with a single negative number at the end of each data line. Now make these changes:

```
1010 DATA 63,66,-1
1020 DATA 60,65,-1
1030 DATA 56,67,-1
1040 DATA 55,55,57,62,64,70,-1
1050 DATA 23,31,55,55,58,61,64,69,-1
1060 DATA 21,32,47,67,84,85,-1
1070 DATA 16,33,46,69,83,91,-1
1080 DATA 10,34,60,71,81,101,-1
```

and RUN the program. The IF statement in line 20 branches to the subroutine every time a negative number is read into X1. One is added to the row number and we are returned to line 20 to read in the next data value. The rest of the data is included here in case your computer can't live another day without having its very own dragon!

```
* 1090 DATA 3,36,50,68,80,117,-1
  1100 DATA 9,38,57,69,79,126,-1
  1110 DATA 13,39,56,71,78,121,-1
  1120 DATA 14,41,55,68,76,116,-1
  1130 DATA 14,42,54,66,74,113,-1
  1140 DATA 12,43,53,67,72,111,-1
  1150 DATA 10,45,52,64,69,112,-1
  1160 DATA 3,125,-1
  1170 DATA 12,115,-1
  1180 DATA 14,44,48,64,67,112,-1
  1190 DATA 14,42,46,65,69,109,-1
  1200 DATA 14,40,45,66,71,110,-1
  1210 DATA 12,39,44,68,73,118,-1
  1220 DATA 7,38,43,67,74,107,-1
  1230 DATA 17,37,42,66,76,101,-1
  1240 DATA 22,37,42,72,79,99,-1
  1250 DATA 22,36,41,72,81,102,-1
  1260 DATA 20,36,40,72,83,109,-1
  1270 DATA 14,35,40,78,85,100,-1
  1280 DATA 25,35,40,78,87,98,119,121,-1
  1290 DATA 31,34,40,85,90,95,118,125,-1
  1300 DATA 32,34,40,85,92,97,113,126,-1
  1310 DATA 32,33,40,86,95,101,113,120,-1
  1320 DATA 32,32,40,92,113,119,-1
  1330 DATA 41,92,110,118,-1
  1340 DATA 37,92,110,117,-1
  1350 DATA 35,93,110,116,-1
  1360 DATA 33,75,82,99,105,116,-1
  1370 DATA 32,38,54,72,88,99,105,114,-1
  1380 DATA 32,37,61,67,90,100,104,114,-1
  1390 DATA 32,36,62,67,92,113,-1
  1400 DATA 32,35,63,69,94,111,-1
  1410 DATA 31,35,65,72,96,109,-1
  1420 DATA 22,41,55,78,99,106,-1
  1430 DATA 19,22,29,33,39,44,52,55,63,69,76,79,-1
  1440 DATA 25,30,59,64,-1
  1450 DATA 23,25,58,59
```

ure 3.9   The dragon.

Simple Animation

ow Is It Done?

imation is the art of creating the illusion of motion with our graphic displays. How
it done? Simple, really. All we have to do is continuously change our display so that
e eye perceives it as motion. Animated cartoons are created with a series of frames,
ch one differing only slightly from the next. When these frames are shown in rapid
ccession, our eyes "see" movement.

e key word here is *rapid*. Television uses about 60 frames per second, so our eyes
e accustomed to that kind of speed. Unfortunately, working with an interpretive
nguage like BASIC, we do not always have access to that kind of speed. You'll
tice that most of the good arcade programs are written in machine language. The
oblem with BASIC is that *every* program line has to be translated into machine
nguage *every* time it is executed by the computer. Although the translation is fast
ough for most applications, it greatly limits the type of animation we can produce
ing BASIC.

we are fortunate enough to be working with an application in which only a small
rtion of the screen has to be animated at any given time, speed is no problem. Take
e case of moving a single graphic dot around the screen. Type

```
EW
Ø  Y=Ø
Ø  CLS
Ø  FOR X=1 TO 126
Ø  SET(X,Y) : RESET(X-1,Y)
Ø  NEXT X
JN
```

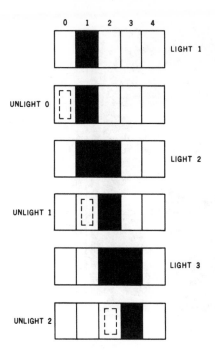

Figure 3.10   A moving dot.

The motion is due to the RESET statement. Every time a new rectangle is lit, the on
to its left is erased. The motion seems fairly continuous; it will certainly pass for a
bouncing ball in a ping-pong game. But what would happen if we tried to move a
larger object across the screen? Change the following lines:

```
30 FOR X=1 TO 40 : FOR Y=1 TO 10
50 NEXT Y : NEXT X
```

and RUN. Here we are trying to move a vertical bar sideways, but the motion appear
jerky at best. To get a feel for the way the size of the bar can affect the continuity of
motion, try

```
10 INPUT "N="; N
30 FOR X=1 TO 40 : FOR Y=1 TO N
60 GOTO 10
```

RUN it and try different values for N, especially numbers between 1 and 10. The
lesson in this exercise is that SET and RESET are of limited use when we try to
animate large objects, but that they work quite well for smaller ones. Large objects
can be effectively animated, even in BASIC—you will see more on this later. For
now, let's see what we can do with SET and RESET.

First, we will take a single point and move it randomly around the screen. Type

```
NEW
10 X=64 : Y=24 : CLS
20 H=RND(3)-2 : K=RND(3)-2
100 RESET(X,Y) : X=X+H : Y=Y+K : SET(X,Y) : GOTO
RUN
```

Line 10 clears the screen and establishes the starting point at (64,24). The
RND (3) - 2 in line 20 selects a − 1,0, or 1 for H and K, which are then added to X
and Y to determine the position of the next point.

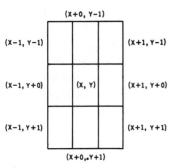

Figure 3.11   Random motion.

In line 100, the old point is erased, the new position calculated, and the new point
plotted. Of course, without some kind of control, the point will eventually run off the
screen, but that will be rectified shortly.

Keyboard Control With INKEY$

The I N P U T statement is not adequate for real-time keyboard control of motion.
Every time an I N P U T is executed, the screen display freezes in anticipation of
operator input. In addition, the program cannot continue until the (**ENTER**) key is
pressed. Fortunately, to sidestep these drawbacks, the TRS-80 is equipped with an
I N K E Y $ function. The I N K E Y $ function continually strobes the keyboard. When
a key is depressed, the ASCII value of that key is stored in the I N K E Y $ buffer.
Because this buffer is only one byte long, each time a new key is depressed, its ASCII
value replaces the one previously stored in the buffer. So we can test the buffer for the
ASCII value of the last key to be depressed. All of this can happen without disturbing
the screen display.

One other quirk of this function is that each time we test the buffer location, it is
emptied. It will stay empty until another key is hit. Let's add this function to our
program so that you can control the motion of the dot with the four arrow keys.

Add

```
20 REM
30 I$=INKEY$ : IF I$="" THEN 80
80 REM
```

but don't R U N it yet! The first part of line 30 tests the I N K E Y $ buffer (which also
clears it) and stores the value in the string variable I $. If the buffer was blank, then
no key has been depressed since our last test and we jump to line 80. If an arrow key
has been depressed, we'll have to adjust H and K to direct the dot in the proper
direction. This is done by adding

```
40 IF ASC(I$)=8 H=-1: K=0: GOTO 80
50 IF ASC(I$)=9 H=1: K=0: GOTO 80
60 IF ASC(I$)=10 H=0: K=1: GOTO 80
70 IF I$="[" H=0: K=-1      (Press ⬆ for "[")
RUN
```

Press the arrow keys to change the direction of the moving dot. You are controlling the animation! The animation will continue until the dot runs off the edge of the screen. If the ⬇ key is pressed, ASC(I$) will equal 8. H and K are given values in line 40 so that the SET statement in line 100 will produce motion to the left. Motion in three other directions is achieved in a similar fashion. Notice that diagonal movement could be produced by introducing four new keys and by adjusting H and K. (We left this out to make the program a little easier and faster.)

Patrolling The Borders

A few refinements and we'll have ourselves a real game program. First, we will eliminate the RESET in line 100 so that the dot leaves a trail. Second, we'll add a screen border. Type

```
10 X=64 : Y=24 : CLS : GOSUB 110
100 X=X+H : Y=Y+K : SET(X,Y) : GOTO 20
110 FOR J=0 TO 127: SET(J,3) : SET(J,47)
120 IF J<48 SET(0,J) : SET(127,J)
130 NEXT J : RETURN
RUN
```

Yes, the border is *supposed* to look strange. Now, we will add a rule to the game: No crashing into the border or any part of your tail. The program can enforce this rule with

```
80 IF H=0 AND K=0 SET(X,Y): GOTO 30
90 IF POINT(X+H,Y+K) PRINT@ 980, "YOU LOSE
    BUSTER!";: GOTO 140
140 GOTO 140
```

The POINT function is a companion to the SET and RESET statements. It checks the location specified by the two arguments to see if it is lit or not. If that location is lit, the POINT function is TRUE. Conversely, if it is not, the POINT function is FALSE. In our program, if the next location is already lit, we are about to crash into a wall or a portion of the tail, so we'd lose. We have line 80 to protect us from losing before any keys are depressed when H and K are still zero.

If the object of the game is to go as long as we can without bumping into something, then it might help to insert some kind of timer. Add

```
10 X=64 : Y=24 : CLS : GOSUB 110 : T=0
20 T=T+1 : PRINT@ 28, "TIME:" INT(T/10);
90 IF POINT(X+H,Y+K) PRINT@ 980, "YOU LOSE!
    TIME:" INT(T/10);:
    GOTO 140
RUN
```

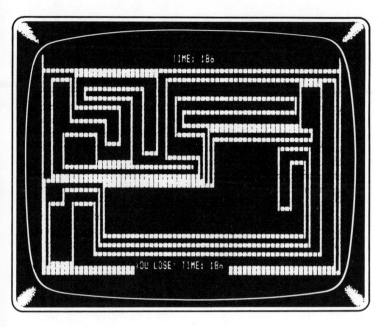

Figure 3.12   A game display.

Your final listing should look like this:

```
*10 X=64 : Y=24 : CLS : GOSUB 110 : T=0
 20 T=T+1 : PRINT@ 28, "TIME:" INT(T/10);
 30 I$=INKEY$ : IF I$="" THEN 80
 40 IF ASC(I$)=8 H=-1: K=0: GOTO 80
 50 IF ASC(I$)=9 H=1: K=0: GOTO 80
 60 IF ASC(I$)=10 H=0: K=1: GOTO 80
 70 IF I$="[" H=0: K=-1
 80 IF H=0 AND K=0 SET (X,Y): GOTO 30
 90 IF POINT(X+H,Y+K) PRINT@ 980, "YOU LOSE!
    TIME:" INT(T/10);: GOTO 140
 100 X=X+H : Y=Y+K : SET(X,Y) : GOTO 20
 110 FOR J=0 TO 127: SET(J,3) : SET(J,47)
 120 IF J<48 SET(0,J) : SET(127,J)
 130 NEXT J : RETURN
 140 GOTO 140
```

Many refinements could be made to beef up the game somewhat:

- vary the size of the border
- include diagonal motion
- place random obstacles on the screen
- add control keys and a moving dot for another player
- create boxes with varying point values that randomly appear and disappear (first
player to the box gets the points or penalty)

If you have small children, you could make the game fairly kid-proof by adding

```
5  ON ERROR GOTO 150
150 RUN
```

Get busy. Modifying programs can be a valuable learning aid as well as pure and simple fun.

Warp Factor 3

Let's look at another example of how lighting up rectangles can give a feeling of animation. For this example, imagine yourself sitting at the helm of the Enterprise as you zip past the stars at warp 3. You guessed it: We are going to create a viewport complete with moving stars (you will have to supply the Romulans and Klingons). Man your stations!

First we will set the stage for the animation by designating variables, clearing the screen, and drawing and labeling the viewscreen. Type

```
NEW
10 DEFINT A-Z : CLS
20 FOR I=20 TO 107 : SET(I,10) : SET(I,37) : NEXT I
30 FOR I=10 TO 37 : SET(20,I) : SET(107,I) : NEXT I
40 PRINT@ 854, "ENTERPRISE VIEWSCREEN"
```

and RUN. Line 10, of course, defines all variables to be integers. Now what we would like to do is to choose a dot randomly located near the center of the screen and move it away from the center. By using (64,24) as the center, we can create a point near the center by adding

```
70 X=53+RND(21)
80 Y=19+RND(9)
100 SET(X,Y)
```

Line 70 gives us a horizontal range from 54 to 74 and line 80 gives a vertical range from 20 to 28. RUN it a few times to be sure that the point created is reasonably close to the center of the screen. (You may wish to modify the ranges later to suit your taste.) Now to add the motion. Change the last part of the listing to

```
50 RESET(X,Y)
60 IF X+H>20 AND X+H<107 AND Y+K>10 AND Y+K<37
   GOTO 90
70 X=53+RND(21) : H=X-64 : IF H=0 THEN 70
80 Y=19+RND(9) : K=Y-24 : GOTO 100
90 X=X+H : Y=Y+K
100 SET(X,Y)
110 GOTO 50
```

Use the editor if necessary, and RUN it. Because the computer initializes X and Y to zero, line 50 erases (0,0) and line 60 is ignored. Lines 70 and 80 choose values for the point (X,Y) and calculate H and K which will be the horizontal and vertical distances the dot will move. The GOTO in line 80 sends control to 100 where the first point is lit. The GOTO in line 110 then sends control to line 50 where the same point is immediately erased. You might think this is a bit strange, but it has to be done to simulate motion. Now you must quickly calculate the next position for the dot and light it. Line 60 first checks to see if the new position will still be inside the viewport. If not, control goes to line 70 where a new point is generated. If it is, we hop to line 90 to calculate the next position and then SET the point in line 100. As long as the point stays within the viewport, the sequence of

```
Calculate  —      90 X=X+H : Y=Y+K
      SET  —     100 SET(X,Y)
and RESET  —         RESET(X,Y)
```

ontinues. Otherwise, we start over again with a new point.

o far, so good. Unfortunately, there is often more than one star visible on the
nterprise viewscreen. To make our display a bit more realistic, we'll have to add a
:w more stars. Nothing could be easier. All we have to do is create a loop from line
0 to line 100, and add subscripts to the variables X, Y, H, and K. To keep the motion
airly smooth, we will settle for three moving stars. Edit the program to

```
10 DEFINT A-Z : CLS
20 FOR I=20 TO 107 : SET(I,10) : SET(I,37) : NEXT I
30 FOR I=10 TO 37 : SET(20,I) : SET(107,I) : NEXT I
40 PRINT@854, "ENTERPRISE VIEWSCREEN"
50 FOR I=1 TO 3 : RESET(X(I),Y(I))
60 IF X(I)+H(I)>20 AND X(I)+H(I)<107 AND
   Y(I)+K(I)>10 AND Y(I)+K(I)<37 GOTO 90
70 X(I)=53+RND(21) : H(I)=X(I)-64 : IF H(I)=0 THEN 70
80 Y(I)=19+RND(9) : K(I)=Y(I)-24 : GOTO 100
90 X(I)=X(I)+H(I): Y(I)=Y(I)+K(I)
100 SET(X(I),Y(I)) : NEXT I
110 GOTO 50
```

RUN it and may the force be with you. (Oops. Spock informs me that the Admiral has
 desk job waiting for anyone caught using Star Wars lingo on this vessel!)

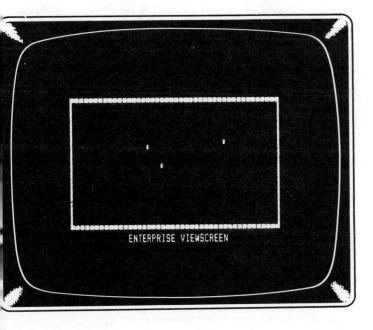

igure 3.13   Moving stars.

Using Strings

ASCII Code

his chapter, we will investigate several ways of creating graphics through the use
strings of characters and codes. Because we are going to push your knowledge of
SIC to the limit (or at least give it a gentle shove), we need first to lay the
undwork.

ere comes a time in the lives of all BASIC programmers when they realize that lots
mysterious symbols that cannot be displayed by pressing a key on the keyboard are
ing somewhere inside the computer. They know, for example, that there are
phics characters running around in the character generator, but there are no
phics keys. How do you get those symbols to display on the screen or a printer
hout keys? Let's see . . .

intable Symbols

ery displayable symbol is assigned a number according to the American Standard
de for Information Interchange (ASCII). There are 128 codes used ranging from 0
127 decimal. The numbers from 32 to 127 represent printable symbols.

ASCII PRINTING CODES . D = DECIMAL

D	CHR$(D)	D	CHR$(D)	D	CHR$(D)
32		64	@	96	'
33	!	65	A	97	a
34	"	66	B	98	b
35	#	67	C	99	c
36	$	68	D	100	d
37	%	69	E	101	e
38	&	70	F	102	f
39	'	71	G	103	g
40	(	72	H	104	h
41	)	73	I	105	i
42	*	74	J	106	j
43	+	75	K	107	k
44	,	76	L	108	l
45	—	77	M	109	m
46	.	78	N	110	n
47	/	79	O	111	o
48	0	80	P	112	p
49	1	81	Q	113	q
50	2	82	R	114	r
51	3	83	S	115	s
52	4	84	T	116	t
53	5	85	U	117	u
54	6	86	V	118	v
55	7	87	W	119	w
56	8	88	X	120	x
57	9	89	Y	121	y
58	:	90	Z	122	z
59	;	91	♠ or [	123	{
60	<	92	♥ or /	124	|
61	=	93	♦ or]	125	}
62	>	94	♣ or ^	126	~
63	?	95	—	127	±

MODEL III   MODEL I

gure 4.1   Standard ASCII symbols.

Most of these symbols can be displayed by pressing a key on the keyboard, with onl
a few exceptions. Try pressing the left arrow key to display a left arrow. No luck. T
key causes the cursor to back up and erase a previously typed character. So how do
get the left arrow symbol to print on the screen? This is where the ASCII chart come
in handy. Any of the symbols shown in the chart (with the exception of lowercase
symbols if your machine doesn't have lowercase capability) can be displayed on the
screen by typing PRINT CHR$(N), where N is the ASCII number of the symbo
you wish to display. To display the left arrow character (right bracket on the Model
III) type PRINT CHR$(93). Even the standard keyboard characters can be
displayed this way. Type

```
PRINT "BUTTER" : PRINT CHR$(80)CHR$(65)CHR$(82)
       "KAY"
```

Can you tell them apart?

If you find yourself wondering what code number is generated by pressing a particu
key, use

```
NEW
10 A$=INKEY$: IF A$="" THEN 10
20 PRINT ASC(A$)
30 GOTO 10
RUN
```

Press some of the special keys such as (CLEAR), (ENTER), and the arrow keys, with ar
without the (SHIFT) key.

Control Codes

ASCII numbers 0 through 31 are used as *control codes*. They control activities such
as moving the cursor around the screen, erasing parts of the screen, and converting
double-width characters.

Dec.	Hex.	Control Code
8	08	Backspace and erase
9	09	Tab (0, 8, 16, 24, . . .)
10	0A	Move cursor to start of next line and erase line
13	0D	Move cursor to start of next line and erase line
14	0E	Cursor on
15	0F	Cursor off
* 21	15	Swap space compression/ special characters
* 22	16	Swap special/alternate characters
23	17	Double-size characters
24	18	Backspace without erasing
25	19	Advance cursor

*Model III only

Dec.	Hex.	Control Code
26	1A	Move cursor down
27	1B	Move cursor up
28	1C	Move cursor to upper left corner
29	1D	Cursor to start of line
30	1E	Erase to end of line
31	1F	Erase to end of display

Figure 4.2   Control codes.

Control codes can also be implemented in BASIC with the CHR$ function. Type

```
NEW
10 PRINT "PRESS ANY KEY TO ERASE THIS LINE";
20 A$=INKEY$
30 IF A$="" THEN 20
40 PRINT CHR$(29) CHR$(30)
RUN
```

Control code 29 moves the cursor to the beginning of the line, and code 30 erases the line. These two codes can be lots of fun. Try this on an unsuspecting friend:

```
NEW
5 CLS : PRINT CHR$(23)
10 FOR J=1 TO 3
20 READ X$: PRINT X$;
30 FOR I=1 TO 100 : NEXT I
40 PRINT CHR$(29) CHR$(30);
50 NEXT J
60 RESTORE: GOTO 10
70 DATA I, LOVE, YOU
RUN
```

Line 5 clears the screen. CHR$(23) sets the screen in double-width mode, a dandy trick to remember. A word is read and printed in line 20; line 30 pauses while we admire the word. Line 40 erases the word and line 50 sends us back for the next word. When all three words are read, line 60 restores the DATA pointer and starts the whole process again.

Moving The Cursor

Codes 24 through 27 are very useful in creating graphics. These codes move the cursor one position in any direction. Type:

```
NEW
10 CLS: PRINT
20 PRINT "1";
30 PRINT CHR$(27)"2";
40 PRINT CHR$(26)"3";
50 PRINT CHR$(26)CHR$(24)CHR$(24)"4"
```

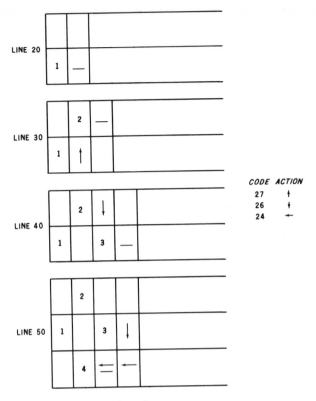

Figure 4.3   Cursor motion codes.

As each character is printed, the cursor automatically moves right. You can then use control codes to move the cursor to the position in which the next character is to be printed. Code 27 moves the cursor up, 26 moves it down, and 24 moves it to the left.

Special Foreign Characters

The Model III also has a hidden set of characters from foreign alphabets.

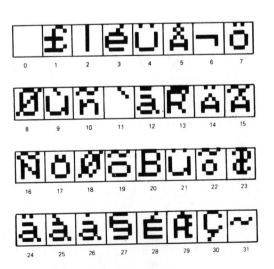

Figure 4.4   Model III foreign character set.

is accessed via the POKE statement. To see the foreign character set, enter

```
NEW
10 CLS: FOR I=0 TO 31
20 POKE 15360+2*I,I: NEXT I
30 GOTO 30
RUN
```

You may want to explore this set of characters after we discuss the POKE statement
(n Chapter 5.)

Graphic Codes

The TRS-80 features its own extension of the ASCII code, namely, the decimal
numbers from 128 to 255. The first sixty-four of these numbers identify the TRS-80
graphic character set.

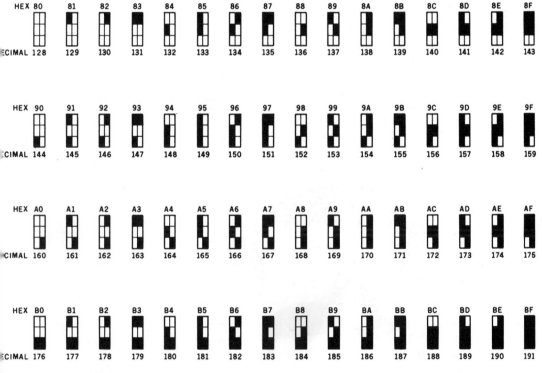

Figure 4.5 Graphic characters.

To display all of them on the screen type

```
NEW
10 CLS : FOR C=128 TO 191
20 IF C=8*INT(C/8) PRINT
30 PRINT CHR$(C); C"   ";    (two spaces)
40 NEXT C
50 GOTO 60
```

and RUN. Not bad! The ASCII numbers are converted into symbols by the CHR$ function in line 30. If you want to display the keyboard characters as well, change the 128 in line 10 to 32. Then add

```
40 IF C=127 INPUT A$
```

and RUN. Line 40 will cause the program to pause; so press the (ENTER) key to continue. Remember that unless you have the lowercase modification, all symbols will be displayed as uppercase. If you *do* have the lowercase mod, it has to be activated by using (SHIFT) (ZERO) on the Model III, or by loading a SYSTEM tape or from DOS by typing LCDVR on the Model I.

Now you can create your own graphic figures. Just refer to figure 4.5. Try this:

```
PRINT CHR$(166)CHR$(179)CHR$(153)
```

or

```
NEW
10 CLS
20 PRINT CHR$(189)CHR$(144)
30 PRINT CHR$(191)CHR$(135)
40 PRINT CHR$(129)
RUN
```

Let's assume that we have a figure already drawn on a video display worksheet, and that we are ready to translate it to character codes. If the ASCII chart is available, we can determine the codes by searching the chart for each character.

Figure 4.6   A sample figure.

Figure 4.6 consists of three characters.

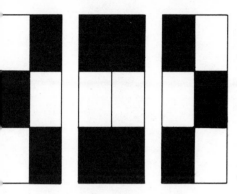

Figure 4.7   The graphic characters.

Look on the ASCII chart to find the matching figures. You should find codes 166, 179, and 153. In the event that the ASCII chart is not readily accessible, you can calculate the codes by remembering the following pattern:

1	2
4	8
16	32

Figure 4.8   The pattern for calculating graphic codes.

Each of the six positions of a graphic character is assigned a number. For any graphic character, the code is the sum of the numbers associated with the blocks to be lit *plus* 128. For example, the first graphic character in figure 4.7 uses blocks 2,4, and 32. Its code is 128 + 2 + 4 + 32, which equals 166. The second one is 128 + 1 + 2 + 16 + 32, or 179, and the third is 128 + 1 + 8 + 16, or 153. See if you can determine the codes for this figure:

Figure 4.9   A quiz figure.

Notice that it might be easier to subtract from 191 for nearly solid characters. The codes are as follows:

$$191 - 8 = 183$$
$$128 + 4 + 8 = 140$$
$$191 - 4 = 187$$

Space Compression Codes

The rest of the codes, 192 through 255, are space compression codes. These enable us to print from 0 to 63 spaces with a single character. Try

```
NEW
10 FOR I=192 TO 200
20 PRINT I; "ONE" CHR$(I) "TWO" I-192
30 NEXT
RUN
```

The CHR$ function prints blank spaces between the words "ONE" and "TWO". The number of blanks is I − 192.

It's easy to calculate the space compression code needed to print a desired number of blank spaces. Just add 192 to the desired number of blanks. Suppose you want to flash a message 'YOU WIN !' at the end of a game. The message is nine characters long. To blank it out, we need a code of 9 + 192 = 201. Type

```
NEW
10 CLS
20 PRINT@ 400, CHR$(201)
30 FOR I=1 TO 20 : NEXT
40 PRINT@ 400, "YOU WIN!"
50 FOR I=1 TO 20 : NEXT
60 GOTO 20
RUN
```

Of course, you could let the computer calculate the code needed for you. Type

```
NEW
10 CLS
```

```
20 INPUT "ENTER YOUR NAME"; A$
30 W$="YOU WIN "
40 PRINT@ 400, "!!!!! "W$; A$ " !!!!!"
50 PRINT@ 406, CHR$(192 + 8 + LEN(A$));
60 FOR I=1 TO 40 : NEXT I
70 PRINT@ 406, W$; A$;
80 GOTO 50
RUN
```

Line 50 calculates just the right number of blank spaces. It adds 8 for W$ as well as
enough for A$. The trailing semicolons in lines 50 and 70 ensure that the exclamation
marks remain.

Model III Trickery

Time out for a special word to Model III users.

The Model III has two more special character sets we can display with CHR$. They
share the same ASCII numbers as the space compression codes: 192 through 255.
Now, how can that be? A 192 either represents a space compression code or it
doesn't. Make up your mind! Well, the trick is that only one of the three sets of
characters is active at a given time. When the machine is "booted up" (computerese
for switched on), the space compression codes are the active set, just like the Model I.
Using ASCII codes 192 through 255 gives us space compression characters. To see
what a mess these codes can make on the screen, type

```
NEW
10 CLS: PRINT CHR$(23)
20 FOR I=192 TO 255
30 PRINT I; CHR$(I);
40 NEXT I
RUN
```

But try this one on for size:

```
PRINT CHR$(21)
RUN
```

Wow! Look at all those nifty characters! Greek letters, faces, a rocket—something for
nearly everyone. The CHR$(23) in line 10 set the screen to double width so that
you can get a good look at them. CHR$(21) is the code that activated this set and
retired the space compression codes. So, how do we get the space compression codes
back? Use CHR$(21) again:

```
PRINT CHR$(21)
RUN
```

CHR$(21) switches back and forth between the two sets. Where does the third
character set fit into all this? It has been waiting patiently in the dugout all this time. It
can be sent in as a pinch hitter for the special character set. Type

```
PRINT CHR$(22)
```

GREEK LETTERS
FACES   192
ROCKET   255

Now our special character set is inactive, and the new set is about to take the field. Enter

```
PRINT CHR$(21)
RUN
```

Surprise—Japanese Kana characters! Now what would happen if we tried this:

```
PRINT CHR$(22)
RUN
```

Back to the original special character set. So, CHR$(22) alternates between the special character set and Kana characters. CHR$(21) alternates between the space compression codes and the currently active special character set. Whew, we've finally got that straightened out! Try playing around with these. Maybe you'll understand it better than we do.

ASCII numbers 192 − 255 are used throughout the book as space compression codes. If you are having trouble with a program, check to make sure that the special character sets are *not* active.

2 Use Of Strings

One of the most dynamic graphic techniques is the use of *string variables*. A string variable is formed by appending a $ to a numeric variable name. Examples are A$ and S4$. Each variable can hold up to 255 (*not* 256 !) characters. Look at the following example:

```
           1          2          3          4          5
1234567890123456789012345678901234567890123456789012345678901234567890
ST$="............THIS VARIABLE CAN HOLD UP TO...............
...............TWO HUNDRED FIFTY-FIVE CHARACTERS............
..........................!!.WOW.!!.........................
..............THAT'S ALMOST 4 LINES OF INFORMATION..........
...............  ..........."
```

Once the information is stored in the variable, it can be recalled with the PRINT or PRINT@ statement. PRINT ST$ displays the information on the screen. Some useful functions and statements associated with string use are:

```
                    CLEAR
                    DEFSTR
                    STRING$
                    CHR$
            +  (concatenation)
                    MID$
                    LEFT$
                    RIGHT$
                    LEN
```

EFT$

ne of the first tricks to learn as a BASIC programmer is to use the L E F T $ function
look at the first character of a string. Look at the following way of soliciting a
s/no response:

```
  PRINT "MAIN PROGRAM"
             .
             .
             .
0  PRINT "END OF MAIN PROGRAM"
Ø  INPUT "WOULD YOU LIKE TO TRY AGAIN"; A$
0  IF A$="YES" GOTO 10
Ø  IF A$="NO" END
Ø  PRINT "USE YES OR NO ONLY" : GOTO 510
N
```

e program responds to YES or NO, but what would happen if you felt like
swering with a simple Y or N or even NOT TODAY, PAL? One way to allow
ch more flexibility is to compare the first character of the response with Y and N as

```
  PRINT "MAIN PROGRAM"
           .
           .
Ø  PRINT "END OF MAIN PROGRAM"
Ø  INPUT "WOULD YOU LIKE TO TRY AGAIN"; A$
Ø  IF LEFT$(A$,1)="Y" GOTO 10
Ø  IF LEFT$(A$,1)<>"N" PRINT "USE Y OR N" : GOTO 510
Ø  END
```

y input that starts with Y will start the program again. Conversely, any input that
rts with N will stop it.

ID$, LEN

unction that allows us to pick a group of characters right out of the middle of a
ng is M I D $. It can be used to add a bit of variety when displaying text. Try

```
W
CLS
 READ A$
 IF A$="END" END
 FOR I=1 TO LEN(A$)
 PRINT MID$(A$,I,1);
 FOR T=1 TO 40: NEXT T
 NEXT I : PRINT
 GOTO 10
 DATA "THIS IS LINE ONE OF THE SCROLLING DEMO."
 DATA "IT IS JUST AS EASY TO USE DATA STATEMENTS"
Ø DATA "AS PRINT STATEMENTS."
Ø DATA END
N
```

Each string of data is read into A$. The MID$ function in line 40 selects one character from position I in the string A$. Each character is printed until the end of the string is reached. The LEN function in line 30 returns the length of the string A$. Line 50 provides the desired delay between characters.

CHR$, STRING$

Two of the functions that receive heavy-duty use in graphics are CHR$ and STRING$. Recall that the CHR$ function allows us to display any of the 255 character codes available on the TRS-80 with PRINT CHR$(N), where N is the number of the code we desire. The function STRING$ will repeat any one of these codes up to 255 times. Try

```
CLEAR 255: PRINT STRING$(255,191)
```

(We will get to CLEAR shortly). These two functions can be combined with the PRINT@ statement in a variety of applications. A good example of their utility can be demonstrated in printing oversized numbers and letters. First, design the characters on the video display worksheet.

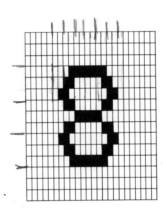

Figure 4.10   An oversized eight.

The number 8 shown here uses 18 graphic characters arranged in three rows and six columns. Each row can be printed using character codes and strings of character codes. The entire figure can be printed almost anywhere on the screen. The position specified with the PRINT@ statement. Type

```
NEW
10 CLS: INPUT P
20 PRINT@ P,
   CHR$(160)CHR$(158)STRING$(2,131)CHR$(139)CHR$(1
30 PRINT@ P+64,
   CHR$(128)CHR$(179)STRING$(2,140)CHR$(166)CHR$(1
40 PRINT@ P+128,
   CHR$(130)CHR$(173)STRING$(2,176)CHR$(184)CHR$(1
RUN
```

ype in any number between 0 and 889. The upper left corner of the 8 will be printed
ere while the rest will be printed on successive lines.

or another demonstration of the power of STRING$ and PRINT@ type

```
EW
Ø CLEAR 200
Ø R=RND(159)+32: A$=STRING$(64,R)
Ø IF RND(2)>1 THEN FOR X=Ø TO 1023 STEP 64 ELSE
  FOR X=960 TO Ø STEP -64
Ø PRINT@ X, A$;
Ø ,NEXT X: GOTO 20
UN
```

ine 10 reserves room in memory for string handling, whereas line 20 chooses a
ndom character from the ASCII chart. The first 32 codes are skipped because they
e control codes. A$ is set equal to a string of 64 of this character, enough to fill up
he row. The RND function in line 30 determines whether the printing will start at the
p or the bottom of the screen. Line 40 does the actual printing of A$. The
OR/NEXT loop marches us up or down the screen until the GOTO in line 50 starts
e entire process again.

lear

efore you can make extensive use of strings in a BASIC program, memory must be
served. BASIC automatically reserves 50 characters as a scratch-pad for use in
orking with strings. If 50 characters are not enough, you will get an OUT OF
TRING SPACE error message. Change line 10 in the previous program to
Ø CLEAR 50 and RUN it. Yes, sir! Got to CLEAR enough string space.

ow does one determine the size of the string work space necessary for a given
ogram? Sorry, no easy answers here, but we will tackle the problem in Chapter 7.
r now, your best bet is to CLEAR plenty of room for string use, especially if you
e doing a lot of string manipulation (e.g., sorting, concatenating).

EFSTR

ne more note on string use before we charge into concatenation. If you get tired of
ping a dollar sign on the end of every string variable, the DEFSTR statement will
me in handy. DEFSTR can change the type of any variable or range of variables to
ring variables. For example, type

```
EFSTR A
1="I AM A STRING VARIABLE"
RINT A1
```

ok Ma, no $ on A1. The DEFSTR statement defines any variable starting with A
a string variable. Of course, this doesn't work if the variable is followed by a
meric type declaration (!, #, or %). Try DEFSTR A%. It gives us a syntax error.
ho would want an integer precision numeric string anyway!

You can also define a range of variables to be strings. Type

```
DEFSTR T-Z
U="STRING"
PRINT U
```

From now on, all variables starting with a letter from "T" to "Z" are string variable unless a type declaration is added.

3 Building Strings With Concatenation

The real power of string graphics is about to be unveiled, so take good notes. Much o that power derives from the simple fact that strings may be joined (concatenated) wit a plus sign. Try typing this:

```
NEW
10 CLEAR 1000 : DEFSTR A-Z
20 A="STRING"
30 C=CHR$(183)+A+CHR$(187)
40 PRINT C
RUN
```

Three strings—CHR$(183), A, and CHR$(187)—are concatenated in line 30 and the new string created is stored in the string variable C. That's only the first step. The building process can be repeated by changing line 30 to

```
30 C=C+CHR$(183)+A+CHR$(187)
```

and adding

```
50 INPUT I: GOTO 30
RUN
```

Press (ENTER) whenever you see the question mark. Each time line 30 is executed, eight characters are added to the end of string C. The string C will continue to expan until the string space allocated in line 10 is used up, or until the limit on the length of string variable is exceeded. Considering that up to 255 character codes (nearly a quarter of the screen) can be stored in one string variable, there is quite a lot of powe here.

How To Build Your Own

Techniques for building strings are as numerous and varied as BASIC programmers themselves, so they cannot all be presented here. We will show enough examples, however, to give you an idea of the variety of approaches you can take in building your own strings.

A real natural for this sort of thing is to store the information in DATA statements an read it into strings. Type

```
NEW
10 DEFSTR S: READ N
20 FOR I=1 TO N
30 READ A: S=S+CHR$(A)
40 NEXT I
50 READ S1: PRINT S,S1
60 DATA 12,174,156,191,141,174,159,175,157,174,159,
   191,132
70 DATA TRAIN
RUN
```

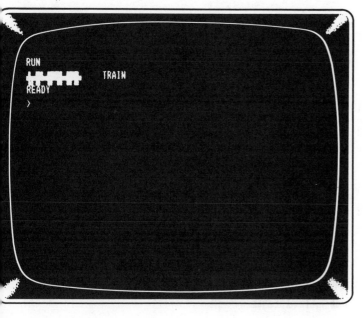

gure 4.11   On the track with strings.

he character codes are stored in line 60 and are added to string S in line 30.

Moving The Cursor

fter you have explored all the exciting (?) possibilities of one-line graphics, you
aduate to multiple-line figures. This requires moving the cursor from line to line.
'e have seen this done with the PRINT@ statement, but that won't help us much
hile we're building strings. Control codes to the rescue. Remember early in this
apter how we used the ASCII character codes 24-27 to move the cursor? Well, by
mbining these codes with graphic codes, it is possible to store a many-lined figure
a single string variable. Type

```
NEW
10 DEFSTR A : CLS
20 A=CHR$(149)+CHR$(26)+CHR$(24)
30 FOR I=1 TO 3 : A=A+A : NEXT
40 PRINT A
RUN
```

Line 30 links together several versions of the original string A. When the string is printed in line 50, the codes 26 and 24 move the cursor down and to the left each time the graphic code 149 is printed. This positions the cursor so that the next graphic code printed will be directly below the previous one. Thus, we have a vertical line stored in one string.

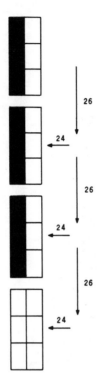

Figure 4.12   The making of a vertical line.

Once a graphic string is built, it can be printed almost anywhere on the screen (but watch out for the borders). Change line 50 to

```
50 PRINT@ L,A
```

and add

```
40 INPUT L: CLS
60 GOTO 40
RUN
```

As you can see, the cursor motion codes are very useful in building strings. Use them

Go With The Flow

If the figure to be drawn is a bit more horizontal, we can use the natural flow to the right to aid us in the drawing. Notice that the space compression codes instead of multiple backspaces are used in the following example. Try

```
EW
 CLEAR 300 : DEFSTR A : FOR I=1 TO 31
 READ B : A=A+CHR$(B): NEXT I
 INPUT "ENTER SCREEN POSITION (0-1023)"; P
 CLS : PRINT@ P, A : GOTO 30
 DATA 160,156,140,172,144,184,140,140,180,247
 DATA 191,195,130,195,170,149,246
 DATA 130,137,164,144,194,176,140,131,243
 DATA 199,130,137,131,249
JN
```

...ies 10 and 20 build a single string, A, out of the numbers in the DATA statements.
...nes 30 and 40 input the desired screen position and print the figure. The data greater
...an 191 are space compression codes; they greatly reduce the number of characters
...quired to print this heart. Save this program—we will use it later in this chapter.

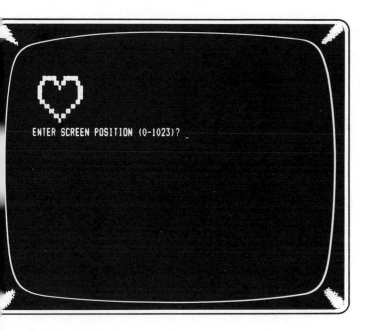

ENTER SCREEN POSITION (0-1023)?

...ure 4.13   A heart.

...ing The BASIC Editor

...other way to add cursor motion to your strings is to use the editing features of
...ASIC. Type

```
EW
 CLS
 A$="123   4"
 PRINT@ 400, A$;
 GOTO 40
```

...wo blank spaces in line 20.) RUN it just to be sure there is nothing up our sleeves.

Your output should look like this: 1̄23   4. We are about to use a devious ploy so that the string A$ prints like this:

```
41
32
```

To do this, we will have to insert control codes between the numbers in line 20 using the built-in BASIC editor. When we are finished, the line should be stored in memory as

```
1↓←2←←3↓←4
```

Figure 4.14   Embedded cursor control codes.

The arrows indicate cursor motion codes. The codes could be added in the following manner:

```
20  A$="1"+CHR$(26)+CHR$(24)+"2"+...
```

but, hang on to your hats, there is an easier way. These three control codes can be entered directly from the keyboard. It will jumble up the listing a bit, but it will require fewer CHR$.

Detour For Model I Owners

Before we get into the editing, however, we'll have to take a special detour for Model I owners with the old ROM chip. In Chapter 2, we found that the new and old ROM chips handled the TAB statement differently. Another difference is the way in which CHR$(26), the cursor down character, is generated from the keyboard. Those of you with the old chip can use (SHIFT) and ⊙ keys. Those with the new ROM or Model III use (SHIFT) ⊙ ''Z''.

In the editing to follow, old ROM folks will have to ignore the (Z). When the instructions call for a (SHIFT) ⊙ (Z), use (SHIFT) ⊙ instead.

Back Again

On to editing. The line we are about to edit is

```
20  A$="123    4"
```

Follow the instructions very carefully. If you make a mistake, retype line 20 and start again. Don't try to patch up a partially edited line. Press (ENTER) *only* at the end of the editing session. Enter edit mode with EDIT 20 (ENTER). Type

```
S2I
(SHIFT) ⊙Z (SHIFT)( ↑ (SHIFT)⊙
S3I
```

SHIFT(◀) SHIFT(◀) SHIFT(◆)
(SPACEBAR)2C
SHIFT(◆) SHIFT(◀)
ENTER

Note that the role of the (SHIFT) (◆) depends on the mode. It terminates input in the insert mode, but it acts like CHR$(27) in the change mode. Now RUN the program. Your output should look like this:

1
2

Type

CLEAR
LIST

To see how line 20 has changed. It should appear as 20 A$=4". Where did all those numbers go? Believe it or not, they *are* there. To see them, type EDIT 20 and S-L-O-W-L-Y space through the line watching how the cursor moves. If you miss it the first time, press (L) (while you're still in the editing mode) and try, try again.

Substrings

Another technique used in building graphic strings is assigning useful graphic codes to variables. These variables can then be used to build large graphic strings. As an example, enter

```
NEW
10 CLEAR 100 : DEFSTR A-Z: CLS
20 A=CHR$(179): B=CHR$(160)
30 C=CHR$(175)+A+CHR$(159)
40 D=CHR$(183)+A
50 X=B+STRING$(3,176)+D+D+CHR$(191)+B+CHR$(26)+STRING$(10,24)
60 X=X+CHR$(138)+C+STRING$(2,143)+C+CHR$(131)
70 PRINT X
RUN
```

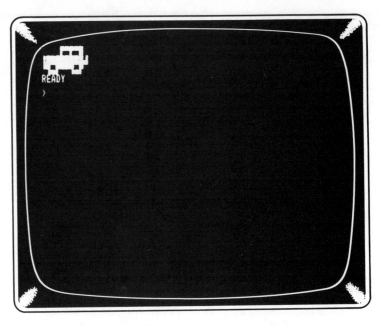

Figure 4.15   On the road with substrings.

Notice how codes 2 6 and 2 4 are used at the end of line 50 to create a two-line figure.

Intermediate Variables And String Arrays

Another idea for building several large but similar figures is to store similar portions of the figures in intermediate variables. The final figures can first be created from the intermediate variables, then stored in string arrays for easy access. This technique is particularly useful in printing oversized numbers in that many of the digits share common features.

We will start by creating a set of ten figures each three characters high by five wide.

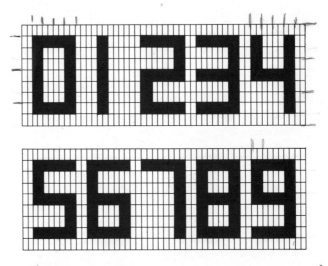

Figure 4.16   Large digits.

ur goal will be to store the digits in the string array N$(Ø)-N$(9). This way,
ey can easily be recalled by number. Next, we must identify substrings that are
ommon to several figures. The figures are designed so that there is quite a bit of
uplication.

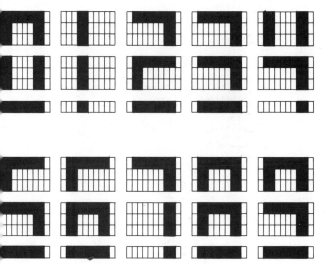

gure 4.17   An exploded view of the large digits.

tart with

```
EW
Ø CLEAR 300: DEFSTR A-Z : DEFINT J,K
Ø CLS
Ø M=CHR$(26)+STRING$(4,24)
```

ine 30 will take care of the cursor motion necessary to keep the three rows of each
gure lined up. The character codes used by several of the figures are

```
Ø X=CHR$(128): Y=CHR$(131): Z=CHR$(191)
```

he intermediate strings necessary are

```
Ø A=X+Y+X+X : B=X+X+X+Y : C=X+Z+X+X
Ø D=X+X+X+Z : E=Y+Y+Y+Z : F=Z+Y+Y+Z
Ø G=Z+X+X+Z : H=Z+Y+Y+Y : I=Y+Y+Y+Y
```

ee figure 4.18.

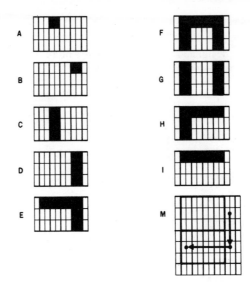

Figure 4.18   Intermediate strings.

Merging these substrings into the final figures will be a breeze now that the hard work
is done. The substrings must be separated by the cursor motion string, M. Add

```
240 N(0)=F+M+G+M+I
250 N(1)=C+M+C+M+A
260 N(2)=E+M+H+M+I
270 N(3)=E+M+E+M+I
280 N(4)=G+M+E+M+B
290 N(5)=H+M+E+M+I
300 N(6)=H+M+F+M+I
310 N(7)=E+M+D+M+B
320 N(8)=F+M+F+M+I
330 N(9)=F+M+E+M+I
```

You now have a set of large digits that can be called by number as needed. And
because they are stored as strings, they can be printed nearly anywhere on the screen
with PRINT@. The applications for oversized numbers are virtually endless;
displaying a digital clock, math drills and games are just a few.

A very simple example of how to use these numbers is the following:

```
*340 FOR J=0 TO 900 STEP 192
 350 FOR K=0 TO 55 STEP 5
 360 PRINT@ (J+K), N(RND(10)-1);
 370 NEXT K : NEXT J
 380 GOTO 340
 RUN
```

4 Controlling Screen Position

Fluttering Heart

Once graphic figures are stored in string variables, duplicating and moving them around is a cinch with the PRINT@ statement. Reload the heart program (figure 4.13), and delete lines 30 and 40. The remaining program loads the entire heart into the string variable A. By varying the position at which the heart is printed, we can duplicate it all over the screen. Add

```
100 PRINT@ RND(1023), A$
130 GOTO 100
RUN
```

Sure gets crowded in a hurry, eh? Add

```
110 CLS
RUN
```

to get a fresh screen each time. Whoa, Nelly! That's a bit fast! To slow it down, add

```
110 FOR I=1 TO 20: NEXT
120 CLS: FOR I=1 TO 20: NEXT
RUN
```

Controlled Animation

Now for the animation that all you game freaks have been waiting for. Actually most of the work (storing the figures in strings) is already done, but we need to exercise more control over the motion. The random fluttering of the heart is too sporadic for most applications.

One clever way to move a figure slowly across the screen is to buffer the edges of your figure with blank spaces. Printing the figure in an adjacent position will cause it to erase the previous character. Try

```
NEW
10 CLS: FOR I=1 TO 22
20 READ N : A$=A$+CHR$(N)
30 NEXT I
40 FOR P=0 TO 50
50 PRINT@ P, A$;
60 REM
70 NEXT P
80 DATA 128,160,158,163,143,167,180,128,160,182,246
90 DATA 176,178,189,176,179,184,191,184,191,135,128
RUN
```

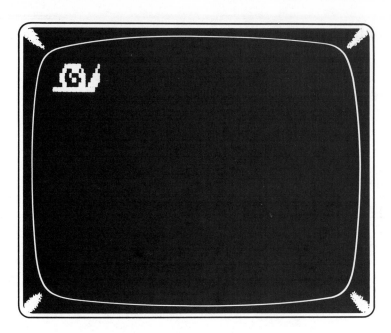

Figure 4.19   A snail.

What a cutie! Lines 10 through 30 build the string A$ from the data statements; lines 40 through 70 move the snail from print position 0 to 50. If your snails seem to be slower than ours, add

```
60 FOR I=1 TO 60: NEXT I
RUN
```

There, that will slow it down. To make it move backwards use

```
40 FOR P=50 TO 0 STEP -1
RUN
```

Getting Fancy

What happens if we just let our snail friend traipse on into the edge of the screen? Try it:

```
40 FOR P=0 TO 62
RUN
```

Poor thing. Fragmented at such an early age. (Escargots Provençal, anyone?)

But, with a little advance planning in the way the string is constructed, we can at least give our snail a graceful exit off the screen. If the figure is stored in the string column-by-column instead of the easier row-by-row format, we can use substring functions to print only part of the snail as it creeps toward the end of a line. In order to do this, we will need cursor motion strings so that the snail can be printed column-by-column. Add

```
5 CLEAR 180: D$=CHR$(24)+CHR$(26): U$=CHR$(27)
```

D$ will move the cursor down with the necessary backspace, and U$ will move it
up.

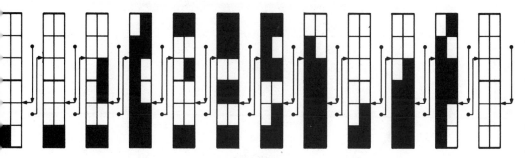

Figure 4.20   String reorganization.

The DATA will have to be reorganized to match:

```
80 DATA 128,144,128,176,160,178,158,189,163,176,143,179
90 DATA 167,184,180,191,128,184,160,191,182,135,128,128
```

The cursor motion strings can be inserted as the graphic codes are read in:

```
10 CLS: FOR I=1 TO 12
20 READ N, M: A$=A$+CHR$(N)+D$+CHR$(M)+U$
```

We still have to chop off the right part of the figure as it approaches the right side of
the screen. Do so with

```
50 IF P>52 PRINT@ P, LEFT$(A$,(64-P)*4); ELSE
    PRINT@ P, A$;
RUN
```

This line prints only the left portion of the figure as it nears the edge of the screen.
Yes, yes—it *is* a lot of work, but that is the sacrifice one must make in order to be
creative. So, happy snails to you, and, smooth snailing.

PEEK, POKE, And Other Oddities

Memory-Mapped Video

PEEK/POKE

So far, we have looked at several methods of creating graphics on the screen, including SET/RESET, PRINT, and PRINT@. Another one for our collection is PEEK/POKE.

The PEEK and POKE instructions enable us to examine and modify the contents of memory locations without leaving BASIC. PEEK, as the name implies, is like a peak window into the inner workings of the TRS-80. It allows us to look at the contents of any memory location, including the read-only memory (ROM) area. The ROM portion of memory is where the BASIC language and operating system are stored. With the POKE instruction, we can alter any of the random-access memory locations from 15360 (3C00 HEX) to the end of memory. Using PEEK and POKE, we can write machine language programs, modify the screen display, monitor the use of peripherals, change the contents of variables . . . . in short, we can really gum up the works if we set our minds to it! The amazing thing about PEEK and POKE is that they enable us to do all these things from BASIC.

The Memory Map

So, what does modifying memory locations have to do with graphics? Everything!

The memory of the TRS-80 is used for many purposes, as indicated in figure 5.1. The 1024 characters displayed on the screen are stored in memory locations 15360 − 16383 (3C00 − 3FFF HEX). Location 15360 corresponds to print position 0, and location 16383 to 1023. Any changes to this area of memory are immediately reflected on the screen as well. Let's see how this works. Enter

```
NEW
10 CLS : PRINT "A"
20 N=PEEK(15360)
30 PRINT N,CHR$(N)
RUN
```

The PRINT statement in line 10 prints an A in print position 0, which automatically places the ASCII code for A, 65 (41 HEX), in memory location 15360. Of course, it is stored in memory in binary form. The PEEK instruction in line 30 reads this value, converts it to decimal, and stores it in the variable N. The CHR$ function is used to convert the code back to the original symbol. (Note that lower case mods will give different results.)

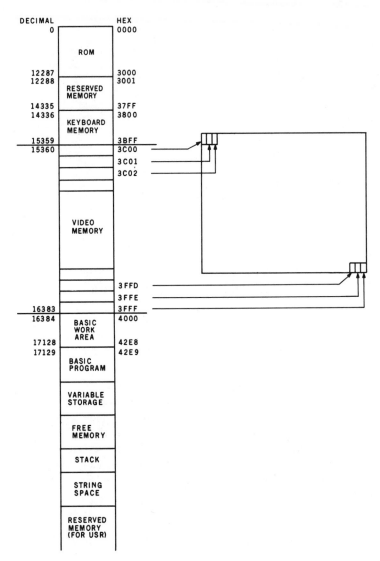

Figure 5.1 A memory-mapped video display.

To change the A to a B, we can poke the ASCII code for B, 66, into location 15360 (top left corner of the screen). Add

```
20 POKE 15360, 66
RUN
```

Line 30 then reads the 66 from location 15360, and line 40 prints it.

!!!WARNING!!! CARELESS POKING MAY BE HAZARDOUS TO YOUR PROGRAM'S HEALTH! Don't poke any locations except the screen section of memory unless you know what you are doing. The chances of hurting your computer are slim, but it is easy to lose a program.

To poke a character into any of the 1024 screen locations, use 15360 plus the PRINT@ number of the desired location. We can simulate a PRINT@ 400, "*" statement with

```
CLS: POKE 15360+400, 42
```

The 42 is the ASCII code for *.)

POKE vs. PRINT

Although POKE can be used to display many of the same characters as the PRINT statement, it reacts quite differently to some of the ASCII codes. The next program will enable you to experiment with poking different ASCII codes to the screen. The POKE statement controls the screen position.

```
NEW
10 CLS: S=15360
20 FOR I=129 TO 191
30 PRINT CHR$(28);
40 INPUT N
50 POKE S+I, N
60 NEXT I
RUN
```

Type in numbers from 0 to 255, and this program will poke them into consecutive screen locations. Note that the control and space compression codes do not function in the same manner as when they are displayed with the PRINT statement. Also, Model owners who have not activated the lower case modification will find a lot of duplication. Codes 0 through 31 act like 64 through 95, and codes 96 through 127 behave like 32 through 63.

Animation

In the previous chapter, we discussed using string functions to control animation. The POKE statement can be used as an alternative, but it is more awkward to use when large amounts of data have to be moved quickly. Recall the original snail program in Chapter 4. The snail was stored in A$, then printed in a loop:

```
FOR P=0 TO 50
PRINT@ P, A$;
NEXT P
```

One could accomplish the same thing with the POKE statement. (Don't type this.)

```
10 DEFINT X: CLS
20 FOR X=15360 TO 15410
30 POKE X, 32 : POKE X+1, 164
40 POKE X+2, 176 : POKE X+3, 176
50 POKE X+4, 176 : POKE X+5, 141
60 POKE X+6, 140 : POKE X+64, 32
70 POKE X+65, 138 : POKE X+66, 131
80 POKE X+67, 131 : POKE X+68, 139
90 NEXT
100 GOTO 100
```

The POKE statement gets the same job done, but for larger figures, the speed of animation would be slower. Consequently, POKE is best suited to a supporting role in animation.

Graphic Subroutines — Large Numbers Revisited

Where speed is not crucial, POKE can be used in subroutines to create large figures without using up string space. The large number program could easily be written with POKE instructions. As an example, the subroutine to print an eight would be like this:

```
NEW
10 ' MAIN PROGRAM
20 CLS: I=15840
30 GOSUB 1800
40 ' CONTINUE
50 GOTO 50
1800 POKE I, 160: POKE I+1, 158: POKE I+2, 131:
     POKE I+3, 131: POKE I+4, 139: POKE I+5, 180
1810 POKE I+64, 128: POKE I+65, 179: POKE I+66, 14
     POKE I+67, 140: POKE I+68, 166: POKE I+69, 14
1820 POKE I+128, 130: POKE I+129, 173: POKE I+130,
     176 POKE I+131, 176: POKE I+132, 184: POKE
     I+133, 135
1830 RETURN
RUN
```

Using strings to print this figure uses less code. The main advantage of using POKE is that it does not use up string space.

Cursor Movement

It is easy to overlook the fact that the POKE statement has no effect on the cursor position. The cursor stays at the last position printed (*not* poked!) regardless of where we poke characters on the screen. As a result, we have to specify each position to be poked. Compare the above routine with a version using PRINT:

```
1800 PRINT@ I, CHR$(160)CHR$(158)CHR$(131)...
1810 PRINT@ I+64, CHR$(128)CHR$(179)CHR$(140)...
                         .
                         .
                         .
```

Each time a character is printed, the cursor moves to the right, ready to print the next character.

Sometimes, this feature of the POKE statement can be advantageous. It means that we can make updates to the screen without changing the location of the cursor. The following short routine demonstrates this feature of POKE:

```
NEW
10 CLS
20 PRINT@ 400, "WHERE ARE YOU ";
30 POKE 15360+960, 42
```

```
Ø PRINT "CURSOR?"
UN
```

he POKE in line 30 doesn't disrupt the continuity of printing in lines 20 and 40.

PEEK And POKE At Pressure Points

o far in this chapter, we have seen the POKE statement come up short when used as
n alternative to the PRINT@ statement and string animation techniques. As
rustrating as it may seem, it is good to know the limitations as well as the strengths of
ae tools at our disposal. We are now going to explore some of the unique aspects of
*OKE and its companion statement, PEEK.

hese statements allow BASIC programmers to probe and change almost any portion
f memory at will. If used with care, they can give us access to places in memory that
ontrol important functions. You have already seen how we can control the video
isplay portion of memory. In this section, we will explore other locations used to
ontrol graphics.

Double-Width Characters

he memory areas in figure 5.1 labeled RESERVED contain several tables and status
ndicators used by BASIC. The Model I uses these areas somewhat differently from
he Model III. For example, location 16445 indicates the width of the characters on
he screen for the Model I, whereas location 16912 does this as well as several other
hings for the Model III. When the computer is first turned on, characters are normal
vidth and location 16445 contains a 0; location 16912 contains a 40. To check this,
ype

```
JEW
PRINT PEEK(16445)          Model I
PRINT PEEK(16912)          Model III
```

iee, we wouldn't kid you! Now try this:

```
PRINT CHR$(23)
PRINT PEEK(16445)          Model I
PRINT PEEK(16912)          Model III
```

The entire screen goes into double-width mode when CHR$(23) is printed, and the
values at these locations change. Returning to normal width can be achieved by
pressing the (CLEAR) key or by typing CLS. Unfortunately, both of these methods
clear the screen as well as change to normal character width. There may be times
when you want to change character width without clearing the screen. As you may
have guessed, we can return to normal character width without clearing the screen by
poking the original values in these locations. Enter

```
PRINT CHR$(23)
PRINT "XXXXX"
```

Everything on the screen is in double width. Now try

```
POKE 16445, 0              Model I
POKE 16912, 40             Model III
```

Hooray! Back to normal character width. Notice that everything that was printed while the screen was in double-width mode is printed in every other character position. In a similar fashion we could use

```
POKE 16445, 8              Model I
POKE 16912, 44             Model III
```

to go to double width instead of PRINT CHR$(23). Now to flex our new muscle in a BASIC program. Enter

```
NEW
10 CLS : J=1
20 PRINT@ 400, "TERMS -$850"
30 FOR I=1 TO 200 : NEXT
40 J=-J
50 POKE 16445, 8           Model I
50 POKE 16912, 44          Model III
70 GOTO 30
RUN
```

So, what happened to the double-width mode we were promised in line 50? Press **(BREAK)** to find out. Surprise! It was in double-width mode all the time, just too embarrassed to admit it. For some reason, this poking works in immediate mode, but not in a program. Hang on, there is a way to remedy the situation. Change line 50 to

```
50 POKE 16445, 8 : OUT 255, 8          Model I
50 POKE 16912, 44: OUT 236, 4          Model III
RUN
```

Amazing! Now we will alternate between the two modes. Change to

```
50 IF J<0 POKE 16445, 8 : OUT 255, 8   Model I
60 IF J>0 POKE 16445, 0 : OUT 255, 0   Model I
50 IF J<0 POKE 16912, 44: OUT 236, 4   Model III
60 IF J>0 POKE 16912, 40: OUT 236, 0   Model III
RUN
```

That's more like it. For most applications, CHR$(23) is the easiest way to enter double-width character mode, and CLS is the easiest way to return to normal width. When you don't want the screen cleared, use the appropriate POKE-OUT combination in place of CLS.

INPUT With PEEK

So far, we have seen two ways of entering information into a program from the keyboard: INPUT and INKEY$. The INPUT statement is the bread-and-butter method of input, and INKEY$ is best suited to situations where real-time interaction is needed. A third method of input involves using the PEEK statement to test the keyboard section of memory. This section of memory is closely tied to the keyboard,

uch like the video section of memory and the video display. Using PEEK in this
ay is similar to using INKEY$, but there are some important differences. If you
st can't wait to get a complete rundown on this method, skip to the last part of
hapter 7. The rest of us will settle for a simple example at this point. Enter the
ollowing:

```
EW
Ø CLS: L=15360
Ø G=L
Ø POKE L, 191
Ø POKE G, 32: GOTO 20
UN
```

o PEEKs yet! These lines just set up the flashing ''cursor'' we are going to move
ith PEEK. Line 10 clears the screen and sets the POKE location to the start of
creen memory. Line 20 sets up G as a second POKE location. Line 70 puts a solid
raphic character in location L, and line 90 replaces it with a blank space to simulate a
ashing cursor.

Ve are going to move the ''cursor'' by means of the four arrow keys. The keyboard
nemory cell that we will use to test for the arrow keys is 14420. It reacts to the
eyboard as follows:

KEY DEPRESSED	CONTENTS OF 14420
no key depressed	0
up arrow	8
down arrow	16
left arrow	32
right arrow	64

o move the cursor, we need to peek at location 14420 to see which key is depressed
nd change L accordingly. Change as follows:

```
Ø R=PEEK(14420): G=L
Ø IF R=64 L=L+1: IF L>16383 L=16383
UN
```

Depress the ⬤ key. As long as you hold down that key, the cursor moves to the
ight. Release it, and the motion stops. Try that with INKEY$! Motion is created in
ine 60 by adding one to L as long as the right arrow is depressed. The end of line 60
rotects us from straying to other parts of memory and destroying the program.
Motion in the other three directions can be added with

```
3Ø IF R=8 L=L-64: IF L<15360 L=L+64
4Ø IF R=16 L=L+64: IF L>16383 L=L-64
5Ø IF R=32 L=L-1: IF L<15360 L=15360
```

Check these lines carefully before you RUN the whole thing. The listing should be
his:

```
1Ø CLS: L=15360
2Ø R=PEEK(14420): G=L
3Ø IF R=8 L=L-64: IF L<15360 L=L+64
4Ø IF R=16 L=L+64: IF L>16383 L=L-64
5Ø IF R=32 L=L-1: IF L<15360 L=15360
```

```
60 IF R=64 L=L+1:  IF L>16383 L=16383
70 POKE L, 191
90 POKE G, 32:  GOTO 20
```

Why Change A Good Thing?

Only the arrow keys and the (BREAK) key should have any effect on the program at this point. With a few modifications, we can have the cursor leave a trail of any keyboard character as it moves. Change lines 10, 70, and 90 and add 80 so that the program looks like this:

```
10 CLS: L=15360: POKE 16537, 32
20 R=PEEK(14420): G=L
30 IF R=8 L=L-64:  IF L<15360 L=L+64
40 IF R=16 L=L+64:  IF L>16383 L=L-64
50 IF R=32 L=L-1:  IF L<15360 L=15360
60 IF R=64 L=L+1:  IF L>16383 L=16383
70 POKE L, 191: I=PEEK(16537)
80 IF I<>8 AND I<>9 AND I<>10 AND I<>91 B=I
90 POKE G, B:  GOTO 20
RUN
```

Press a key, any key, then use the arrow keys to duplicate that character around the screen. To erase, use the (SPACEBAR). The quiz for the day is to figure out why this works!

For Thrill Seekers Only

For some real excitement, delete the second IF statement in line 40 (save the program before you do this; you are about to lose it!). RUN the program, and be sure to use the (←) key. We *told* you to be careful where you are poking! Now you've done it! That IF test protected the rest of memory from our merciless flashing cursor. You will have to reset the whole works if you want to use it again.

Controlling Strings

As you have seen, strings are quite a versatile tool to the graphic programmer. We have stuffed them with alphanumeric characters, graphic characters, control codes, and space compression codes. Could there possibly be anything that we have overlooked? Yes and no. No, there is nothing new to put into strings. Yes, there are new ways to put items in a string and lots of applications that no one has even thought of yet. One string-packing technique we have not yet covered is finding the location of a string in memory and poking in the values we want. Then we can use strings to hold look-up tables, machine language programs, and so forth.

The TRS-80 operating system keeps a three-byte index to each string variable used in a BASIC program. One byte holds the length of the string, and the other two bytes contain the memory location of the string itself.

```
               BYTE 1: LENGTH
INDEX          BYTE 2: LOCA-
               BYTE 3: TION


               BYTE ?: C
               BYTE ?: O
               BYTE ?: N
TRING          BYTE ?: T
               BYTE ?: E
               BYTE ?: N
               BYTE ?: T
               BYTE ?: S
```

Figure 5.2   The string variable three-byte index.

The variable pointer function, VARPTR, allows us to find the location of the index of any variable. To see how it works, type

```
NEW
10 CLEAR : A$="STRING"
20 V=VARPTR(A$) : PRINT V
```

The number printed is the location of the first byte of the index to A$, not the starting location of A$ itself. We have to examine bytes two and three of the index to find out where A$ is hiding. Add

```
30 LE=PEEK(V)
40 LSB=PEEK(V+1)
50 MSB=PEEK(V+2)
60 PRINT LE, LSB, MSB
RUN
```

The length of A$ is six. In lines 40 and 50, LSB and MSB are used to store the least significant byte and most significant byte of the location of A$. If the PEEK instruction displayed numbers in hexadecimal, we could simply place them side by side—MSB LSB—to get the location of A$ in HEX. For example, if LSB = 05H and MSB = 28H, then the location of A$ would be 2805H. Working in decimal, the location is calculated by multiplying MSB by 256 and adding the result to LSB. Add

```
70 L=LSB+MSB*256
80 PRINT L
LIST
RUN
```

Now all we have to do is to peek into our memory starting at location L to see what is stored in A$. Enter

```
90 FOR I=L TO L+LE-1
100 PRINT CHR$(PEEK(I))
110 NEXT I
RUN
```

Isn't that terrific?

You should be aware of a couple of pitfalls in using the VARPTR function. Strings stored in the string pool space tend to move around a lot, so you should always use VARPTR to check their position before examining the contents. Also, note that the PEEK instruction works on addresses up to 32767. If the string variable is at a higher numbered location, use PEEK (desired addressed − 65536).

3 String Packing

Dummy Strings

Now that we know how to locate string variables in memory, we can look at another way to fill them up with graphic codes. Keeping in mind that we don't want the string to wander around in memory, we will start by setting up a dummy string. We'll need to be careful to keep the value unchanged. Enter

```
NEW
10 DEFSTR A : CLS
20 A=":::::"
```

(Use 5 colons or any other character in line 20.)

We are going to find out where A is located, then poke graphic characters into the string, thus replacing the five colons. The location is easy. Add

```
30 L=PEEK(VARPTR(A)+1) + 256*PEEK(VARPTR(A)+2)
```

Line 30 calculates the location of A using bytes two and three of the index to A. It is just a compact version of lines 20 through 70 in the previous program.

Now we will set up a loop to ask for graphic character codes (128 through 191), then poke them into location L. Add

```
40 FOR I=1 TO LEN(A)
50 INPUT "GRAPHIC CODE"; N
60 POKE L+I-1, N
70 PRINT@ 480, A
80 NEXT I
RUN
```

Answer the five prompts with the numbers

$$141 \quad 140 \quad 140 \quad 191 \quad 140$$

You have just created your first Boeing 747. Not bad, but can it fly in formation? Enter

```
CLS: FOR P=0 TO 900 STEP 68: PRINT@ P, A: NEXT
```

This method of poking graphic characters in strings can be used to create larger diagrams. Simply redo line 20 using the desired number of dummy characters. As long as we don't use a LET statement to reassign different values to A, we can poke away at it all day.

Graphics Editor

Packing strings with graphic codes is so useful that several companies market programs to aid in entering characters into strings. Here is a simplified version. It is designed to be appended to the end of any program, either by typing it in or by merging it with the host program on a disk system. It will allow us to enter codes into several strings of our host program, provided that we have entered the appropriate number of dummy characters in the original strings. Type

```
NEW
60000  N$="": CLS: INPUT "ENTER VARIABLE NAME"; X$
60010  INPUT "ENTER SCREEN POSITION"; PO
60020  P=PEEK(16548)+256*PEEK(16549)
60030  N=PEEK(P)+256*PEEK(P+1): IF PEEK(P+4)=ASC(X$)
       GOTO 60050
60040  IF PEEK(N)+256*PEEK(N+1)=0 PRINT "VARIABLE
       NOT IN PROGRAM": GOTO 60010 ELSE P=N:
       GOTO 60030
60050  N1=INT((P+7)/256) : POKE VARPTR(N$)+1,
       P+7-256*N1: POKE VARPTR(N$)+2, N1:POKE
       VARPTR(N$), N-P-7
60060  CLS: FOR I=P+4 TO N-2: PRINT CHR$(PEEK(I));
       : NEXT I
60070  FOR I=P+4 TO N-2: PRINT@ 200, "DECIMAL:"; :
       X=PEEK(I)
60080  PRINT@ 208, X; TAB(22)"CHARACTER: "; : IF
       X>31 AND X<192 PRINT CHR$(X), ELSE PRINT
       "CONTROL",
60090  IF I-P-6>0 PRINT@ PO, LEFT$(N$,I-P-6);
60100  X$="": PRINT@ 234, "NEW"; : INPUT X$
60110  IF X$"" THEN 60130 ELSE IF ASC(X$)=91 AND
       I>P+4 I=I-1 : GOTO 60070
60120  X=VAL(X$): IF X=0 END ELSE IF X<0 OR X>255
       PRINT@ 33, "ERROR": GOTO 60090 ELSE POKE I, X
60130  NEXT
```

There are several techniques of interest in this program. First, lines 60020 through 60040 direct the search for the variable name by following the line number pointers embedded in the BASIC program. Second, N$ is a dummy variable used to display the contents of the variable being edited. Line 60050 recreates the index to N$ so that it points to the variable entered in line 60000. The use of a dummy variable allows the graphics editor to modify several different program lines.

Let's use the editor to store figure 5.3 in a string variable.

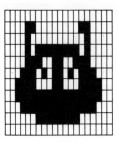

Figure 5.3   Bright eyes.

We have to add a dummy string with enough characters to contain the figure. Enter

```
10 A$="12345678901234567890123456 7"
```

Using the editor, we can poke graphic and space compression codes into A$. Type RUN 60000. Answer the prompt with A. The program will search line-by-line for a line starting with A. When the A is located, the program asks where it should display the figure. Use 410 for now. We can then edit the line character-by-character. The editing features are the following:

(ENTER)	Skip to next character
(◄) (ENTER)	Backspace through line
Ø	End editing before end of line
1<=NUMBER<=255	Change character to this code

Control codes and space compression codes are displayed as CONTROL. Use the (◄) to correct mistakes, and (Ø) to quit before the end of the line.

As soon as the variable A is located, the editor will display the line at the top of the screen and give you the opportunity to change the line character-by-character. Do not change the first few characters. Press **(ENTER)** until the first 1 is displayed. Then type these numbers, each followed by **(ENTER)**:

```
128  128  151  176  176  176  176  171  249
184  191  137  170  149  134  191  180  248
139  143  191  191  191  191  143  135  128
```

Most are graphic codes, but 249 and 248 represent space compression codes. Now type LIST 10. On the Model III, the figure will be listed as entered. On the Model I, it will be a mess! When Model I BASIC lists any line, it interprets all codes greater than 127 as BASIC key words. Don't worry, A$ will still print a nice graphics figure as long as you don't try to edit the line or save it on disk with the A option. To show off the figure, add

```
20 CLS: P=480
30 IF RND(2)=1 P1=1 ELSE P1=-1
40 FOR I=1 TO RND(20)
50 P=P+P1 : PRINT@ P, A$
60 NEXT I
70 GOTO 30
RUN
```

The editor can be used to create several graphic strings in one program. Use RUN 60000 to access the editor.

OUT Statement

he OUT statement is used to send information to any one of 256 ports available on
e TRS-80, numbered 0 through 255. Unfortunately, the only port used on the Model
s port 255, the cassette recorder. (If you are interested in taking advantage of the
her ports, see *Controlling the World*, by David A. Lien, Compusoft Publishing,
ic.) On the Model III, we can use any of the ports.

ou have already seen one use of the OUT statement in this chapter. Remember, it
ot us back to normal character width when combined with the correct POKE
atement. The OUT statement can also be used to create some crazy graphics effects.
nter the following program, and let loose your imagination:

```
EW
Ø CLS: INPUT I,J
Ø FOR L=1 TO 40
Ø OUT 236, I                (Model I, use OUT 255, I)
Ø FOR X=1 TO 8: NEXT X
Ø OUT 236, J                (Model I, use OUT 255, J)
Ø NEXT L: GOTO 10
UN
```

nter the following pairs of numbers:

Model I		Model III	
,Ø	Changes character width	4,Ø	4,4
,Ø	Wow! Sound, such as it is	2,Ø	Ø,2
,5	Listen closely for this one	2,2	6,2
,5	Sound and wavy display	6,Ø	

ou'll find these fairly typical of other combinations, but don't let me stop you from
xperimenting. Listen for the OUT statement in the next chapter.

Machine Language Graphics And Sound

Using Machine Language With BASIC

Why Machine Language?

We were just getting used to BASIC, so why throw this at us now? Because BASIC is a *slow* language, and animated graphics depend on speed. We spent all that time learning about building strings so that we could squeeze every last bit of speed out of BASIC. Unfortunately, there are going to be times when BASIC just can't perform, especially when machine language programs can run hundreds of times faster than BASIC programs.

Do we have to learn machine language? Of course not. We could probably spend years developing applications using the techniques we have developed to this point and never even miss machine language. If it turns out that speed is important but machine language is not our cup of tea, we can run out and buy one of those programs that compiles BASIC programs into machine code. In any event, feel free to skip this chapter without any loss of continuity. It will be waiting for you if you ever decide to take the leap. For those of us who are going to press on, we'll have to decide just how to approach this topic. Should we investigate assembly language or should we confine the discussion to how machine language routines can be used in conjunction with BASIC? The latter approach seems to be the easiest way to get our feet wet. Do we hear any nays? Good. The ayes have it.

Where Do We Put The Darned Thing?

We have several options. We can store our machine language routines in high memory by reserving space for them when we enter BASIC. We can store them in low memory and relocate the BASIC program to make room for them. For small routines, we can even store them right in the midst of the BASIC program itself. That's right! In fact, you have already seen the technique. Simply poke them into string variables. Now why didn't we think of that? The string variable approach is the one we will use in this chapter. If you write your own machine language programs using this approach, they must be relocatable.

Sample Program

Let us begin by poking a small 12-byte routine into a string variable. This will also be a good review of the VARPTR function. Enter

```
NEW
Ø M$="SCREENSCROLL"
Ø V=VARPTR(M$)
```

```
40 LS=PEEK(V+1): MS=PEEK(V+2)
50 L=LS + 256*MS
60
70 FOR I=0 TO 11
80 READ N
90 POKE L+I, N
100 NEXT I
110 DATA 33,191,63,17,255,63,1,192,3,237,184,201
```

In this program, M$ is the dummy string where the routine will be stored. V is the location of the three-byte index that points to the location of M$ while L is the location of the first character, S, in M$. Lines 70-100 read the machine language program from the DATA statement and poke it into M$ starting at location L. RUN the program, then LIST it. If everything went according to plan, line 20 should be a real mess. It looks like this on the Model I:

```
20 M$="!USING?ISA?VARPTRMKS$CLEARINKEY$"
```

It is even worse on the Model III. Don't worry. In its efforts to list line 20, BASIC interprets some of these numbers as normal parts of a BASIC program. The Model I interprets them as codes for keywords, and the Model III prints them as normal ASC characters, including the graphic characters. But it works. Boy, did we pull a fast one!

USR

Once the machine language program is written and stored in memory, executing it from BASIC is a breeze. First, tell the machine where the routine is located in memory. Second, execute it.

Whenever we are operating without a disk, we must poke the starting location of the routine into memory cells 16526 and 16527. Remember that the location of a string variable is stored in bytes two and three of its index. We have to transfer the least significant byte of the index to 16526 and the most significant byte to 16527:

```
POKE 16526, LS : POKE 16527, MS
```

Disk users must use the DEFUSR statement DEFUSR=L. Now, we don't know if you have a disk, but your computer does. Why don't you ask it? Type

```
IF PEEK(16396)=201 PRINT "OF COURSE NOT,
   SILLY" ELSE
PRINT "SURE DO"
```

Clever little beast. Location 16396 contains a 201 on power up only on a nondisk system. So we can take care of either case by adding

```
60 IF PEEK(16396)=201 POKE 16526, LS : POKE 16527
   MS ELSE DEFUSR=L
```

Now the machine knows where to find the routine.

Next, we have to execute the machine language program. All machine language programs are executed from BASIC with the USR function. Enter

```
130  X=USR(1)
```

The USR function allows us to pass information to and from the machine language routine. The 1 is passed to the machine language program, and the variable X will contain any information passed back to the BASIC program. Neither of these is used by the routine currently stored in M$. We simply want to execute the program. Before we RUN it, add

```
120  PRINT@ 64, "HEY, IT WORKED!"
140  GOTO 140
```

Then type CLS:RUN. What happened? When the USR function is called, the machine language routine is executed. This particular program causes the entire screen to scroll downward one line. Each line is copied to the line below it. The copy sequence is: line 15 copied to 16, 14 to 15, 13 to 14, . . ., and finally line 1 copied to line 2. So there are two copies of line 1 after the routine executes. To see it execute several times, change line 130 to:

```
130  FOR I=1 TO 16: X=USR(1): NEXT I
```

Then type

```
LIST
RUN
```

The screen scrolls downward 16 times, and the top line is replicated down the screen. For an interesting effect, add

```
140  PRINT@ 960,: LIST
RUN
```

The duplication of the top line can be used to clear the screen from the top down. Enter

```
10  CLEAR 100
120  PRINT@ 0, STRING$(64,32);
RUN
```

In fact, it can be used to move anything down the screen. Change these lines:

```
140  GOTO 140
120  CLS : PRINT@ 0, STRING$(64,191);
RUN
```

See if you can dream up your own applications for this routine.

Entering The Data

Take another look at line 110:

```
110  DATA 33,191,63,17,255,63,1,192,3,237,184,201
```

It's a safe bet that most machine language programs don't start out as a string of decimal numbers. In fact, you will usually find them listed in hexadecimal form. The above routine originally looked like this:

```
HEX CODE              MNEMONICS
21BF3F                LD  HL,3FBF
11FF3F                LD  DE,3FFF
01C003                LD  BC,03C0
EDB8                  LDDR
C9                    RET
```

There has to be an easy way to translate programs from hex into decimal. One tried and true method is to get out your ''T.I. Programmer'' calculator and convert the numbers one at a time:

```
HEX                   DECIMAL
21                    33
BF                    191
3F                    63
 .                     .
 .                     .
etc.                  etc.
```

Another method if you have Disk BASIC is to use hex notation—&H21 for 21H, for example—but there is a much easier way if you are willing to type a few extra lines into your program. Why not enter the data in hex form and let the computer do the translation for you?

Add these lines to the current program:

```
*10 CLEAR 100: DEFSTR S
 70 I=1: READ S: IF S="END" GOTO 120
 80 GOSUB 100: IF S1<>" " THEN N=D*16: I=I+1:
    GOSUB 100: N=N+D: POKE L, N: L=L+1
 90 I=I+1: IF I< LEN(S) THEN 80 ELSE 70
100 S1=MID$(S,I,1): D=ASC(S1)-48+7*(S1>"9"): RETU
110 DATA 21BF3F 11FF3F 01C003 EDB8 C9
115 DATA END
```

RUN it to be sure it works the same. You'll notice that it takes a little longer poking the values into the string, but that's a small price to pay for the added convenience. Besides, the USR routine works just as fast.

Lines 70 through 100 read data in hex form, convert it to decimal, and poke it into the dummy string. The hex bytes in the DATA statements can be separated by commas or spaces, and grouped as you see fit. END must be on a separate DATA line or separated by a comma.

Retype line 20 to read as follows:

```
20 M$="SCREENSCROLL"
```

The final listing of the screen scroll program should look like this:

```
10 CLEAR 100: DEFSTR S
20 M$="SCREENSCROLL"
```

```
    V=VARPTR(M$)
    LS=PEEK(V+1): MS=PEEK(V+2)
    L=LS + 256*MS
    IF PEEK(16396)=201 POKE 16526, LS : POKE 16527,
    MS ELSE DEFUSR=L
    I=1: READ S: IF S="END" GOTO 120
    GOSUB 100: IF S1<>" " THEN N=D*16: I=I+1:
    GOSUB 100: N=N+D: POKE L, N: L=L+1
    I=I+1: IF I< LEN(S) THEN 80 ELSE 70
100 S1=MID$(S,I,1): D=ASC(S1)-48+7*(S1>"9"): RETURN
110 DATA 21BF3F 11FF3F 01C003 EDB8 C9
115 DATA END
120 CLS : PRINT@ 0, STRING$(64,191);
130 FOR I=1 TO 16: X=USR(1): NEXT I
140 GOTO 140
```

...ve this program as HEXENTRY on cassette or disk, as we are going to use it in the ...xt section.

Creating Your Own

..., this is not going to be a crash course in Z-80 machine language. We are about to ...n through another example so that you can appreciate the hex entry routine and be ...prised of certain problems in using strings to store machine language programs.

...cture yourself in your easy chair thumbing through your favorite Z-80 magazine. ...a page 3, there is a machine language routine that you have been losing sleep over ...r several weeks. So, you naturally load in our HEXENTRY program (did you save ...') and prepare to enter the routine from the magazine.

... make the program a little more general, change line 120 to

```
120 INPUT "PRESS <ENTER> FOR USR ROUTINE"; I$
```

...e hex routine is listed in the magazine as

```
    21DF3D              LXI H,3DDF
    3699                LD (HL),99
    C9                  RET
```

... you quickly go to work on lines 20 and 110. Let's see, there are six bytes to enter:
... DF 3D 36 99 C9. So, line 20 should be

```
    M$="123456"
```

...d thanks to lines 70 through 100, we can enter line 110 as

```
110 DATA 21DF3D 3699 C9
```

...e how easy that is! Because we don't know what this routine will do yet, try it with a
...S first:

```
130 CLS: X=USR(1)
```
...JN

Well, what did you expect? A fireworks display from six bytes of machine code? At least it worked and was easy to enter.

Passing Values

One useful feature of the USR function is that it allows us to send one integer variabl to the machine language routine and bring one back. In the current setup, we are sending a 1 in line 130 and storing the returned value in X. Unfortunately, the machine language routine isn't taking advantage of either feature. In order to receive the 1, the machine language routine must execute a CALL 0A7F (CD 7F 0A). The 1 will then show up in the HL register. In order to send a value back to the BASI program, the machine language routine must store the value in the HL register pair and execute a JP 0A9A (C3 9A 0A) in place of the normal return (C9).

Let's send a screen location to the machine language program so that we can control where the graphic character is printed. Type

```
110 DATA CD7F0A 3699 C9
120 INPUT "ENTER A SCREEN LOCATION 15360-16320";
130 CLS: X=USR(N)
140 GOTO 120
RUN
```

Enter as many values in the indicated range as you like. To pass a value to the BASIC program, make these changes:

```
20 M$="12345678"
110 DATA CD7F0A 3699 C39A0A
135 PRINT@N-15298, X;
RUN
```

Line 135 prints the value received in X. Your listing should now be as follows:

```
10  CLEAR 100: DEFSTR S
20  M$="12345678"              (a mess)
30  V=VARPTR(M$)
40  LS=PEEK(V+1): MS=PEEK(V+2)
50  L=LS + 256*MS
60  IF PEEK(16396)=201 POKE 16526,LS : POKE 16527,
    MS ELSE DEFUSR=L
70  I=1: READ S: IF S="END" GOTO 120
80  GOSUB 100: IF S1<>" " THEN N=D*16: I=I+1:
    GOSUB 100: N=N+D: POKE L, N: L=L+1
90  I=I+1:IF I< LEN(S) THEN 80 ELSE 70
100 S1=MID$(S,I,1): D=ASC(S1)-48+7*(S1>"9"): RETU
110 DATA CD7F0A 3699 C3A90A
115 DATA END
120 PRINT: INPUT "ENTER SCREEN LOCATION
    ,15360-16320"; N
130 CLS: X=USR(N)
135 PRINT@ N-15298, X;
140 GOTO 120
```

aveat Emptor

oring machine language routines in strings has its drawbacks. Listings can be very
tidy, and we must avoid using Ø in our machine code. BASIC uses zeros to mark
e end of a program line. If we poke a zero right in the middle of a string, BASIC will
terpret everything to the right of the zero as a separate program line with its own line
mber. Once a zero value has been poked into the string, the program will not run
rrectly a second time; a fresh version of the program must be loaded.

f course, there is a fairly neat solution to this problem. Use the STRING$ function
define our dummy string:

```
Ø M$=STRING$(30,Ø)
```

oom for 30 bytes.)

efining M$ with the STRING$ function forces the string to be stored in the string
ol area, not in the midst of the BASIC program. This will not only clean up the
ting, but also allows us to throw anything into the string. (Well, *almost* anything.)

re you ready for the bad news ? We must take a few precautions in using this
ethod.

rst, we must clear sufficient string pool space for the string. A good rule of thumb is
use twice as many bytes as are necessary for the string.

cond, be aware that strings stored in the string pool space do not always stay put.
e string pool area is periodically reorganized as variables are reassigned. (For a
tter understanding of how this is done, see Chapter 7.) To protect against losing a
GR routine, always recalculate the location of the dummy string variable just before
ing the USR command. It can be very embarrassing to attempt to run a machine
nguage program that has moved on to greener pastures!

ird, note that the string pool space is in high memory. If you are using a 32 K or
K system, your dummy strings will be stored way above the 32767 limit of the
EEK and POKE statements. If you intend to use this method with a large system,
u must change line 50 to

```
Ø L= LS + 256*MS : IF L>32767 L=L-65536
```

fact, the only program changes necessary to use the string pool space on the current
ogram are the ones mentioned for lines 20 and 50. Try it. And, this would be
other good time to save the program.

Some Graphic Routines

raphic Character Reverse

e scope of this book does not permit a complete investigation of machine language
aphic techniques; however, there are a few routines that may prove particularly
eful. One is a complete screen whiteout. Another is a routine that reverses all
aphic characters on the screen (i.e., resets all lit blocks and sets all unlit blocks).

Here is one written by the one and only James Garon and modified by your authors:*

LABEL	HEX	MNEMONICS	COMMENTS
	21FF3F	LD HL,3FFF	LOAD HL WITH END OF SCREEN
	063C	LD B,3C	USED LATER TO SEE IF DONE
START	7E	LD A,(HL)	GET NEXT BYTE FROM SCREEN
	FE80	CP 80	IS IT A GRAPHIC BYTE?
	3808	JR C	JUMP IF NOT TO NEXT
	FEC0	CP C0	SPACE COMPRESSION CODE?
	3004	JR NC	JUMP IF SO TO NEXT
	2F	CPL	REVERSE CHARACTER
	C640	ADD 40	RESTORE GRAPHIC BIT
	77	LD (HL),A	SEND CHARACTER TO SCREEN
NEXT	2B	DEC HL	POINT TO NEXT LOCATION
	7C	LD A,H	PREPARE FOR END TEST
	B8	CP B	STILL ON THE SCREEN?
	30EE	JR NC	IF SO, BACK TO START
	C9	RET	RETURN TO BASIC

This routine requires a dummy string of 24 bytes. It alters ASCII codes between 127 and 192 only, so it does not harm text or special character sets. To see what it can do, enter the routine in the DATA lines, then change the following lines:

```
120 CLS: FOR I=1 TO 100:
    PRINT@ RND(1023), CHR$(31+RND(224));: NEXT
130 PRINT@ 960, "PRESS ANY KEY TO REVERSE GRAPHIC
140 I$=INKEY$: IF I$<>"" X=USR(1)
150 GOTO 140
```

Delete line 135 and RUN.

On the Model III, type PRINT CHR$(21) in immediate mode to activate the special character set.

ROM Routines

One way to ease into programming in machine language is to use routines that are already stored in the read-only memory. Keep in mind that this approach can be very unrewarding if you move your program to a machine with a newer ROM in which the location of your favorite ROM routine is different. That problem aside, ROM routines can greatly shorten your code and cut down on programming time. The rest of the routines discussed in this section will be of this type. To use them, you will need to know three things: where they are located, what input they require, and what they do.

Display Character

At location 0033H, there is a routine that will send the byte stored in register A to the current cursor position. You can manipulate the cursor position by changing location 4020H and 4021H. We will use this routine to white out the screen. The CLS in line

*Reprinted with permission of Softside Publishing, © 1980

...0 will position the cursor for us at the top left corner of the screen. The program
...ting is as follows:

```
3EBF                    LD A, BFH
CD3300                  CALL 0033H
18F9                    JR. -6
```

...EBF loads the A register with BFH (191 — solid graphics character).
...03300 calls the display routine.
...8F9 jumps back to the first line

...e call to 0033H increments the cursor position, so that the entire screen will be
...vered. Unfortunately, this routine gets us into an infinite loop, so we must find a
...ay to exit the USR routine.

...eyboard Control

...rtunately, we can add a type of INKEY$ function by a call to 035BH. If a key is
...pressed, its value will be stored in the A register. If no key is depressed, the A
...gister will contain a zero. The new code needed is this:

```
CD5B03                  CALL 035BH
FE00                    CP 0H
C0                      RETNZ
18F3                    JR -13
```

...e first line calls the INKEY$ routine. FE00 compares the value returned to the A
...gister with zero. If a key has been pressed, control is returned to the BASIC
...ogram. Otherwise, the program jumps back to the beginning. The changes needed
...e these:

```
...LETE 130-150
..0 DATA 3EBF CD3300 CD5B03 FE00 C0 18F3
..0 X=USR(1)
..N
```

...ss the (SPACEBAR) to exit the USR routine.

...ne Delay

...now have a smooth exit from the routine, but the interference on the screen is
...turbing, isn't it. We can clean it up with a short time delay. This routine is located
...0H and requires only that you store a loop counter in the BC register pair. The
...essary changes are these:

```
010001                  LD BC,0100H
CD6000                  CALL 0060H
18ED                    JR -19
```

...ange line 110 to

```
..0 DATA 3EBF CD3300 010001 CD6000 CD5B03 FE00
    C0 18ED
..N
```

...w we are getting somewhere!

Random Numbers

Randomizing is often a welcome addition to break up any monotony in the display. We can choose a random character by replacing 3EBF with

```
21A000                    LD HL, 00A0H
CDCC14                    CALL 14CCH
CD7F0A                    CALL 0A7FH
7D                        LD A, L
C620                      ADD 20H
```

and by changing 18ED to 18E3. The random number routine works by placing an integer value in the A register, followed by calls to 14CCH and 0A7FH. A random number from one to the value in A will be placed in locations 4121H and 4122H as well as in the HL register pair. We will use the routine to place a random number from 1 to 160 in HL. By transferring the value in L to A and then adding 32, we change the range to 33 through 192. This keeps control codes from disturbing the display. Change line 110 to

```
110 DATA 21A000 CDCC14 CD7F0A 7D C620 CD3300 0100
    CD6000 CD5B03 FE00 C0 18E3
RUN
```

(Don't forget to change the last byte.)

That's all for ROM routines.

3 Machine Language Sound Routines

Hang on to your seats! We are about to enter the realm of bust-your-eardrums sound to augment your graphic displays. What's our rationale? First, sound can greatly enhance the impact of your programs (and that, after all, is what this book is all about), and second, sound routines are no more difficult to implement than other machine routines; the same techniques can be employed.

The Connection

The sound is sent out the cassette port through the AUX plug of the cassette cable. The easiest way to hear the sound is to plug this cable into a small amplifier. Radio Shack's catalog #277-1008 would be a good bet, and it should cost only about $15. Just plug it in, turn up the volume, and get on with the programming.

If you don't want to make that investment, you can prepare your cassette for CSAV and record sound on tape. Rewind the tape and remove the earplug to listen to the sound. To hear the sound as it is being recorded, replace the earphone plug with the earphone that came with the recorder. Don't place the earplug in your ear—the sound can be quite *loud*! If you don't necessarily want to record your melodious creations, you'll have to fool the recorder into thinking that it has a cassette in it. Remove the cassette and depress the cassette sensor before you press (PLAY) and (RECORD). You will find the sensor at the left rear of the cassette area in a CTR-41 recorder.

Music Maestro

es, yes, this chapter *is* on machine language, but we will start out by generating
und from BASIC. Sound is generated by sending alternating positive and negative
•ltages to a speaker. The speaker cone then vibrates according to the frequency of
e change between the two voltages. The faster the change, the higher the note; the
›wer the oscillation, the lower the note will sound.

•sitive and negative voltages are sent with the OUT command. Prepare your
nplifier or cassette and enter the following:

```
EW
∅ DEFINT A-Z
∅ OUT 255, 1
∅ OUT 255, 2
∅ GOTO 40
JN
```

ipee—noise! Press (BREAK) to stop it. Controlling the duration of the tone is simple.
dd

```
᠈ INPUT D
᠈ FOR I=1 TO D
᠈ NEXT I
᠈ GOTO 20
(ST
JN
```

• control the length of the tone, enter numbers from zero to whatever you can
•erate. The pitch is controlled by changing the oscillation between the two OUT
•tements. Enter

```
EW
᠈ DEFINT A-Z
᠈ OUT 255, 1
᠈ OUT 255, 2
᠈ GOTO 20
JN
```

d remember that tone. Now add

```
᠈ REM
JN
```

ne 30 slows down the switching between positive and negative voltages, hence a
›wer tone. Why don't we make line 30 into a timing loop to control the pitch? Add

```
᠈ FOR T=1TO1: NEXT T
JN
```

y goodness! That's too low. And the larger the loop, the lower the tone would be.
›, how do we raise the pitch in BASIC? Try

```
OUT255, 1: OUT255, 2: GOTO 5
JN
```

ll sounds like a baritone. Afraid that's about as fast as BASIC can pedal.

Machine Language To Save The Day

Fortunately, speed is the forté of machine language. With it, we can place a timing delay after each OUT command and still generate a tone so high in pitch that your ear may not even hear it.

Here is a short annotated routine that generates a single tone. The frequency and duration are determined by the argument of the USR function in BASIC. Look at the comments. You'll find that the approach is quite similar to that used in BASIC.

```
       HEX        MNEMONICS                COMMENTS
CD 7F 0A  CALL 0A7FH  LOAD THE USR ARGUMENT INTO THE
                      HL REGISTER: DURATION IN H AND
                      FREQUENCY IN L
CB 24     SLA H       DOUBLE THE DURATION
45        LD B,L      LOAD FREQUENCY INTO REGISTER B
3E 01     LD A,1      PREPARE FOR OUT 255,1 COMMAND
D3 FF     OUT FFH,A   SEND 1 TO CASSETTE PORT
10 FE     DJNZ        TIMING LOOP: DECREMENTS B
                      REGISTER TO ZERO
45        LD B,L      LOAD FREQUENCY INTO REGISTER B
3E 02     LD A,2      PREPARE FOR OUT 255,2 COMMAND
D3 FF     OUT FFH,A   SEND 2 TO CASSETTE PORT
10 FE     DJNZ        TIMING LOOP: DECREMENTS B
                      REGISTER TO ZERO
25        DEC H       H=H-1
20 EF     JRNZ -17D   IF H<>0 JUMP BACK TO THIRD LINE
                      (LD B,L)
C9        RET         RETURN TO BASIC
```

Don't get too hung up on deciphering the machine code. Load the HEXENTRY program from the first section of this chapter (here's hoping you saved it earlier), and make sure that there is string space for 23 bytes in line 20. Enter the sound routine in the DATA line.

A single tone is generated each time a USR function is executed. The desired frequency and duration are sent to the routine via the argument of the USR function. Because we can send only one number to the routine, we can let BASIC combine the two numbers in such a way that the machine language routine can unravel them again. It sounds difficult, but it is actually very easy. Add

```
120 INPUT "ENTER FREQUENCY,DURATION"; F, D
130 X=USR(F+256*D)
140 GOTO 120
RUN
```

The range on the frequency is 0 to 255. One gives the highest pitch, 255 gives a low pitch, and 0 acts like 256 to give the lowest pitch. The range on the duration is 0 to 127. A very short note is obtained from 1, and 127 gives a long note. Finally, 0 acts like a 128. (You should note that lower notes have a longer duration.) Don't exceed the range limitations unless you want unpredictable results.

Note that the system clock causes fuzzy tones. Disk users can correct this by changing the end of line 60 to

```
ELSE DEFUSR = L : CMD"T"
```

ur First Song

e thinking of a good melody while the orchestra tunes:

```
RANDOM
20 X=USR(RND(255)+256*RND(127)): GOTO 120
UN
```

K, here's a good one. Type

```
120 ON ERROR GOTO 220
130 READ F : IF F<0 GOSUB 160 : GOTO 130
140 READ D
150 X=USR(F+256*D): GOTO 130
160 FOR I=1 TO -F: NEXT I: RETURN
170 DATA 111,80,111,80,120,80,120,80,128,120,128,
    80,111,40
180 DATA 120,40,111,80,111,80,120,80,120,80,128,
    120,-20
190 DATA 111,40,128,40,94,80,94,80,100,80,100,80,
    111,60,
200 DATA 100,40,111,60,128,40,140,60,150,60,150,
    60,170,55
210 DATA 170,55,190,80,190,80
220 GOTO 220
RUN
```

he data alternate between frequency and duration. Use negative numbers for a rest.
ake up your own data if you like. If you really get hooked on this, there are many
rdware/software products on the market that give your TRS-80 several
multaneous voices. *Enjoy*!

Special Graphics Considerations

Speed Comparisons

Different Graphic Techniques

Choosing the right graphic technique can be a bit frustrating. Each of the techniques has both advantages and drawbacks. Before you dive into any graphics project, carefully consider the speed required to give the desired effect. Interactive arcade-type games, for example, often require nearly simultaneous animation, keyboard input, and sound output. The speed required is rarely feasible in BASIC; hence the need for machine language. Clever use of string packing and PRINT@ can often be used as an alternative when the action is a little less frantic. POKE can be used effectively in certain situations. And, of course, nothing beats SET and RESET for plain old convenience in plotting functions, even if they *are* slow!

A good means of comparing the relative speeds of the different techniques is to set them hard at work on a nice time-consuming task like painting the screen white. Let's see how the SET statement fares on this one:

```
NEW
10 CLS: CLEAR 260: DEFSTR S
20 INPUT "PRESS <ENTER> WHEN READY"; S
30 FORY=0TO47: FORX=0TO127: SET(X,Y): NEXT: NEXT
40 GOTO 40
RUN
```

Whew! About 40 seconds. That's quite a few nanoseconds! Maybe POKE will be a little faster. Change 30 to

```
30 FORX=15360TO16383: POKEX, 191: NEXT
RUN
```

Six seconds. Better, but still exasperatingly slow for some folks. How about PRINT@? Change

```
30 S=STRING$(255,191):
   PRINT S; S; S; S; STRING$(3,191);: POKE 16383, 191
RUN
```

(Remember, can't PRINT the last screen position.) One second. Not bad at all. And, if you think *that* was fast, sink your fingers into *this* one:

```
NEW
10 IF PEEK(16396)=201 THEN L=16526 ELSE DEFUSR=32756
20 POKE L, 244: POKE L+1, 127
30 CLS: POKE 16561, 243: POKE 16562, 127
40 FOR X=32756 TO 32767: READ N: POKE X, N: NEXT
```

SEVEN

```
50 DATA 62,59,33,255,63,54,191,43,188,32,250,201
60 INPUT "PRESS <ENTER> WHEN READY"; I$
70 X=USR(0)
80 GOTO 80
RUN
```

They just don't make them much faster than that!

Racing Stripes In Program Design?

The particular graphics technique we choose is not the only factor in the speed of our graphic displays. The overall design and implementation of the program can have considerable impact, too. Realize that BASIC is an interpretive language. That is, it not only has to decode each instruction into a series of equivalent machine language instructions, but it also has to search for line numbers and variables and convert all decimal constants and line numbers to binary. Obviously, the less work we give it to do, the faster our programs will execute.

Squeezing the last ounce of speed out of a BASIC program does not always require a total rewrite. Programs typically spend most of their time executing only a small portion of the code. These high-use areas of the program should be streamlined by removing remarks and by using both short variable names and multiple statement lines. Those of you who appreciate well-documented code may cringe at these changes. But where speed is a primary consideration, remarks and single statement lines become unaffordable luxuries.

Defining Variable Types

TRS-80 BASIC uses a wide range of variable types. The variable type can be specified by suffixing the variable name with one of these symbols: $, %, !, #. Or, the type can be defined at the beginning of the program with DEFSTR, DEFINT, DEFSNG, or DEFDBL. The latter approach will increase program speed by reducing the amount of information BASIC has to read. The most important speed consideration with regard to variable types is that BASIC handles integer variables much more efficiently than the default variable type (single precision). Use integer variables to increase execution speed.

Eliminate Constants

Another way to cut down on execution time is to replace often-used constants by variables. It may sound odd, but each constant encountered has to be converted to binary *every time* BASIC reads that line. If the constant is replaced by a variable, it only has to be converted one time. The larger the constant, the greater the savings. Try these examples:

```
                          5    A=123456
10 FOR I=1 TO 2000        10 FOR I=1 TO 2000
20 X=123456+123456        20 X=A+A
30 NEXT                   30 NEXT
```

The Upside-Down Approach

Frequent hopping around to various parts of the program can also be a big time-waster. When speed is important, eliminate jumps to short subroutines. We may have to retype the subroutine a few times, but that is the price we pay for greater speed. Join the statements of the routine together on one line, separating the statements by colons. If the jump to the subroutine is conditional (e.g., IF X>0 GOSUB 2000), then the jump can be eliminated by placing the routine at the end of the IF statement. For example:

```
IF X>0 PRINT Z-16*T: T=T-1: SET(0,0)
```

Routines that are impractical to duplicate are not a total loss. The placing of these routines near the beginning of the program can be a big time-saver. Each time BASIC encounters a GOTO or a GOSUB, it starts searching for the line number from the beginning of the program. It has to translate each line number to binary and compare it to the desired number. Placing often-used routines near the beginning of the program means not only less searching, but also smaller line numbers and therefore, less decoding.

So, how do we organize a program to take advantage of this fact? Start the program off with a jump to high line numbers where all the program initializing will take place. Then jump down to the intermediate line numbers for the main body of the program. Finally, keep all the often-used subroutines near the beginning of the program. Sound crazy? Maybe, but it's just another way to defeat the speed demon without using a BASIC compiler or machine language.

String Organization In Memory

One of the pitfalls of heavy use of strings and arrays is unexpected time delays. A program may be chugging along smoothly, then suddenly freeze for a minute or two for no apparent reason. The culprit is likely to be variable reorganization in memory. Try this sample program:

```
NEW
10 DIM M$(5000)
20 PRINT "INTRODUCING SLOW GRAPHICS"
30 A$=CHR$(166)
40 B$=CHR$(179)
50 C$=CHR$(153)
60 PRINT TAB(12) A$ STRING$(11,B$) C$
RUN
```

Should it take that long to create A$, B$, and C$? Not in our book. RUN it again and notice the delay after line 20 is printed.

The problem boils down to the order in which BASIC variable types are located in memory. All nonsubscripted variables are stored before arrays. In the above program, 15,000 memory cells (3 for each string) are reserved for the string array M$. When the three strings A$, B$, and C$ are subsequently defined, the entire M$ array is shifted upwards to make room for the smaller strings. This causes the inordinate delay. To correct the problem, either move lines 30 through 50 before line 10, or add

```
5 A$="": B$="": C$=""
RUN
```

Merely mentioning the simple strings before the D I M statement is enough to solve the problem. Once space is reserved for the unsubscripted variables, there is no need to move M$.

One Down, One To Go

Unfortunately, subscripted variables are only part of the problem. A major irritation for graphics users is the automatic reorganization of the string pool space. This is a special section of memory set aside for string manipulation. Each time a variable that has been stored in the string area is assigned a new value, a complete new copy of it is stored in the free space area, regardless of the relative sizes of the new and old versions. The memory previously used by that variable becomes an unusable hole in the string storage area. When all the free string space is used up, the holes are recombined to form free space at the bottom of the string storage area, and the variables are shuttled to the top. If there are many holes, the pause during this reorganization can be very lengthy.

A Closer Look

Let's take a closer peek into what causes a string to be stored in the string area in the first place. We can use the function F R E to find out. This function tells us how much of the string pool space is available at any time. It also causes a string area reorganization. Type

```
NEW
10 CLEAR 20
100 PRINT "FREE STRING SPACE="FRE(A$)
RUN
```

No surprises here. We haven't assigned any values to strings, so all 20 memory cells reserved for string use in line 10 should be available. A $ is a dummy string. We would get the same result if B $ were used. Add now

```
20 A$="STRING"
RUN
```

Hold on there! Where is the string A $ hiding if it is not in the string pool space? Variables assigned to literal strings as in line 20 are not stored in the string space. The variable pointer points right to the BASIC program. The string pool space is used only when work must be done to create the string. Try

```
20 A$="STRING$": GOSUB 100
30 A$=LEFT$(A$,7): GOSUB 100
40 B$=A$: GOSUB 100
50 B$="SURPRISE": GOSUB 100
60 LIST
70 END
110 RETURN
RUN
```

Let's take it line by line. Line 20 uses no string pool space because the assignment was made with a literal string. In line 30, a string function LEFT$ is used, causing the resultant string to be stored in string pool area. Line 40 uses seven more string pool locations since A$ was located in the pool space already. Line 50 again uses a literal string (no string manipulation functions). Now, B$ is stored in the program, thus opening up the pool space previously occupied by B$.

Are you ready for the quiz? Put on those thinking caps! What would happen if we changed

```
60 A$=B$: GOSUB 100
```

Sure enough—since the contents of B$ are stored in the program, there is no need to use string pool space for the newest version of A$. So, all the string pool memory is freed.

What can we conclude from this exercise? Probably that the string pool space is used to store variables created by string manipulation functions. This includes LEFT$, RIGHT$, MID$, concatenation (+), and STRING$. So, you can keep strings out of this area by avoiding string functions.

Making Doughnut Holes

Strings are stored in the string pool space from the top down. The following program would store both strings in the string pool space:

```
10 A$="STR"+"ING"
20 B$=A$
```

And would look like this:

```
▶▶▶▶▶▶▶▶STRINGSTRING
        B$       A$
```

The concatenation in line 10 causes A$ to be stored in the string area. If

```
30 B$=A$
```

were added, the string space would look like this:

```
▶▶STRINGSTRINGSTRING
    B$    HOLE   A$
```

The designers of the TRS-80 ROM decided that when strings in the pool space are reassigned, a complete new copy would be made, leaving an unused hole in the string area. This increases the speed of string use since new variables can be deposited in the first unused spot at the bottom of the string area without moving a lot of strings around. Unfortunately, these holes use up a lot of string space. When the operating system runs out of room for new strings, an automatic reorganization takes place. All the holes are moved to the bottom of the string area, and the variables are concatenated at the top. Because this reorganization is very time-consuming, we can't afford to have it take place during a dynamic graphics display.

What can we do to avoid this delay? That depends on your system. If it has plenty of memory, an easy way to avoid the reorganization delay is to clear as much room as possible for the string pool. If you don't have much extra memory to play with, try

1) using numeric variables instead of strings when possible.
2) storing strings with the LET or READ statements.
3) minimizing the use of concatenation and substring functions such as LEFT$, MID$, and RIGHT$.
4) using space compression codes when storing blank spaces.

3 Input

Fundamental to the implementation of graphics on the video screen is user control of the action. A whole new level of appreciation is added when the user can interact with the program. Beginning programmers are usually introduced to the INPUT statement as the means of telling the computer what they want. INPUT allows a prompting message, displays a question mark on the screen, and accepts numerical or string information from the keyboard *as long as* the input is terminated with the (ENTER) key. The last feature is where the utility of the INPUT statement comes up short. INPUT not only forces a ? on the screen, but it also locks the program in a loop waiting for user input. Everything on the screen freezes until (ENTER) is pressed. Ducks aren't supposed to stand still at the penny arcade. For real-time action, INPUT is put out.

Here Comes INKEY$

INKEY$ is a string function that enables us to receive information from the keyboard without requiring the use of the (ENTER) key. Using INKEY$, we can make virtually any key perform special functions. We can use the arrow keys to move a figure around the screen, or the (SPACEBAR) to activate a laser cannon.

How does it work? Location 16537 is a one-byte buffer that stores the ASCII value of any key that is depressed. The value stays in the buffer until another key is depressed or until the INKEY$ function is used. When another key is depressed, its value replaces the one previously stored there. So the buffer stores only the value of the most recently pressed key. When the INKEY$ function is invoked, the value stored in the buffer is transferred to the INKEY$ function, and the buffer is emptied. The INKEY$ function can then be evaluated, printed, or stored in another string variable. Here is an example of its use:

```
NEW
10 A$=INKEY$
20 IF A$="" GOTO 10 ELSE PRINT "WE GOT ONE,
   MA!",, A$, ASC(A$)
30 GOTO 10
RUN
```

The buffer starts out empty. As long as no key is depressed, the program goes back to recheck the buffer. When a key is depressed, its character value is stored in A$ and printed. Note that if the key is an action key, printing A$ causes that action to occur.

Try some of the control keys. You should find that they generate these values:

KEY	NO SHIFT	SHIFT
◖	8	24
◗	9	25
◉	10	26
◉	91	27
(BREAK)	1	1
(CLEAR)	31	31
(ENTER)	13	13

Flashing Cursor

Using INKEY$, we can choose any character we want for our cursor and also have it flash. This is very useful in a business or an educational setting where attention must be directed to different locations on the screen. We must first find the current location of the cursor. Try

```
NEW
100 CLEAR 200: CLS: PRINT@ 400, "ENTER:";
110 P=PEEK(16416)+256*PEEK(16417)  : L=P
RUN
PRINT L
```

L is used as the current cursor location, and P is the starting position of the input. For the moment, they are the same. The number printed should be in the range 15360 to 16383. For a little more convenience, let's put it in the range 0 through 1023. Use

```
110 P=PEEK(16416)+256*(PEEK(16417)-60)  : L=P
RUN
PRINT L
```

Now we print the cursor with a pause (use any character you want):

```
120 PRINT@ L, CHR$(143); : FOR I=1 TO 10: NEXT
```

Test for a key:

```
130 I$=INKEY$ : IF I$<>"" THEN 160
```

Print a blank if no key has been pressed yet:

```
140 PRINT@ L, " "; : FOR I=1 TO 10: NEXT
```

Give them another chance:

```
150 I$=INKEY$ : IF I$="" GOTO 120
160 PRINT@ L, I$
RUN
```

Model III owners can turn on a blinking cursor with POKE 16412,0. The blink can be turned off by poking a non-zero number to 16412. In addition, the cursor character can be changed by poking the ASCII number of the desired character to 16419.

Multicharacter INKEY$

If more than one character is to be entered, we can store it in string A$ with

```
160 I=ASC(I$)
170 IF I=13 THEN 210
190 A$=A$+I$ : PRINT@ P, A$
200 L=L+1: GOTO 120
210 PRINT@ P+64, A$
RUN
```

In fact, we could even limit the number of characters acceptable in A$ by changing line 200 to

```
200 IF LEN(A$)<10 L=L+1: GOTO 120
RUN
```

Or, make the limit a variable that can be changed at different points in the program.

The numbering of this program segment starts with 100 to emphasize that it is best used as a subroutine. Call it whenever you want a flashing cursor and greater control of the input. And, speaking of greater control. . . .

Error Trapping

Another advantage that INKEY$ has over INPUT is the ability to protect against certain operator errors. A very easy way to do this is to add

```
180 IF I<32 GOTO 120
RUN
```

This line protects against any unwanted linefeeds, screen clears, and so on. Of course, we can handle each code individually if we choose. For example, let's give our operator the ability to erase mistakes with the left arrow key:

```
160 I=ASC(I$): IF I=8 AND LEN(A$)>0 A$=LEFT$(A$
     ,LEN(A$)-1): PRINT@ P, A$+CHR$(30): L=L-1
RUN
```

Press the (◀) to erase the previous character and press (ENTER) to terminate input. Voilà.

A Better Mousetrap

The INKEY$ function has one major flaw: There is no way to repeat a key entry simply by holding the key down. Once a key is depressed, it must be released then pressed again for the INKEY$ buffer to sense it. Try holding down the (◀) in the current program to erase two or three characters at a time. Any luck? What good is a great computer like the TRS-80 if it doesn't have the smarts to repeat a key until it is released! All we have to do is roll up our sleeves and dig a little deeper into the forbidden zone of the reserved RAM area to find what we are looking for.

Change line 160 to

```
160 I=ASC(I$): IF PEEK(14400)=32 AND LEN(A$)>0
    A$=LEFT$(A$,LEN(A$)-1): PRINT@ P, A$+CHR$(30):
    L=L-1: GOTO 160
RUN
```

Enter several characters, then hold down the left arrow and watch it repeat! How sweet it is. By the way, this would be a good time to save the input program.

How It Works

If you have an ounce of curiosity in you, you'll want to know how this works and how to apply it to your own programs. Each time a key on the keyboard is pressed, it changes the contents of a fixed memory location. Location 14400, for example, contains a zero when no key is depressed. The value changes to 32 when the ⬤ is pressed, and stays that way until the key is released.

In fact, every one of the 52 keys on the entire keyboard is linked to a specific memory cell somewhat like the video display. There is one major difference: Whereas each video display memory cell corresponds to one screen position, keyboard memory cells may correspond to several of the 52 keys. Keyboard memory extends from 14336 (3800H) to 15359 (3BFFH); however, eight of these locations contain all the information we will need. These eight locations and their corresponding keys are shown in figure 7.1.

Value Address	1	2	4	8	16	32	64	128
14337	@	A	B	C	D	E	F	G
14338	H	I	J	K	L	M	N	O
14340	P	Q	R	S	T	U	V	W
14344	X	Y	Z					
14352	0	1	2	3	4	5	6	7
14368	8	9	*:	+;	<,	=-	>.	?/
14400	ENTER	CLEAR	BREAK					SPACE
14464	SHIFT							

Figure 7.1 Keyboard memory.

Each row of the table represents one of the eight memory locations. The keys that affect each memory location are listed across the row, and the values corresponding to the keys are listed at the top of the table. Each time a key is pressed, its "value" is added to the current contents of the appropriate memory location. To see how this works, enter

```
NEW
10 CLS
20 PRINT@ 480, PEEK(14337): GOTO 20
RUN
```

Refer to the first row in figure 7.1. When no keys are pressed, location 14337 contains a zero. Press the (@). As long as you hold it down, memory cell 14337 contains a one. Release the key, and it returns to zero. Now for some scientific experiments. Simultaneously press the (B) and (C) keys. What do you get? Yup, $4 + 8 = 12$. When more than one key is pressed, you get the sum of the values corresponding to the depressed keys. If all the keys in the first row of the chart were simultaneously depressed, 14337 would show a 255. Go ahead and try it; no one is looking.

The numbers at the top of the chart were not randomly chosen. Each one is a power of 2, and represents one bit in the value stored at a given location. When you press a key, it sets a bit in the appropriate memory location. Thus, every combination of keys has a unique numeric representation.

Play Ball

Moving a ball around the screen under operator control is now almost child's play. First, we have to position the ball (have it your way—the graphic block) and interrogate location 14400. Enter

```
NEW
10 CLS: DEFINT A-Z
30 Y=22: X=64
40 SET(X,Y): V=PEEK(14400)
50 RESET(X,Y): IF V=0 THEN 40
```

Next, we have to take the desired action when an arrow is pressed:

```
60 IF V AND 8 Y=Y-1
70 IF V AND 16 Y=Y+1
80 IF V AND 32 X=X-1
90 IF V AND 64 X=X+1
100 GOTO 40
RUN
```

The arrow keys will move the dot in any of four directions. In fact, the AND operator used in lines 60 through 90 allows diagonal movement if two or more keys are pressed. And, of course, we have the sought-after repeat feature.

A few more changes, and we might soon be on the mound in Dodger stadium facing Henry Aaron. Change

```
20 PRINT@ 510, CHR$(191) CHR$(191);
30 Y=22: X=1
100 IF X<128 THEN 40
RUN
```

Line 20 is home plate.) Try out all the combinations. Show 'em your curveball, fastball, screwball, changeup, yes, even your yoyo-ball.

Now use this idea for your own applications. If the repeat feature is a bit too fast, slow it down with

```
35 IF V=PEEK(14400) FOR K=1 TO 20: NEXT K
```

This statement checks to see if the value in 14400 has changed since the last loop. If it hasn't, a short delay is added.

Watch Out For Button Pushers

There are times during the execution of a computer program that keyboard interruption from the operator is particularly undesirable. This is especially true during disk access. One way to protect your programs is to totally disable the keyboard. That's right. With a simple POKE, you can render the operator virtually helpless. (Don't remind him or her about the ON/OFF switch!) Save the current program, and type

```
NEW
10 POKE 16396, 165          (For Model III)
        16405, 0            (For Level II)
        23886, 0            (For TRSDOS 2.3)
        23461, 0            (For NEWDOS+)
    CMD"B","OFF"            (For Model III TRSDOS)
20 FOR I=1 TO 1000: PRINT I;:
30 POKE 16396, 201          (For Model III)
        16405, 1            (For Level II)
        23886, 1            (For TRSDOS 2.3)
        23461, 1            (For NEWDOS+)
    CMD"B","ON"             (For Model III TRSDOS)
40 FOR I=1 TO 1000: PRINT I;:
RUN
```

POKE 16405,0 disables the entire keyboard, including the (BREAK) key. Try breaking the program during its first count to 1000. POKE 16405,1 reenables the keyboard during the second loop. This method can be dangerous if the program somehow gets waylaid before reaching the second POKE. Change line 20 to

```
20 INPUT A
RUN
```

Oops! Just lost the program. Even the reset button can't save us now. The only way out is to reboot BASIC. The same thing could happen with unanticipated I/O errors, syntax errors, and so forth. If you disable the (BREAK) key, be sure to trap for errors with the ON ERROR GOTO statement.

An Alternative — For Level II Users Only

If your computer is without disk, there is a safer way to disable the (BREAK) key without the risk of losing anything.

Enter

```
10 POKE 16396, 165
20 INPUT A$
30 GOTO 20
RUN
```

The keyboard is totally accessible, except for the (BREAK) key. So, how do you get out of this infinite loop? Easy. Use (SHIFT) (BREAK). And, if you want to reinstate the normal functioning of the (BREAK) key, change line 10 to

```
10 POKE 16396, 201
RUN
```

If you want to totally disable the (BREAK) key, use POKE 16396,23

Off The Wall

While we are in the neighborhood, the keyboard section of memory can be used to generate some interesting graphic patterns. Try

```
NEW
10 FOR I=14336 TO 14464
20 PRINT CHR$(PEEK(I));
30 NEXT I: GOTO 10
RUN
```

Press any combination of keys. Don't be bashful. It may be months until all the possibilities can be cataloged.

APPLICATION

Geometric Shapes And Function Plots

Lines

Mathematicians are going to love this chapter. We will cover topics that terrorize high-school students across the land every day. But don't fret if you are not among the chosen few who daydream about rational functions and conic sections. Your TRS-80 will teach you everything you always wanted to know about graphics but were afraid to ask. Experiment and persevere.

Straight Lines

The easiest lines we can draw on the TRS-80 screen are horizontal and vertical ones. They can be drawn with SET statements and FOR/NEXT loops. Let's review one way of drawing a horizontal line across the middle of the screen. We need to pick a particular row, let's say row 24, and light up graphic blocks in each column (0 - 127) in that row. The SET statement necessary is SET(X,24), where X ranges from 0 to 127:

```
Ø FOR X=Ø TO 127
Ø SET(X,24)
Ø NEXT X
```

A vertical line could be drawn just as easily by selecting a column, say 50, and using

```
Ø FOR Y=Ø TO 47
Ø SET(5Ø,Y)
Ø NEXT Y
```

Screen Border

A typical application is to draw a border around the screen. This requires four lines and could be done using four loops; however, we managed to do it with only one loop in Chapter 3. Here is a modified version of that program:

```
Ø CLS
Ø FOR X=Ø TO 127
Ø SET(X,Ø): SET(X,47)
Ø IF X<48 SET(Ø,X): SET(127,X)
Ø NEXT X
Ø GOTO 6Ø
```

Is there a faster way to draw this screen border? But of course! Use PRINT or POKE instead of SET. To use the PRINT statement, we need to consider that each of the four lines is composed of different graphic characters:

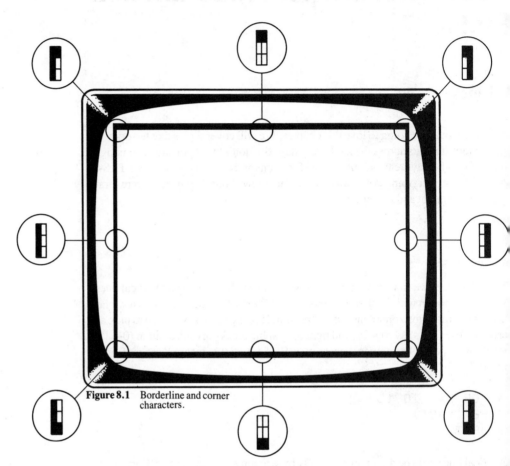

Figure 8.1   Borderline and corner characters.

As you can see, the four corners are made of different characters as well. We'll need to calculate the ASCII value of each of these characters. Recall the value of each of the six graphic blocks:

1	2
4	8
16	32

Figure 8.2   Graphic code pattern.

To create the graphic character for the upper left corner, we will light up the blocks with values 1, 2, 4, and 16. The ASCII value of this character is $128 + 1 + 2 + 4 + 16 = 151$. The other values are calculated in a similar fashion.

Now we can type in the program. First, the top row:

```
NEW
10 CLS: CLEAR 200
20 PRINT@ 0, CHR$(151)STRING$(62,131)CHR$(171);
```

Next, the sides:

```
30 FOR I=1 TO 14
40 PRINT@ I*64, CHR$(149)CHR$(254)CHR$(170);
50 NEXT I
```

Finally, the bottom row:

```
60 PRINT@ 960, CHR$(181)STRING$(62,176)CHR$(186);
70 GOTO 70
```

OK, RUN this to see what kind of speed difference there is. Oh my! Caught by the old screen scroll trick again. The problem appears to be in line 60, right? Remember, every time we PRINT to location 1023, we can expect retaliation from the machine. We'll have to resort to the POKE statement again. Change line 60 to

```
60 PRINT@ 960, CHR$(181)STRING$(62,176);;:
   POKE 16383, 186
RUN
```

You should notice a definite increase in speed over our original attempt using the SET statement. Why? The SET statement lights only one graphics block at a time, but the PRINT statement lights two blocks at a time while plotting the rows, and three at a time while plotting the columns. Wasn't it worth the extra headache?

Picky, Picky, Picky

In line 40, CHR$(254) was used to position the cursor at the right edge of the screen. It also prints 62 spaces in the middle of the screen, obliterating anything in its path. To test this, add

```
15 PRINT@ 416, "1"
RUN
```

If you wish to preserve the screen, change line 40 to

```
40 PRINT@ I*64, CHR$(149);: PRINT@ I*64+63, CHR$(170);
RUN
```

This version uses a second PRINT@ statement to move the cursor to the right edge of the screen.

Not-So-Straight Lines

Lines that are not strictly horizontal or vertical deserve special attention on a computer. After all, rectangles are poor excuses for dots. These lines are bound to appear awkward due to the low resolution, but they can still be used effectively for many applications. Recall that horizontal and vertical lines can be drawn with the SET statement by holding one of the arguments constant and by varying the other argument (e.g., (SET(24,Y)). In order to draw "crooked" lines, we must simultaneously change both arguments of the SET statement at the same time. Enter

```
NEW
10 CLS
20 FOR X=0 TO 30
30 SET(X,X)
40 NEXT X
RUN
```

The line is drawn by moving down one position for every move to the right. By changing the relative rates at which the arguments vary, we can change the angle of the line. The easiest way to do this is to choose one of the arguments in line 30 and multiply it by a constant. Type and RUN

```
NEW
10 CLS
60 FOR X=0 TO 127
80 SET(X,X*,2)
90 NEXT X
```

You can experiment with drawing different lines by modifying the program above to read several different constants from a DATA statement. Modify the current program to read

```
10 CLS
20 READ K
30 IF K<0 THEN 150
60 FOR X=0 TO 127
70 IF X*K>47 THEN 100
80 SET(X,X*K)
90 NEXT
100 GOTO 20
150 GOTO 150
160 DATA .01, .1, .2, .5, .8, 1, 5, 10, 30, -1
RUN
```

Change the data statement to anything your heart desires as long as the *last* entry is negative. Note that line 70 protects us from an illegal function call. This program creates the display shown in figure 8.3.

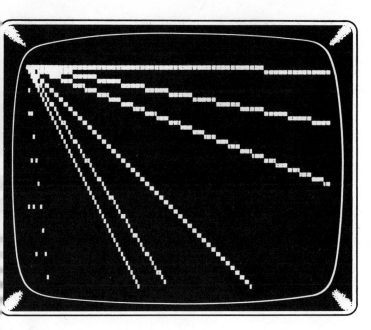

Figure 8.3 Crooked lines.

Values of K from 0 to 1 produce continuous lines. Values of K greater than one give rather sparse results. One way to improve the looks of the lines is to introduce a second loop that draws the line vertically. (Another way to handle this problem will be shown later.) Modify the above program to

```
10  CLS
20  READ K
30  IF K<0 THEN 150
40  IF K<=1 GOSUB 60 ELSE GOSUB 110
50  GOTO 20
60  FOR X=0 TO 127
70  IF X*K>47 THEN 100
80  SET(X,X*K)
90  NEXT
100 RETURN
110 FOR Y=0 TO 47
120 SET(Y/K,Y)
130 NEXT
140 RETURN
150 GOTO 150
160 DATA .004, .2, .8, 1, 2, 5, 70, -1
```

and RUN. Line 40 tests the slope of the line, and sends the program to the appropriate subroutine. Try a few different numbers in the DATA line.

Connect The Dots

There is one glaring limitation in the above program: All the lines start at X = 0, Y = 0. A more versatile program would allow us to specify any two points on the screen, and it would draw a line connecting the points for us. You say this is too much to ask for? My dear (soon-to-be) computer addict! We are dealing with a machine that is the culmination of thousands of years of technological development. We simply have to point it in the right direction! The only two things we will have to teach our quick-learning friend are

1) the formula for the slope (M) of a line connecting two points (X1,Y1) and (X2,Y2):

$$M = (Y2 - Y1)/(X2 - X1)$$

2) the formula for the equation of a line given a point (X1,Y1) and a slope M:

$$Y = M*(X - X1) + Y1$$

To get the ball rolling, we will input the two points (X1 , Y1) and (X2 , Y2):

```
NEW
10 INPUT "FIRST POINT"; X1,Y1
20 INPUT "SECOND POINT"; X2,Y2
30 CLS
```

Then calculate the slope:

```
70 M = (Y2 - Y1)/(X2 - X1)
```

We can now plot the line by letting X vary between X1 and X2, and calculating Y by the above formula. Add

```
100 FOR X = X1 TO X2
110 SET(X,M*(X-X1) + Y1 )
120 NEXT X
130 GOTO 130
RUN
```

Does it work? Sure it does, but it won't draw lines from right to left, and steep lines are very sketchy. Earlier, we used two loops to cope with the problem of steep lines. Another way to handle the same problem is to add a STEP increment to line 100 and change it as the slope of the line changes. For more or less level lines, a STEP of 1 is fine, but for steep lines, a STEP of 1/M will give nice continuous lines. Change line 100 to

```
100 FOR X = X1 TO X2 STEP S
```

and add

```
80 IF ABS(M)>1 S=ABS(1/M) ELSE S=1
```

We also need to account for lines drawn from right to left with

```
90 IF X1>X2 LET S= -S
```

Now we're ready to try out our point connecting program. Go ahead. Take it for a spin. Works fine, doesn't it? Well, it does unless you ask it to draw a vertical line. For some reason, the computer refuses to divide by zero in line 70. We can easily fix that by adding a separate loop to draw vertical lines when X1 = X2:

```
40 IF X2<>X1 THEN 70
50 IF Y1>Y2 THEN S=-1 ELSE S=1
60 FOR Y=Y1 TO Y2 STEP S: SET(X1,Y): NEXT Y: GOTO 130
```

That's better. The final listing should look like this:

```
10 INPUT "FIRST POINT"; X1,Y1
20 INPUT "SECOND POINT"; X2,Y2
30 CLS
40 IF X2<>X1 THEN 70
50 IF Y1>Y2 THEN S=-1 ELSE S=1
60 FOR Y=Y1 TO Y2 STEP S: SET(X1,Y): NEXT Y: GOTO 130
70 M = (Y2 - Y1)/(X2 - X1)
80 IF ABS(M)>1 S=ABS(1/M) ELSE S=1
90 IF X1>X2 LET S= -S
100 FOR X = X1 TO X2 STEP S
110 SET(X,M*(X-X1) + Y1)
120 NEXT X
130 GOTO 130
```

Save the program for future use.

Polygons

The routine that we have created will be an invaluable aid in drawing polygons in that polygons are made by connecting straight line segments end-to-end. Of course we will have to make some modifications, but you should expect that by now! The program must be able to draw lines from point to point around the edge of the polygon. We'll need to create a loop that reads points and draws lines until some end condition is met. For convenience, we will read the endpoints from DATA statements. Also, it would be nice if we had to mention each endpoint only once. The noted changes are

```
10 CLS: ON ERROR GOTO 140
20 READ X2,Y2
30 X1=X2: Y1=Y2: READ X2,Y2 : IF X2<0 THEN 20
130 GOTO 30
140 GOTO 140
150 DATA 6, 27, 20, 27, 13, 21, 6, 27,-1, 0
```

Line 10, of course, both clears the screen and causes it to freeze by sending us to line 140 when there is no more data to read. Line 20 reads the starting point of a new figure. The heart of the modification is line 30. Because we would like to draw several connecting lines, line 30 makes the old endpoint of our figure into the starting point of a new line segment. Then it reads in the new endpoint and checks to see if it is valid. If so, the line is drawn and line 130 sends us back to line 30 where a new point is read and another line drawn. This continues until a negative value is read in for the X coordinate, at which point line 30 sends us to line 20 to start a new figure. Data line 50 will cause three line segments to be drawn:

X1		X2
(6,27)	to	(20,27)
(20,27)	to	(13,21)
(13,21)	to	(6,27)

In short, we've got a triangle. The -1 will allow us to create more figures with additional data.

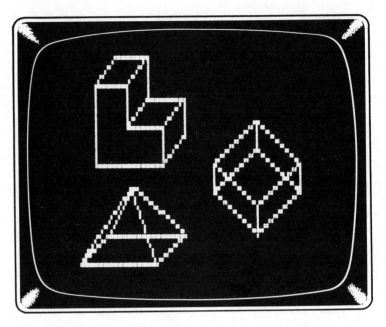

Figure 8.4   Three-dimensional polygons.

As an exercise, you might try adding the data set below. Better yet, make up your own!

```
150 DATA  18,38,6,44,28,28,18,38,50,38,28,28,38,44,
           50,38,-1,0,38,44,6,44,-1,0
160 DATA  98,29,98,23,80,32,62,23,62,29,80,20,98,29
           80,38
170 DATA  62,29,62,23,80,14,98,23,-1,0,80,14,80,20,
           -1,0
180 DATA  80,32,80,38,-1,0
190 DATA  13,6,26,6,35,0,22,0,13,6,13,23,41,23,41,1
200 DATA  50,9,50,17,41,23,-1,0
210 DATA  35,0,35,9,50,9,41,15,26,15,35,9,-1,0
220 DATA  26,6,26,15,-1,0
```

2 Cartesian Coordinate System vs. The TRS-80

X,Y Axes

When we are plotting figures on a two-dimensional surface, it is convenient to have a way to refer to each point. Thanks to a famous mathematician named Descartes, we have one: the Cartesian coordinate system. This system makes use of two perpendicular lines as shown in figure 8.5.

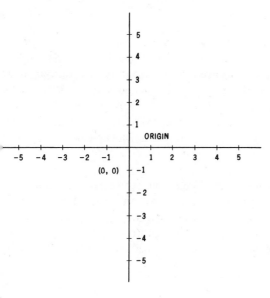

Figure 8.5   The Cartesian coordinate system.

Once the lines (called axes) have been introduced to the plane, each point is referenced by its distance from the two axes. The displacement is calculated in both the horizontal and vertical directions. The point shown in figure 8.6 is named (3,4) because it is 3 units in the positive horizontal direction from the origin, and 4 units in the positive vertical direction from the origin. The two numbers 3 and 4 are called coordinates, and since the axes are typically labeled with X and Y as shown, we will refer to the first number as the X coordinate and the second number as the Y coordinate. So much for the math lesson. On to graphics.

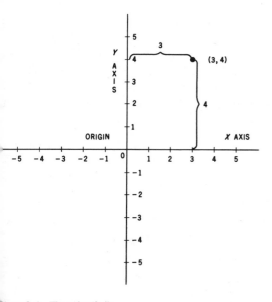

Figure 8.6   The point (3,4).

Cartesian Coordinate System

To draw the Cartesian coordinate system on the TRS-80, we will need two straight lines labeled with number scales. The number scales will have to be flexible in that the range of the X and Y values to be displayed on the screen will vary from graph to graph. For example, we may need to display a range of Y values from -20 to $+20$ in order to clearly understand some graphs, while others can be readily displayed in a range of -4 to $+4$. A reasonable approach that would allow for this variation would be to create a single set of axes and tick marks, and let our number scales change with the application.

The axes could easily be drawn with the SET statement, but we have chosen to PRINT the axes in the example below to make sure you don't doze off! See if you can figure out how strings are used to create the axes and tick marks. Keep in mind that there is no perfect way to write a program. Don't be afraid to try it a new way. If the machine snickers a bit at your attempts, remember that *you* control the ON/OFF button.

Enter this program

```
NEW
10 CLS: CLEAR 200
20 DEFSTR A
40 A=CHR$(140) + CHR$(141) + CHR$(140)
50 PRINT@ 448,;
60 FOR X=1 TO 12
70 PRINT A+STRING$(2,140);
80 NEXT X: PRINT A;
90 PRINT@ 31,;
100 FOR I=1 TO 15
110 PRINT CHR$(157) + CHR$(24) + CHR$(26);
120 NEXT I
130 GOTO 130
RUN
```

Numbering scales should be added to the axes as needed. As an example, add

```
*30 FOR P=0 TO 14 : PRINT@ 28+P*64, 7-P; : NEXT P
 130 PRINT@ 512, "-6    -5    -4    -3    -2    -1";
 140 PRINT@ 548, "1    2    3    4    5    6";
 150 GOTO 150
```

This results in figure 8.7.

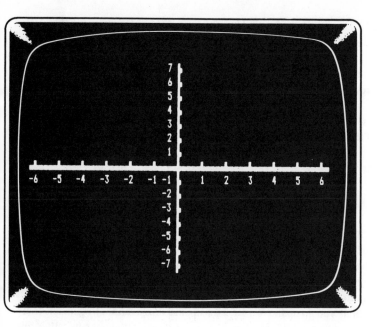

Figure 8.7   A coordinate system.

Plotting Points

All right, so we have a beautiful pair of axes. The question now is how can we plot points on this newly labeled screen? Certainly SET (2 , 3) will not plot the point (2,3). We will have to delve briefly in to the never-never land of mathematics for the answer.

Once we have assigned a coordinate system to the screen, each point (actually, each graphics block) acquires two names. One is its name in terms of our coordinate system; the other is the TRS-80 SET coordinates. For example, the coordinate point (0,0) has SET coordinates (62,22). It would be convenient if we could refer to the point as (0,0) and let the computer do the work of translating it to the proper SET coordinates. This translation is done with a pair of simple equations. For the point (0,0), we can use the equations

$$X1 = X + 62$$
$$Y1 = Y + 22$$

where $X = 0$ and $Y = 0$, and X1 and Y1 are the numbers to be used in the SET statement.

SET (X+62 , Y+22) will translate (0,0) into SET (62 , 22) as desired. Would this system of equations plot the point (2,3) in the appropriate spot? Nope, not even close. See figure 8.7. With $X = 2$ and $Y = 3$, we would get SET (64 , 25). The 64 is not nearly large enough, and the 25 should be much smaller. Don't worry though. We just left out a few minor details. Notice that every labeled unit on the X axis is actually ten graphic blocks. So, to move from $X = 0$ to $X = 2$, we must move 2 times 10, or 20 blocks to the right of $X = 0$. A more accurate equation for our translation in the X direction is

$$X1 = 10*X + 62$$

This will yield X1 = 82 when X = 2. Hurrah! Are you ready to guess the translation for the Y coordinates? Well? . . . . OK Here are three hints:

1) The center is at Y = 22.
2) There are three graphics blocks per Y tick mark (so far you should have
   `Y1 = 3*Y + 22`).
3) (This is the hard one:) Our Y labels increase in the opposite direction from the TRS-80 row numbers.

Now you got it!

```
Y1 = -3*Y + 22
```

The negative sign, of course, flips the Y axis right-side-up. One of the frustrating things about the way our favorite little computer was designed is the vertical numbering scheme used for the SET, RESET, and POINT statements. Zero is at the top of the screen while 47 is at the bottom. This is great for many applications, but not for plotting functions. Every high-school algebra student knows that the numbers should get larger as you go up the Y axis. This upside-down numbering means that any function plotted on the TRS-80 would be upside down without the negative sign in the above equation.

So, what can we do with these equations? Suppose we want to plot a point $(1, -4)$. Simply add

```
150 X=1: Y=-4
170 X1 = 10*X + 62
180 Y1 =-3*Y + 22
190 SET(X1,Y1)
200 GOTO 200
RUN
```

to the coordinate program. RUN it a few times with different X and Y values in line 150. Then try

```
150 X=2.09: Y=1
```

Hmmmmmm. You've spotted a problem. X = 2.09 is closer to 2.1 than 2.0, but the SET statement plots it as 2.0. We might be tempted to ignore such a slight discrepancy, but this round-off error will give us somewhat erratic-looking functions if we don't fix it. We'll have to add .5 to each of the SET arguments so that each point will be plotted at the closest graphic location. This can be done by changing lines 170 and 180 to

```
170 X1 = 10*X +62.5
180 Y1 = -3*Y + 22.5
RUN
```

Graphing Functions

Armed with the appropriate set of translation equations and our updated coordinate program, we can graph almost any function on the TRS-80 screen. Functions are usually given in the form Y = f(X), where f(X) stands for some expression involving X. Typical examples are Y = SIN(X) and Y = 3X-2. We can graph functions like

these by letting X vary between -6 and $+6$ and calculating Y for each new value of
X. This can be done most easily in a FOR / NEXT loop:

```
*150 FOR X = -6 TO 6
 160 Y = 3*X -2
 170 X1 = 10*X + 62.5
 180 Y1 = -3*Y + 22.5
 190 IF Y1>47 OR Y1<0 THEN 210
 200 SET(X1,Y1)
 210 NEXT X
 220 GOTO 220
RUN
```

Line 160 contains the function and line 190 keeps us from plotting off the screen. To
make the plot a bit more continuous, you can take advantage of the optional STEP
parameter in line 150. Change it to

```
150 FOR X =-6 TO 6 STEP .1
RUN
```

Isn't that better? Now, change line 160 to Y = 10*X and try several different
STEP increments. As you can see, small STEP values are required to maintain a
continuous graph for steep functions like Y = 10*X, but this causes a great
reduction in plotting speed. It's the old trade-off between speed and accuracy. You
will have to choose a STEP value that is comfortable for you.

Ready For Take-Off

Now your TRS-80 is almost ready to amaze and dazzle you with some of its awesome
power. First we will set the STEP increment in line 150 to .05 so that the machine
doesn't blind you with its lightning speed (also, in case we run across any steep
functions). Enter any real function that you want in line 160 to see how really clever
your machine can be. Here are some functions to play with. Feel free to change the
STEP increment as you see fit.

```
Y = 6*SIN(X)
Y = 3*SIN(X) + 3*COS(2*X)
Y = ABS(1/4*X)
Y = 2*X - 7
Y = -5
Y = X*X - 4
Y = -X*X + 4
Y = 1/2*X[3 - 4*X
Y = LOG(X)                (X = .01 TO 6)
```

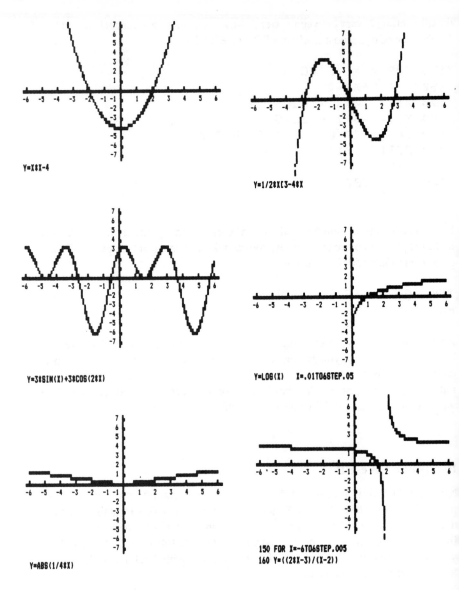

Figure 8.8   Sample functions.

3 Polar Coordinates

The Cartesian rectangular coordinate system is great for plotting all kinds of graphs, but it has an Achilles' heel—circular objects. Sure, you can plot circles, ellipses, cardiods, and such with rectangular coordinates, but their equations are much easier to work with if you use polar coordinates.

A Circle

We'll take a look at plotting a circle using rectangular coordinates before we go polar. First, you would take the equation of a circle:

$$X^2 + Y^2 = R^2$$

nd solve it for Y:

$$Y = \pm\sqrt{R^2 - X^2}$$

'hen plot both positive and negative values of Y as X moves across the diameter of
ne circle.

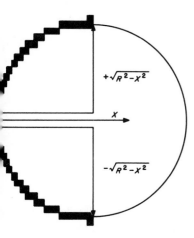

igure 8.9   A rectangular coordinate circle.

Iere is a short program that will get the job done:

```
NEW
Ø CLS : R=4.5
Ø FOR X=-R TO R STEP .1
Ø Y = SQR(R*R - X*X)        (above formula)
Ø SET(64+7*X,24+3*Y)
Ø SET(64+7*X,24-3*Y)
Ø NEXT X
Ø GOTO 70
UN
```

he radius R is defined in line 10. The FOR statement in line 20 causes X to range
om -R to R. The STEP increment determines both the speed with which the figure
drawn and the degree of detail. A small number will take longer and give more
etail. On the other hand, a large number gives less detail, but greater speed. Line 30
alculates the positive value of Y based on the current value of X. Lines 40 and 50 plot
e positive and negative values. Location (64,24) is used as the center of the
ircle, and 7 and 3 are used to adjust for the aspect ratio of the graphics blocks. (You
ouldn't want our circle to look like an egg, now would you?)

Polar Approach

Vhat is a polar coordinate? It is a different way of labeling points in the plane. With
ectangular coordinates, a point is identified by its veritical and horizontal
isplacement from the X and Y axes. With polar coordinates, a point is identified by
s direct distance from the origin and the angle it makes with the positive X axis.

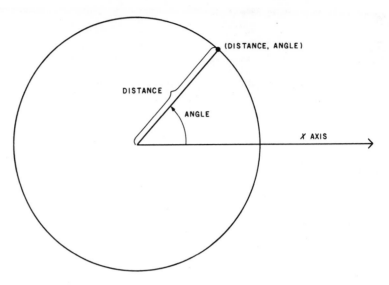

Figure 8.10   Polar coordinates.

If this is getting too technical, hang in there. You can still use the following examples. To plot circular functions, we increment the angle from 0 to 360 degrees (0 to 2 π radians) and let the radius vary as a function of the angle.

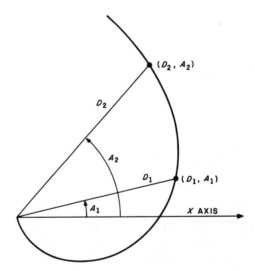

Figure 8.11   Radius (distance) as a function of the angle.

The SET statement only understands X and Y coordinates, but the computer can take care of the translation using the formulas

```
X = RADIUS * COS(ANGLE)
Y = RADIUS * SIN(ANGLE)
```

Once we teach the computer these formulas, we can write functions in polar terms and pretty much forget about rectangular coordinates. The equation for a circle in polar

rms is R = C where C is a constant. Whew, couldn't be much easier. Try this one
n for size:

```
EW
Ø CLS
Ø FOR A=Ø TO 3Ø STEP .Ø2
Ø R=4.5
Ø SET(64+7*R*COS(A), 24+3*R*SIN(A))
Ø NEXT A
Ø GOTO 6Ø
UN
```

is set to a constant in line 30 to create a circle. The angle A is determined in line 20.
ne complete 360-degree revolution around the circle is 6.28 (2 π) radians, but it
ually takes several passes to draw a well-defined picture. Again, the STEP
crement should be adjusted to give the desired balance between speed and detail. If
ou like your circles drawn in a counterclockwise direction, change the second + sign
line 40 to –.

ote that only one SET statement is needed when plotting with polar coordinates.
e used two SET statements when plotting with rectangular coordinates.

etting Dizzy

he real advantage of polar coordinates is the ease with which other circular figures
an be drawn. Other circular figures are drawn by varying the radius with the angle.
hange

```
Ø CLS: ON ERROR GOTO 6Ø
Ø R=A
UN
```

tighter spiral pattern can be generated by

```
Ø R=A*.3
```
                                        Spiral of Archimedes

ubtle changes to line 30 can give surprising results. Try your favorite functions.
ere are some suggestions:

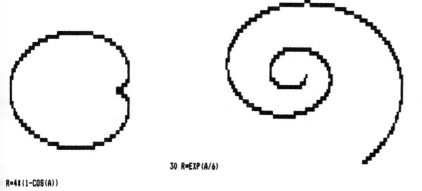

30 R=EXP(A/6)

R=48(1-COS(A))

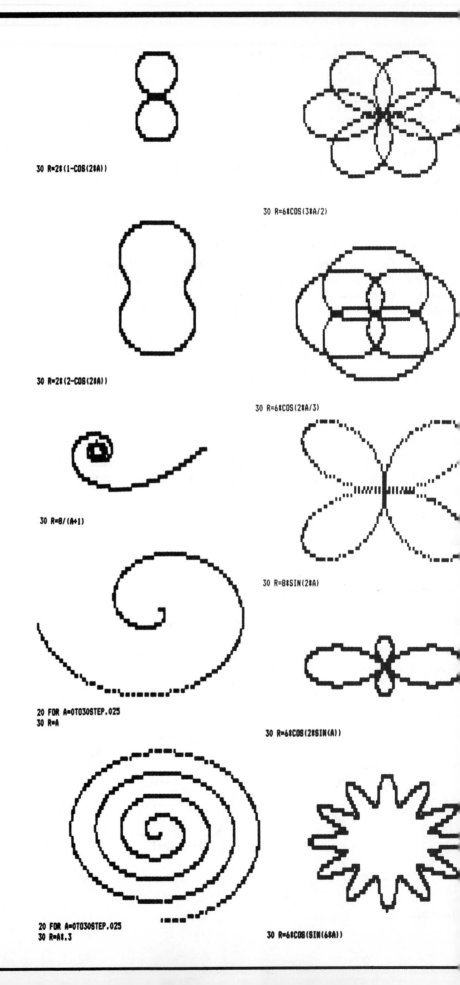

30 R=2$(1-COS(2$A))

30 R=6$COS(3$A/2)

30 R=2$(2-COS(2$A))

30 R=6$COS(2$A/3)

30 R=8/(A+1)

30 R=8$SIN(2$A)

20 FOR A=0TO30STEP.025
30 R=A

30 R=6$COS(2$SIN(A))

20 FOR A=0TO30STEP.025
30 R=A$.3

30 R=6$COS(SIN(6$A))

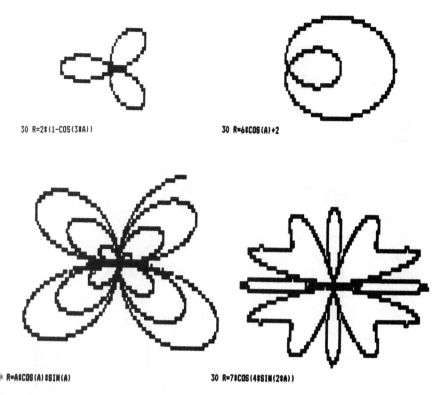

30 R=2*(1-COS(3*A))   30 R=6*COS(A)+2

R=A*COS(A)*SIN(A)   30 R=7*COS(4*SIN(2*A))

Figure 8.12 Polar functions.

```
=A*COS(A)*SIN(A)`
=8*SIN(3*A)               Rose leaf
=6*COS(2*SIN(A))
=6*COS(SIN(6*A))
=7*COS(4*SIN(2*A))
=8*COS(A)*COS(2*A)
=4*(1-COS(A))            Cardioid
=6*COS(A)+2
=EXP(A/6)               Logarithmic spiral
=8/(A+1)                Hyperbolic spiral
=6*COS(2*A/3)
=6*COS(3*A/2)
```

Wouldn't high resolution be nice here? Sigh.

Statistics

Statistics is a study that cuts across many disciplines. Basically, it is used as a tool to help us manage data. There are two main branches of statistics: One, descriptive statistics, endeavors to describe data, whereas the other, inferential statistics, attempts to draw inferences from the data. One guideline of descriptive statistics is that graphic display of information is often more useful in making decisions than long lists or tables of numbers. That's where the computer comes in. We can easily create programs that will transform dull data into readily understood graphs.

Frequency Distributions

Histograms

The histogram is a type of bar graph in which the vertical axis represents frequency and the horizontal axis represents the data being measured. The data items are grouped into intervals and plotted as in figure 9.1.

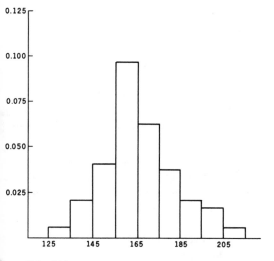

Figure 9.1   A histogram.

In order for a histogram to be of any value, the boundaries between intervals must be labeled. Because this requires more room on the screen than we can readily afford, we will not pursue the histogram here. However, Radio Shack puts out a statistics package that will automatically create labels for you.

Bar Graphs

If there are only a few discrete data items, they can be plotted with a bar graph as in figure 9.2.

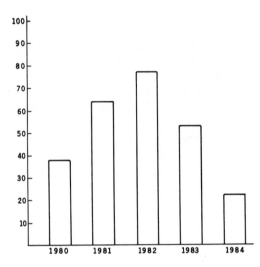

Figure 9.2   A vertical bar graph.

Designing Our Own Bar Graph

Any time we create our own software, design decisions have to be made. The standard trade-offs include speed vs. memory use and flexibility vs. simplicity. What we choose will depend entirely on our needs and the limitations of the system we are working with. For the graph we are about to create, we will

1) use a fixed number of labels on the vertical axis. This will reduce our flexibility but greatly simplify the program.

2) use no labels on the horizontal axis. This will allow for a much greater range of data items — up to 50. If you want to add labels for a particular application, it is easy to do so.

3) enter data from the keyboard. Each column will be drawn as it is entered. A more sophisticated program would allow options of loading and saving data from tape or diskette.

4) employ minimal error checking. This will keep the program short enough to type in and give you something to do for homework.

With these considerations in mind, a sketch of the desired output is the next thing.

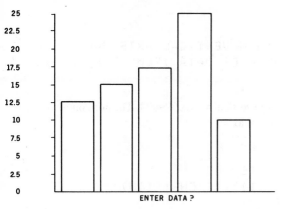

Figure 9.3   A sketch of a bar graph.

O.K., now a quick flowchart.

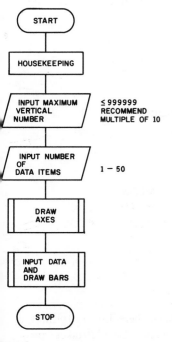

Figure 9.4   A flowchart for bar graphs.

Bring It To Life

The housekeeping is easy:

```
NEW
10 CLEAR 100: CLS
```

Now, the input:

```
20 INPUT "ENTER MAXIMUM VERTICAL AXIS VALUE"; M
30 INPUT "ENTER NUMBER OF DATA ITEMS FOR HORIZONTAL
   AXIS"; N
```

The maximum value allowed for the vertical axis is 999999. The horizontal axis may have up to 50 entries. Add the vertical axis:

```
40 CLS: L=M
50 FOR I=191 TO 767 STEP 64
60 PRINT@ I, L; TAB(11)"-"; CHR$(149)
70 L=L-M/10: NEXT I
80 PRINT@ 832, 0; TAB(12)CHR$(141);
RUN
```

Line 50 creates a loop that controls the position of the items printed in line 60. The values assumed by I are on the right edge of the screen. Because numbers are printed with a leading space, this will ensure that each number is justified on the left of the screen. Line 60 prints a number, tick mark, and part of the vertical axis. Line 70 calculates the numbers on the vertical axis. L starts at the maximum value, M, and decreases by M/10 on each pass of the loop.

And the horizontal axis is almost too easy:

```
90 PRINT@ 845, STRING$(50,140)
```

RUN it to make sure we haven't strayed too far from figure 9.3.

The input is probably the worst part:

```
100 FOR D=0 TO N-1
110 PRINT@ 920, "ENTER DATA"; CHR$(30)
120 PRINT@ 931,;: INPUT X: IF X<=M THEN 140
130 PRINT@ 931, CHR$(30): PRINT@ 938, X "TOO
    LARGE": GOTO 120
140 REM
170 NEXT D
RUN
```

Lines 100 and 170 drive the loop that inputs the N data numbers. Line 110 prints the prompt message, and CHR$(30) clears the data entry line. Line 120 takes care of the input, and line 130 gives an error message if the data exceeds the limit of the vertical axis. Several PRINT@s are needed to reposition the cursor after each use of CHR$(30). The plotting is done in the same loop as the input:

```
140 FOR Y=0 TO INT(X/M*30+.5)
150 FOR Z=0 TO INT(100/N)-2
160 SET(INT(100/N)*D+Z+26,40-Y)
170 NEXT Z: NEXT Y: NEXT D
180 GOTO 180
RUN
```

Notice that (ENTER) will repeat the height of the previous bar.

The Y loop calculates the height of each bar. The Z loop calculates the width of each bar. RUN it a few times, keeping an eye out for where it could be improved.

The final listing should be as follows:

```
*10  CLEAR 100: CLS
 20  INPUT "ENTER MAXIMUM VERTICAL AXIS VALUE"; M
 30  INPUT "ENTER NUMBER OF DATA ITEMS FOR
     HORIZONTAL AXIS"; N
 40  CLS: L=M
 50  FOR I=191 TO 767 STEP 64
 60  PRINT@ I, L; TAB(11)"-"; CHR$(149)
 70  L=L-M/10: NEXT I
 80  PRINT@ 832, 0; TAB(12) CHR$(141);
 90  PRINT@ 845, STRING$(50,140)
100  FOR D=0 TO N-1
110  PRINT@ 920, "ENTER DATA"; CHR$(30)
120  PRINT@ 931,;: INPUT X: IF X<=M THEN 140
130  PRINT@ 931, CHR$(30): PRINT@ 938, X"TOO
     LARGE": GOTO 120
140  FOR Y=0 TO INT(X/M*30+.5)
150  FOR Z=0 TO INT(100/N)-2
160  SET(INT(100/N)*D+Z+26,40-Y)
170  NEXT Z: NEXT Y: NEXT D
180  GOTO 180
```

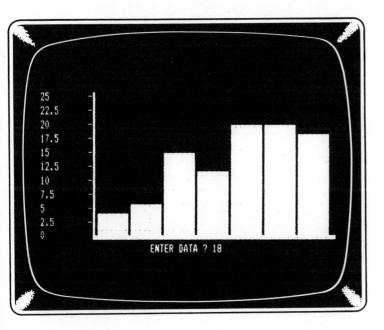

Figure 9.5   A BARGRAPH display.

Save this beastly BARGRAPH program, as it will be used in section 3 of this chapter. Keep in mind that this is a bare-bones program. Many improvements could be made. (See Chapter 11 for a description of elements of a good graph.)

For a change of pace, let's try a different background color. Change

```
DELETE 90
60 PRINT@ I, L; TAB(11)"-"STRING$(50,191)
80 PRINT@ 832, 0; TAB(12)STRING$(50,179)
160 RESET(INT(100/N)*D+Z+25,40-Y)
RUN
```

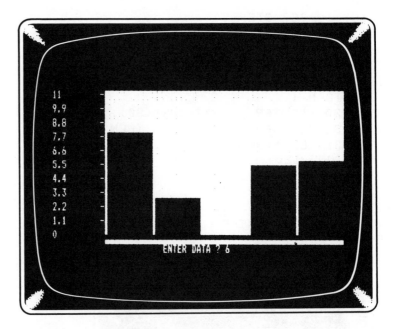

Figure 9.6   A BARGRAPH reverse image.

2 Linear Regression And Correlation

Another area of statistics looks at relations between pairs of variables to see if there is a possibility of a cause-and-effect relationship. As an example, let's look at a recent random sampling of ten TRS-80 users by the PHONY SURVEY CORPORATION (please, a little willing suspension of disbelief!):

WEEKLY CONTACT HOURS WITH TRS-80	HAPPINESS RATING (10 MAX)
25	8
3	3
20	1 (An Apple owner?)
15	4
40	11
8	5
12	6
22	9
0	0 (ouch)
35	9

'e are going to develop a program that will graphically display these pairs of
umbers on a scatter diagram. We will place contact hours on the horizontal axis and
uppiness rating on the vertical axis as shown in figure 9.7

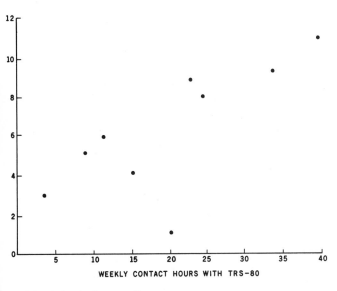

igure 9.7   A sketch of a scatter diagram.

he input approach on this program will differ a bit from the concept in the previous
ue. The earlier program asked for the maximum values to be entered, then plotted
uta as it was entered. It assumed that minimums on both axes were zero. This
rogram, however, will take the approach of storing all data entered in an array and
ill create the number scales using maximum and minimum values from the arrays.

ousekeeping comes first:

```
EW
Ø CLS: DIM X(1Ø), Y(1Ø)
Ø XN=1ØØØØ: YN=1ØØØØ: XM=Ø: YM=Ø
```

his program uses two BASIC statements available only in Disk BASIC:
INE INPUT and INSTRING. LINE INPUT accepts string input with
ommas and quotation marks. INSTRING searches through a string for a specific
ubstring. Nondisk users will be given a different version by and by — be patient.
dd the data entry section:

```
Ø PRINT "ENTER DATA PAIRS SEPARATED BY COMMAS"
Ø I=I+1
Ø LINE INPUT "DATA PAIR:"; A$: A=INSTR(A$,",")
Ø N=I-1: IF A$="" GOTO 18Ø
Ø IF A=Ø PRINT "USE COMMA": GOTO 5Ø
Ø X(I)=VAL(LEFT$(A$,A))
2Ø Y(I)=VAL(MID$(A$,A+1))
7Ø GOTO 4Ø
```

his loop exits to line 180 from line 60. It stores the X values in the array X(I) and
ue Y values in Y(I). The number of data pairs is recorded in N.

If you are employing a nondisk system, use the same lines 30, 40, and 170. But replace lines 50 through 120 with

```
50 PRINT "USE NEGATIVE FIRST VALUE WHEN FINISHED"
60 INPUT "DATA PAIR"; X(I), Y(I)
70 N=I-1: IF X(I)<0 THEN 180
```

Now, we are all together. To calculate the minimum and maximum values of each variable, add

```
100 IF X(I)>XM THEN XM=X(I)
110 IF X(I)<XN THEN XN=X(I)
140 IF Y(I)>YM THEN YM=Y(I)
150 IF Y(I)<YN THEN YN=Y(I)
```

The four variables XM, XN, YM, and YN can be used to create scales for the diagram:

```
*180 CLS: PRINT@ 128,;:
 190 FOR I=1 TO 11: PRINT USING "######.#";
     YM-(YM-YN)/10*(I-1);
 200 PRINT "   -"; CHR$(149): NEXT I
 210 PRINT@ 844, CHR$(131);
 220 PRINT@ 845, STRING$(50,131)
 230 PRINT@ 908,;
 240 FOR I=0 TO 6: PRINT USING "#####.#";
     XN+I/6*(XM-XN);: NEXT I
 250 FOR X=34 TO 118 STEP 14: SET(X,40):NEXT X
 380 GOTO 380
```

If it seems like a lot of code, you're right; it is. And there is more on the way. We are doing a lot of things with this program.

RUN this program. Enter a few pairs of numbers separated by commas on each line. When you are through, press **ENTER** to activate the drawing of the axes. Nondisk users should enter a negative first number to terminate input. The numbers on the horizontal axis should range from the highest X value to the lowest. The numbers on the vertical axis should do the same for the Y values. Plotting the data points is only a matter of adding one line:

```
260 FOR I=1 TO N:
    SET(34+84*(X(I)-XN)/(XM-XN),
    7+(YM-Y(I))/(YM-YN)*30): NEXT I
RUN
```

Enter data pairs using your own data or the weekly contact hours shown above.

Correlation

The two variables are said to be correlated if these dots form a rough straight line. The closer the approximation of a straight line, the higher the correlation. A scatter diagram can help us quickly determine if there is a possible linear relationship between two variables. Naturally, there is a mathematical way to determine the same thing. It is called the "correlation coefficient." We can have our program calculate this number each time a new data pair is added. Add

```
  XS=XS+X(I):  XQ=XQ+X(I)*X(I)
  YS=YS+Y(I):  YQ=YQ+Y(I)*Y(I)
  XY=XY+X(I)*Y(I)
  R1=XY-XS*YS/N  :  R2=XQ-XS*XS/N  :  R3=YQ-YS*YS/N
  R2=SQR(R2)  :  R3=SQR(R3)
  PRINT@ 980, "CORRELATION COEFFICIENT: ";
  PRINT USING "#.####"; R1/R2/R3;
JN
```

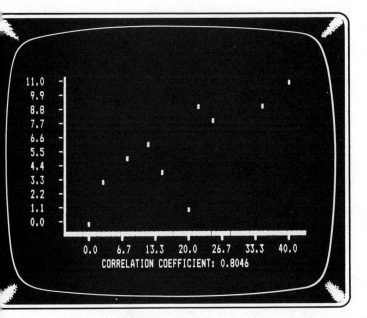

Figure 9.8   A scatter diagram for happiness rating.

ums are accumulated as the data is being entered in lines 90, 130, and 160.
termediate values are calculated in lines 270 and 280. Finally, the correlation
efficient, R, is printed in line 300.

UN this with the weekly contact hours so that we can see what kind of correlation
ere might be in the data. If R is close to positive or negative 1, then there is a high
rrelation. Conversely, if it is close to 0, there is no correlation.

/e knew all along that a dedicated TRS-80 user is a happy one. But a word of caution
 in order: a high correlation between two variables doesn't prove that they neces-
rily affect one another. For example, there is probably a very high correlation
tween the annual production of bananas in Brazil and alcohol sales in the U.S.
very year our sales just keep going up. But somehow, it is hard to believe that
utting down the banana plantations will have much of an effect on alcohol sales,
ght?

ine of Best Fit

or variables that are highly correlated and for which there is a high probability of
ausation, it is useful to find the line that most closely fits the data for purposes of

predictions or estimates. Let's suppose that we run a software house, Al's Plumbing and Programs, with ten employees. (A rich uncle left us his plumbing business.) We are continually bombarded by job-hunters who make all kinds of wild claims. What do? Simple. We have all the current employees write a simple program, and compar the time it took them to do so with their current weekly lines of code produced. Here are the results of the test:

TEST (MINUTES)	WEEKLY LINES OF CODE
45	2010
33	1828
169	75 (a goof-off)
48	2700
29	3684
30	3400

Now add the data to our program. See figure 9.9.

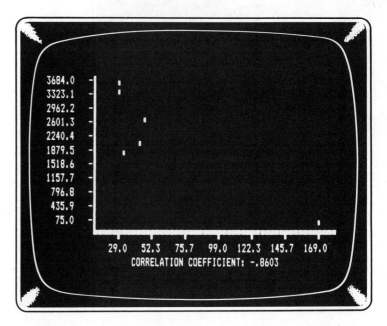

Figure 9.9   A scatter diagram for lines of code.

As you may have guessed, the correlation is rather strong. With a few modifications to the program, we can have the computer calculate and plot the line of best fit. Add

```
310 RM=(XY*N-YS*XS)/(XQ*N-XS*XS)
320 RB=(YS*XQ-XY*XS)/(XQ*N-XS*XS)
```

For you statistics aficionados, RM is the slope of the regression line, and RB is the Y intercept. The equation of the line of best fit is Y = RM * X + RB. Keep typing:

```
330 FOR XT=XN TO XM STEP (XM-XN)/100
340 Y=7+(YM-(RM*XT+RB))/(YM-YN)*30
350 IF Y>37 OR Y<7 THEN 370
```

```
360 SET(34+84*(XT-XN)/(XM-XN),Y)
370 NEXT XT
RUN
```

RUN this program with the test data. The output should look like figure 9.10.

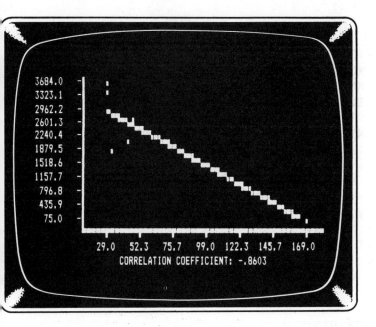

Figure 9.10   The line of best fit.

Now, when a prospective employee walks into our office, we give them the aptitude test. By comparing the results to the line of best fit, we have a reasonable estimate of their productivity. Save this program before we move on. The final listing should be this:

```
10 CLS: DIM X(10), Y(10)
20 XN=10000: YN=10000: XM=0: YM=0
30 PRINT "ENTER DATA PAIRS SEPARATED BY COMMAS"
40 I=I+1
50 LINE INPUT "DATA PAIR:"; A$: A=INSTR(A$,",")
60 N=I-1: IF A$="" GOTO 180
70 IF A=0 PRINT "USE COMMA": GOTO 50
80 X(I)=VAL(LEFT$(A$,A))
90 XS=XS+X(I): XQ=XQ+X(I)*X(I)
100 IF X(I)>XM THEN XM=X(I)
110 IF X(I)<XN THEN XN=X(I)
120 Y(I)=VAL(MID$(A$,A+1))
130 YS=YS+Y(I): YQ=YQ+Y(I)*Y(I)
140 IF Y(I)>YM THEN YM=Y(I)
150 IF Y(I)<YN THEN YN=Y(I)
160 XY=XY+X(I)*Y(I)
170 GOTO 40
180 CLS: PRINT@128,;:
```

```
190 FOR I=1 TO 11: PRINT USING "######.#";
    YM-(YM-YN)/10*(I-1);
200 PRINT "   -"; CHR$(149): NEXT I
210 PRINT@ 844, CHR$(131);
220 PRINT@ 845, STRING$(50,131)
230 PRINT@ 908,;
240 FOR I=0 TO 6: PRINT USING "#####.#"; XN+I/6*
    (XM-XN);: NEXT I
250 FOR X=34 TO 118 STEP 14: SET(X,40): NEXT X
260 FOR I=1 TO N:
    SET(34+84*(X(I)-XN)/(XM-XN), 7+(YM-Y(I)))/(YM-
    YN)*30): NEXT I
270 R1=XY-XS*YS/N : R2=XQ-XS*XS/N : R3=YQ-YS*YS/N
280 R2=SQR(R2) : R3=SQR(R3)
290 PRINT@ 980, "CORRELATION COEFFICIENT: ";
300 PRINT USING "#.####"; R1/R2/R3;
310 RM=(XY*N-YS*XS)/(XQ*N-XS*XS)
320 RB=(YS*XQ-XY*XS)/(XQ*N-XS*XS)
330 FOR XT=XN TO XM STEP (XM-XN)/100
340 Y=7+(YM-(RM*XT+RB))/(YM-YN)*30
350 IF Y>37 OR Y<7 THEN 370
360 SET(34+84*(XT-XN)/(XM-XN),Y)
370 NEXT XT
380 GOTO 380
```

3 Normal Curves

As we said in the introduction to this chapter, inferential statistics is the science of drawing inferences from data. Often, we find that survey results follow a standard bell-shaped pattern.

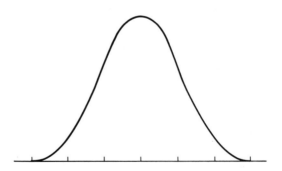

Figure 9.11   A normal curve.

This pattern is called the ''normal curve.'' Using properties of the normal curve and surprisingly small samples statisticians can make very good predictions about populations.

Having a computer at our disposal, we can easily generate a bell-shaped curve by experimenting with the RND function. Our favorite computer is going to simulate rolling three 11-sided dice for us.

Each roll of the dice will give us a number from 3 to 33. By subtracting 3 from the result, the range changes to 0 to 30. As with normal six-sided dice, the probability of getting a very high or a very low sum is much less than the probability of getting a number near the middle, say 15. This occurs because there is only one way to get a 0 $(1 + 1 + 1 - 3)$, but many different ways to get a 15 $(1 + 6 + 11 - 3,$ $1 + 7 + 10 - 3, 1 + 8 + 9 - 3, \ldots 11 + 6 + 1 - 3)$. A graph of these probabilities gives a bell-shaped curve.

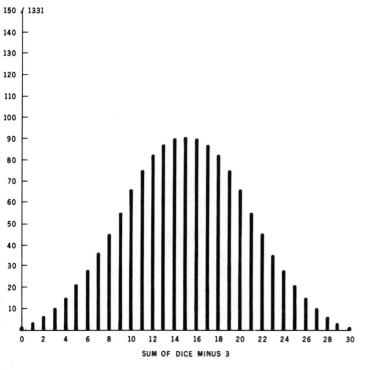

Figure 9.12   Probabilities for three 11-sided dice.

The computer can generate an approximation of this curve by repeated experimentation. The more repetitions, the closer the generated graph will match the probabilities in figure 9.12.

Rather than create a program from scratch, we can modify the BARGRAPH program you saved (you did, didn't you?) earlier in this chapter to do the job for us. Some lines need to be modified:

```
10 CLS: CLEAR 100: DIM R(30): N=30
20 R(R)=R(R)+1: IF M<R(R) THEN M=R(R)
30 GOSUB 40: GOTO 15
40 CLS: L=M: PRINT@ 30, S; "TRIALS";
100 FOR D=0 TO N
110 (Delete)
120 PRINT@ 920,;: X=R(D): IF X<=M THEN 140
180 RETURN
```

We need to add a few new lines:

```
15 FOR T=1 TO 200: R=RND(11)+RND(11)+RND(11)-3
25 S=S+1: PRINT@ 30, S: NEXT T
95 FOR I=0 TO 30 STEP 5: SET(26+3*I,41): PRINT@
   908+1.5*I,I: NEXT I
RUN
```

Line 10 reserves room for 31 variables, R(0) through R(30), to count the frequencies of the different values assigned to R. Lines 15 through 25 make up a loop in which 200 random numbers are calculated and tabulated. The calculation of the random numbers is done in line 15. Three is subtracted from the sum of the three RND functions to change the effective range of R from $3 - 33$ to $0 - 30$. The appropriate variable is incremented by 1 in line 20, and the maximum frequency is updated if necessary. In line 25, the total number of trials is stored in S and printed.

The rest of the BARGRAPH program has been turned into a subroutine from lines 40 to 180. These lines plot the frequencies stored in R(   ). Line 30 calls that routine and returns control to line 15, where the process continues.

This program will run indefinitely, pausing every 200 calculations to display the current results. You can control the frequency of the pauses by changing the limits on T in line 15. You may also want to try changing the RND functions in line 15. But be sure to change the values in line 10 accordingly.

Your final listing should look like this one:

```
*10 CLS: CLEAR 100: DIM R(30): N=30
 15 FOR T=1 TO 200: R=RND(11)+RND(11)+RND(11)-3
 20 R(R)=R(R)+1: IF M<R(R) THEN M=R(R)
 25 S=S+1: PRINT@ 30, S: NEXT T
 30 GOSUB 40: GOTO 15
 40 CLS: L=M: PRINT@ 30, S; "TRIALS";
 50 FOR I=191 TO 767 STEP 64
 60 PRINT@ I, L; TAB(11)"-"; CHR$(149)
 70 L=L-M/10: NEXT I
 80 PRINT@ 832, 0; TAB(12)CHR$(141);
 90 PRINT@ 845, STRING$(50,140)
 95 FOR I=0 TO 30 STEP 5: SET(26+3*I,41): PRINT@
    908+1.5*I,I: NEXT I
100 FOR D=0 TO N
120 PRINT@ 920,;: X=R(D): IF X<=M THEN 140
130 PRINT@ 931, CHR$(30): PRINT@ 938, X "TOO
    LARGE": GOTO 120
140 FOR Y=0 TO INT(X/M*30+.5)
150 FOR Z=0 TO INT(100/N)-2
160 SET(INT(100/N)*D+Z+26,40-Y)
170 NEXT Z: NEXT Y: NEXT D
180 RETURN
```

Computer Assisted Instruction

1 CAI Overview

Computer assisted instruction is, without a doubt, the greatest thing to happen to education since Socrates. Computers aren't going to totally replace all the traditional methods of education, but they are going to make quite an impression. The computer has several advantages that ensure its place in education of the future, namely:

Computers do not get tired.

Programs are easily modified to accommodate new information or teaching styles.

Computer programs are interactive, so they can allow individuals to proceed at their own pace and to cover material selectively.

Computers can generate animated displays on their own video screen as well as control motion pictures and diagrams stored on video disks and cassettes.

If you are a teacher and are worrying about your classroom job being taken over by a computer, don't. Education is usually the last segment of society to wake up to technological advances. It will be a long time before the traditional classroom setting is an anachronism. Besides, there are always students who learn much more quickly from a warm human being than from a collection of integrated silicon wafers.

In this chapter, we will consider a menu-driven approach to presenting educational software. In developing this material, we will include some general graphic display considerations.

Motivation

How can graphics be used in education? The most obvious answer is in diagrams and illustrations. Mind you, our crude black and white graphics cannot compete with color photographs in a flashy textbook, but then photographs do not suddenly spring to life, either. With the techniques we have developed, we can animate words, diagrams—almost anything on the screen. This is a very effective attention-getter and makes up for a whole stack of color glossies. Motion is especially important in stimulating younger students who might have a shorter attention span.

Consider the problem of motivating students to learn a concept like mathematical functions. There are several possible approaches at our fingertips. Mr. White gives his students a list of functions to evaluate for homework. Ms. Jones explains that functions are just like a machine. You put something in one end, and a finished product comes out the other end. She shows them a computer program with an unknown function machine that scoops up the values they enter and spews forth the results.

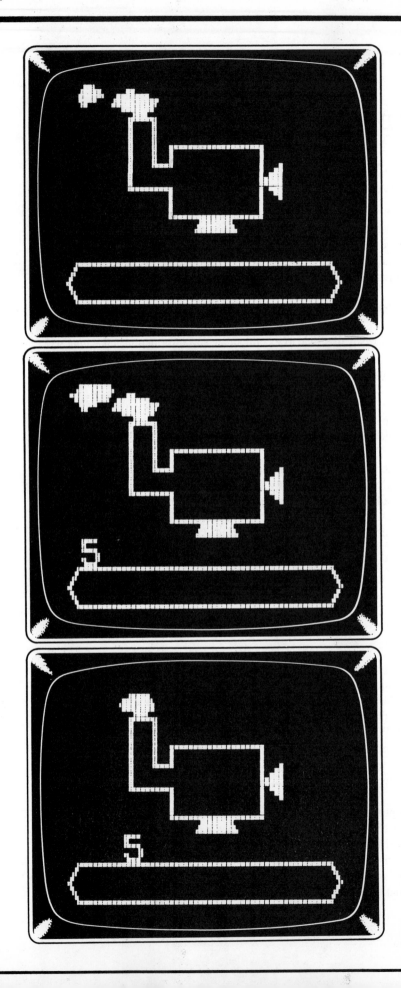

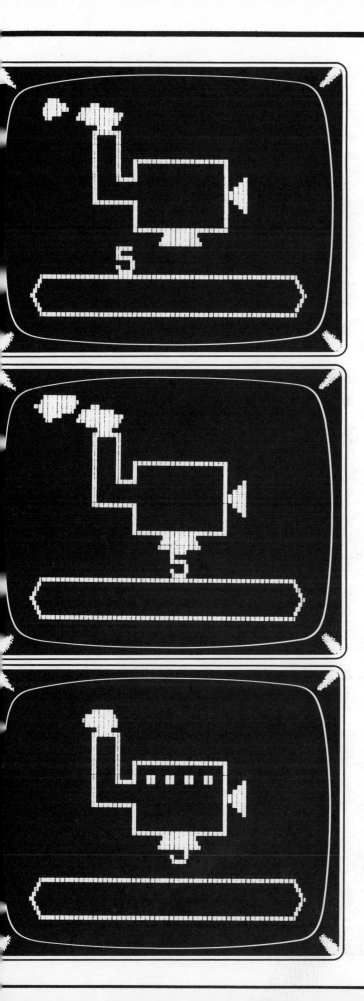

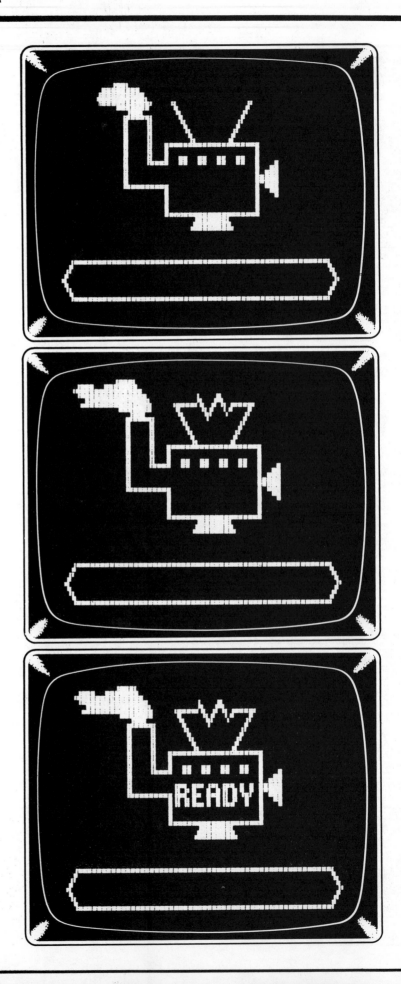

Figure 10.1   A function machine.

e students have to guess what function the machine is using. Her program is
eractive and animated; she has the students in the palm of her hand. You lose, Mr.
hite.

rill and Practice

aphics are often used in drill-and-practice software. Programs that teach music
e recognition, for example, can benefit from graphic display of the notes.

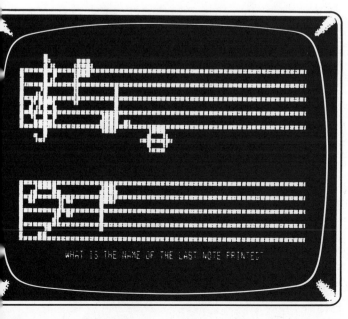

Figure 10.2   Note recognition.

Another classic example of graphics use is provided by programs that develop shape recognition.

Figure 10.3   Shape recognition.

2   Screen Formatting

Menu

A favorite technique used in the designing of educational programs is the offering of menu.

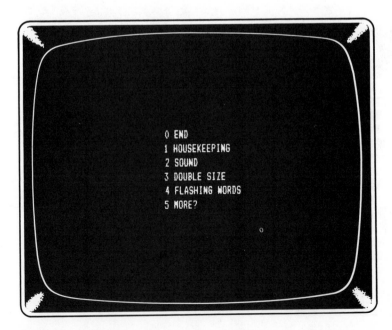

Figure 10.4   A simple menu.

The user can choose an option by pressing a single key. If the program is tutorial in
nature, a menu approach permits immediate access to any portion of the lessons. We
will develop a sample program to illustrate this approach. Our first step will be
formatting the menu. Enter

```
NEW
0 CLEAR 1000
0 N=5: FOR I=0 TO N: READ A$(I): NEXT I
00 CLS
10 R=5: C=24
20 FOR I=0 TO N
30 PRINT@ 64*(R+I)+C, I; A$(I)
40 NEXT I
20 DATA  END, HOUSEKEEPING, SOUND
30 DATA "DOUBLE SIZE", "FLASHING WORDS", MORE?
UN
```

, R, and C determine the number of menu items, the starting row, and the starting
column of the menu list. If you need to update the menu later, edit the DATA lines and
change the values of R and C to suit your tastes.

Title

No menu is complete without a title, so let's give it one. Change

```
00 CLS: A$=N$: GOSUB 240
```

and add

```
0 N$="PROPER PROGRAMMING PRIMER"
10 END
40 L=LEN(A$): P=96-L/2
80 PRINT@ P, A$; : PRINT@ 256,;: RETURN
UN
```

The routine at 240 centers the contents of A$ in row 2. Because that was so easy, let's
give the title a nifty little border. Add

```
50 FOR I=0 TO 2: PRINT@ P-67+64*I,
    CHR$(191)CHR$(192+L+4); CHR$(191);: NEXT
60 PRINT@ P-66, STRING$(L+4,131);
70 PRINT@ P+62, STRING$(L+4,176);
UN
```

Now the routine will not only center but also frame the title.

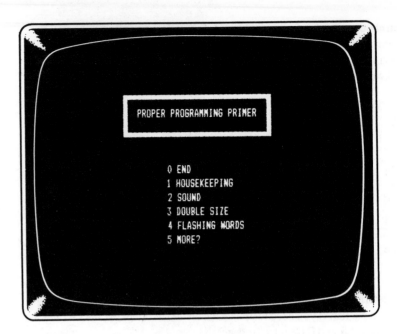

Figure 10.5   A menu title with a frame.

Input

With the menu drawn and ready for use, we have to determine how to make a selection. The input is sometimes done in a subroutine, but we will include it in the main body of the program. A typical approach is to use the INPUT function, but as shown in Chapter 7, INKEY$ gives us much more control and versatility. So, add

```
150 PRINT@ 910, "ENTER SELECTION:";
160 I$=INKEY$: K=VAL(I$): IF I$="0" GOTO 210
170 IF I$="" OR K<1 OR K>N THEN 160
180 PRINT I$
200 GOTO 100
RUN
```

This bit of code will accept only numbers from 0 to N and of course the (BREAK) key. You may want to disable the (BREAK) key as shown in Chapter 7. Protecting your program from wandering fingers is a good idea, especially when the computer will be used by younger students. (Sometimes it is a good idea for older ones, too!)

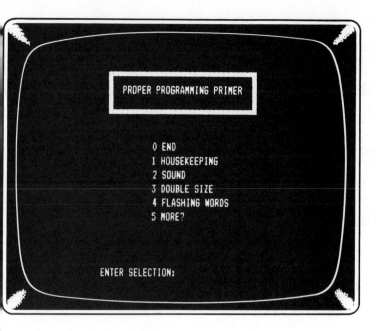

Figure 10.6   A complete menu.

Housekeeping

So far, the menu won't take us anywhere. We need to add an `ON  GOSUB` statement to direct us to various portions of the program. Add

```
190 ON K GOSUB 500, 600
500 CLS: A$=A$(1): R=2: GOSUB 240
540 RETURN
600 CLS: A$=A$(2): R=2: GOSUB 240
560 RETURN
RUN
```

Line 190 directs us to line 500 if K is 1 and to 600 if K is 2, but the titles disappear before we can read them. We need to add a routine that will pause before returning to the menu. Add

```
290 PRINT@ 920, "PRESS ENTER";: INPUT X: RETURN
```

and change

```
540 GOSUB 290: RETURN
560 GOSUB 290: RETURN
RUN
```

And now, we will create one more useful routine, a time delay:

```
300 FOR I=1 TO T: NEXT I : RETURN
310 PRINT "CREATE USEFUL ROUTINES THAT CAN BE USED
    BY EACH MODULE"
320 INPUT "SAMPLE TIME DELAY, ENTER A NUMBER"; T
330 GOSUB 300: PRINT"WE ARE BACK"
LIST
RUN
```

The size of T controls the time of the delay. Try both large and small numbers.

The listing at this point should be:

```
*10  CLEAR 1000
 80  N=5: FOR I=0 TO N: READ A$(I): NEXT I
 90  N$="PROPER PROGRAMMING PRIMER"
100  CLS: A$=N$: GOSUB 240
110  R=5: C=24
120  FOR I=0 TO N
130  PRINT@ 64*(R+I)+C, I; A$(I)
140  NEXT I
150  PRINT@ 910, "ENTER SELECTION:";
160  I$=INKEY$: K=VAL(I$): IF I$="0" GOTO 210
170  IF I$="" OR K<1 OR K>N THEN 160
180  PRINT I$
190  ON  K GOSUB 500, 600
200  GOTO 100
210  END
220  DATA  END, HOUSEKEEPING, SOUND
230  DATA "DOUBLE SIZE", "FLASHING WORDS", MORE?
240  L=LEN(A$): P=96-L/2
250  FOR I=0 TO 2: PRINT@ P-67+64*I,
        CHR$(191)CHR$(192+L+4); CHR$(191);: NEXT
260  PRINT@ P-66, STRING$(L+4,131);
270  PRINT@ P+62, STRING$(L+4,176);
280  PRINT@ P, A$; : PRINT@ 256,; : RETURN
290  PRINT@ 920, "PRESS ENTER"; : INPUT X: RETURN
300  FOR I=1 TO T: NEXT I : RETURN
500  CLS: A$=A$(1): R=2: GOSUB 240
510  PRINT "CREATE USEFUL ROUTINES THAT CAN BE
        USED BY EACH MODULE"
520  INPUT "SAMPLE TIME DELAY, ENTER A NUMBER"; T
530  GOSUB 300: PRINT "WE ARE BACK"
540  GOSUB 290: RETURN
600  CLS: A$=A$(2): R=2: GOSUB 240
660  GOSUB 290: RETURN
```

3 Grabbing Their Attention

One of the most important uses of graphics in an educational environment is getting people's attention. Let's face it: Books put people to sleep (hey, wake up out there!). Classroom instructors are well known for their contribution to the rest periods of America's student population. It would be a shame if computer programs fell into the same rut. The television generation has come to expect dazzling special effects; this creates quite a challenge for programmers and educators.

Sound

Several attention-getting techniques are worth considering. Sound is always a good way to drive a point home, so we will start there. Connect an amplifier to your cassette AUX plug, and add

```
Ø M$=STRING$(24,1): V=VARPTR(M$)
Ø LS=PEEK(V+1): MS=PEEK(V+2)
Ø L=LS+256*MS: IF L>32767 L=L-65536
Ø FOR I=L TO L+20: READ X: POKE I, X: NEXT I
Ø DATA 205,127,10,69,62,1,211,255,16,254,69,62,2,
        211,255,16,254,37,32,239,201
Ø IF PEEK(16396)=201 POKE 16526, LS: POKE 16527,
  MS ELSE DEFUSRØ=L
```

CAUTION! Because we are dealing with PEEK and POKE instructions, it would be a good idea to save this program before it is run.

RUN it to work out any bugs. Lines 20 through 70 place a sound routine in memory. We can access it with the USR function. Add

```
10 FOR I=1 TO 8: X=USR(2000): NEXT: RETURN
10 PRINT "SAMPLE SOUNDS:"
20 INPUT "1"; X: GOSUB 310
UN
```

Choose menu option 2, then press (ENTER) to hear the sound. The USR function is placed in a subroutine at line 310 so that it can be called from other portions of the program. There's more:

```
320 FOR I=1 TO 6: X=USR(20): X=USR(30): NEXT: RETURN
330 FOR I=20 TO 10 STEP-2: X=USR(I): NEXT: RETURN
340 FOR I=1 TO 3: X=USR(56): NEXT
350 X=USR(76): X=USR(68): X=USR(84): RETURN
630 INPUT"2"; X: GOSUB 320
640 INPUT"3"; X: GOSUB 330
650 INPUT"4"; X: GOSUB 340
RUN
```

These routines can be used in other portions of the program.

Large Characters

Normal-width characters are not adequate for all applications. Obviously, double-width characters are much easier to read. The following changes will prepare a double-width screen for us. Change

```
90 ON K GOSUB 500, 600, 700
```

and add

```
00 CLS: PRINTCHR$(23)TAB(10)A$(3)
10 PRINT STRING$(32,42)
90 GOSUB 290: GOSUB 340: RETURN
UN
```

Note the 32-character limit on the screen. Say, isn't it time for your weekly quiz? Add

```
20 PRINT "QUIZ TIME": PRINT
30 PRINT "DOUBLE SIZED CHARACTERS:"
40 PRINT "1 ARE EASIER TO READ"
```

```
750 PRINT "2 GIVE ME A HEADACHE"
760 INPUT "ANSWER"; X
770 IF X<>1 GOSUB 320: GOTO 700
780 GOSUB 330
RUN
```

Sound routines are used to reinforce the appropriate response. If the sound associated with an incorrect response is obnoxious enough, it will encourage a higher proportion of correct answers. But it may discourage use of the program, so, have a heart!

Bright Lights

Here is another technique that uses some of our subroutines:

```
*190 ON K GOSUB 500, 600, 700, 800
 800 CLS: A$=A$(4): GOSUB 240
 810 PRINT "DRAW ATTENTION TO IMPORTANT WORDS OR
     PHRASES WITH"
 820 PRINT "A LITTLE FLASHY RAZZLE DAZZLE:"
 830 FOR J=1 TO 10: PRINT@ 329, "     ";
 840 GOSUB 310: PRINT@ 329, "FLASH";
 850 T=20: GOSUB 300: NEXT J
 860 GOSUB 290: RETURN
RUN
```

Figure 10.7   Flashing words submenu.

The final listing is (take a deep breath here, folks):

```
10 CLEAR 1000
20 M$=STRING$(24,1): V=VARPTR(M$)
30 LS=PEEK(V+1): MS=PEEK(V+2)
40 L=LS+256*MS: IF L>32767 L=L-65536
50 FOR I=L TO L+20: READ X: POKE I, X: NEXT I
60 DATA 205,127,10,69,62,1,211,255,16,254,69,62,2,
        211,255, 16,254,37,32,239,201
70 IF PEEK(16396)=201 POKE 16526, LS: POKE 16527,
   MS ELSE DEFUSR0=L
80 N=5: FOR I=0 TO N: READ A$(I): NEXT I
90 N$="PROPER PROGRAMMING PRIMER"
100 CLS: A$=N$: GOSUB 240
110 R=5: C=24
120 FOR I=0 TO N
130 PRINT@ 64*(R+I)+C, I; A$(I)
140 NEXT I
150 PRINT@ 910, "ENTER SELECTION:";
160 I$=INKEY$: K=VAL(I$): IF I$="0" GOTO 210
170 IF I$="" OR K<1 OR K>N THEN 160
180 PRINT I$
190 ON  K GOSUB 500, 600, 700, 800
200 GOTO 100
210 END
220 DATA  END, HOUSEKEEPING, SOUND
230 DATA "DOUBLE SIZE", "FLASHING WORDS", MORE?
240 L=LEN(A$): P=96-L/2
250 FOR I=0 TO 2: PRINT@ P-67+64*I,
    CHR$(191)CHR$(192+L+4); CHR$(191);: NEXT
260 PRINT@ P-66, STRING$(L+4,131);
270 PRINT@ P+62, STRING$(L+4,176);
280 PRINT@ P, A$; : PRINT@ 256,;: RETURN
290 PRINT@ 920, "PRESS ENTER";: INPUT X: RETURN
300 FOR I=1 TO T: NEXT I : RETURN
310 FOR I=1 TO 8: X=USR(2000): NEXT: RETURN
320 FOR I=1 TO 6: X=USR(20): X=USR(30): NEXT: RETURN
330 FOR I=20 TO 10 STEP-2: X=USR(I): NEXT: RETURN
340 FOR I=1 TO 3: X=USR(56): NEXT
350 X=USR(76): X=USR(68): X=USR(84): RETURN
500 CLS: A$=A$(1): R=2: GOSUB 240
510 PRINT "CREATE USEFUL ROUTINES THAT CAN BE USED
    BY EACH MODULE"
520 INPUT "SAMPLE TIME DELAY, ENTER A NUMBER"; T
530 GOSUB 300: PRINT "WE ARE BACK"
540 GOSUB 290: RETURN
600 CLS: A$=A$(2): R=2: GOSUB 240
610 PRINT "SAMPLE SOUNDS:"
620 INPUT "1"; X: GOSUB 310
630 INPUT "2"; X: GOSUB 320
640 INPUT "3"; X: GOSUB 330
650 INPUT "4"; X: GOSUB 340
660 GOSUB 290: RETURN
700 CLS: PRINT CHR$(23)TAB(10)A$(3)
710 PRINT STRING$(32,42)
720 PRINT "QUIZ TIME": PRINT
```

```
730 PRINT "DOUBLE SIZED CHARACTERS:"
740 PRINT "1 ARE EASIER TO READ"
750 PRINT "2 GIVE ME A HEADACHE"
760 INPUT "ANSWER"; X
770 IF X<>1 GOSUB 320: GOTO 700
780 GOSUB 330
790 GOSUB 290: GOSUB 340: RETURN
800 CLS: A$=A$(4): GOSUB 240
810 PRINT "DRAW ATTENTION TO IMPORTANT WORDS OR
    PHRASES WITH"
820 PRINT "A LITTLE FLASHY RAZZLE DAZZLE:"
830 FOR J=1 TO 10: PRINT@ 329, "        ";
840 GOSUB 310: PRINT@ 329, "FLASH";
850 T=20: GOSUB 300: NEXT J
860 GOSUB 290: RETURN
```

Visual Aids

Introduction To Visual Aids

is often difficult to make meaningful decisions based on large groups of numbers.
raphs and charts can be used to show relationships that might otherwise go
nnoticed. In this chapter, we will look at several different ways of displaying
umerical information with charts and diagrams, including several types of graphs,
ie charts, and pictograms. All of these can be implemented on the TRS-80 with the
chniques discussed in previous chapters.

he types of graphs covered in this chapter can be applied to many areas: advertising,
anagement, sports, you name it. We will present sample programs to create some
amples, and show diagrams of others.

Standard Format

lements Of A Typical Graph

he title should be concise and interesting, and it should clearly indicate the content
d scope of the chart. By convention, it is centered at the top. The following lines
sition a sample title:

```
Ø CLS: CLEAR 100
Ø A$ = "BYTE AND NYBBLE SALES: 1980 - 1987"
Ø PRINT TAB((63-LEN(A$))/2); A$;
UN
```

he source should be included both to give validity to the data and to respect the rights
f the originator of the information. The source is usually located in the bottom left
rner of the display. Add

```
Ø PRINT@ 898, "SOURCE:      BYTE AND NYBBLE SOFTWARE";
99 GOTO 499
UN
```

border can be added if desired:

```
Ø FOR I=1 TO 15: PRINT CHR$(191)CHR$(254)CHR$(191);:
   NEXT
Ø PRINT@ 1, STRING$(62,131);
Ø PRINT@ 129, STRING$(62,140);
Ø PRINT@ 960, CHR$(191)STRING$(62,176);
Ø POKE 16383, 191: PRINT@ 65,;
UN
```

Because of the space compression code used in line 20, this sample border must be printed before going ahead with the title and source. If all the trailing semicolons are in place, the screen should look like figure 11.1.

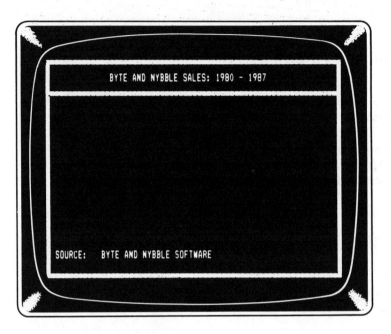

Figure 11.1   Elements of a typical graph.

A legend is used when clarification is necessary. It consists of a sample of the characters used in the diagram, followed by a definition of each character. Usually, it is placed in the bottom right corner, but it can be placed anywhere, as long as it does not interfere with the rest of the diagram. The PRINT@ statement can be used to position the legend. Figure 11.2 shows sample legends.

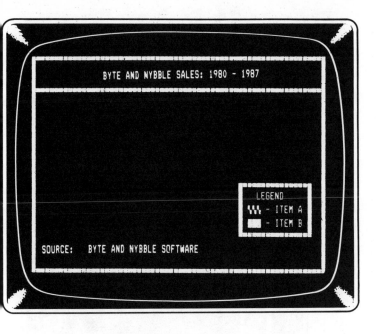

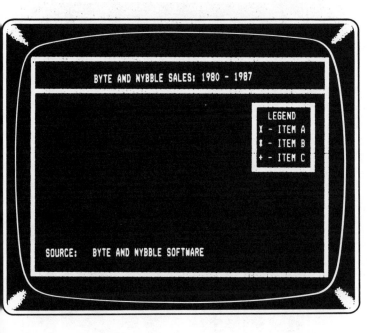

Figure 11.2   Sample legends.

Choosing The Right Form

One of the first steps in graphically presenting data is to decide on the type of diagram that will best express the significant features of the data. Polygonal charts best represent changes in quantities over time. Bar graphs and pictograms could be used to depict changes over time as well as quantities at a fixed point in time. Histograms are employed to display frequencies for grouped data. To compare quantities pie charts serve well. Both maps and pie charts are usually restricted to a single time period. Figure 11.3 shows examples of some of these typical visual aids.

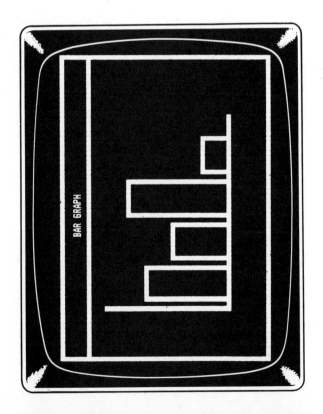

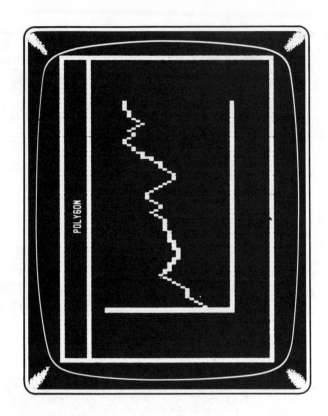

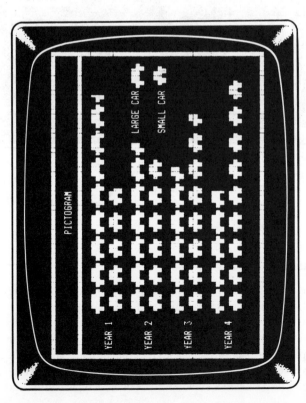

Figure 11-3.   Typical visual aids

3 Sample Programs

Pie Charts

Pie charts show parts of a whole. They describe a single point in time rather than changes over time. For this reason, they are not well suited for projections. It is important that the title include the point in time that the pie chart represents. The major parts of a pie chart are:

1) a circle divided into parts
2) labels to identify parts (optional raw data can be printed near the label for precision)
3) percentages for quick, easy comparisons

We will add a pie chart to our screen border:

```
100 FOR A=0 TO 7 STEP .02
110 SET(63+34.5*COS(A), 26+15*SIN(A))
120 NEXT A: X2=63: Y2=26
RUN
```

Lines 100 through 120 draw the circle. With the help of the line drawing program developed in Chapter 8, we can divide the pie as needed. We will include the program as a subroutine using (63,26) for (X2,Y2). Add

```
500 IF X1<>X2 THEN 530
510 IF Y1<Y2 THEN S=1 ELSE S=-1
520 FOR Y=Y1 TO Y2 STEP S: SET(X1,Y): NEXTY: RETURN
530 M=(Y2-Y1)/(X2-X1)
540 IF ABS(M)>1 S=ABS(1/M) ELSE S=1
550 IF X1>X2 THEN S=-S
560 FOR X=X1 TO X2 STEP S
570 SET(X,M*(X-X1)+Y1)
580 NEXT X: RETURN
```

To use this routine, the program must supply the points (X1,Y1) on the circle. Try

```
*130 READ X1,Y1 : IF X1=0 THEN 499
 140 GOSUB 500: GOTO 130
 150 DATA 63,11,88,15,28,26,75,38,0,0
 RUN
```

This program draws figure 11.4

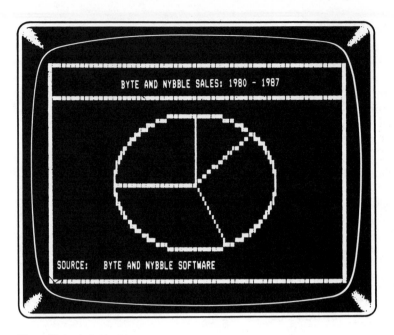

Figure 11.4   A pie chart.

The next figure will help in estimating the points on the circumference. The coordinates are given for 10 percent divisions of the circle.

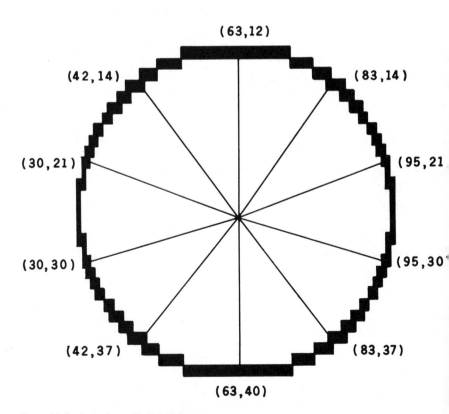

Figure 11.5   A pie chart with 10% divisions.

Labels

Labels are generally located outside the circle and percentages inside. Labels should
be short (preferably only one or two words) and should accurately describe the portion
that they represent. By using the video display sheet you can easily add the
labels and percentages as needed.

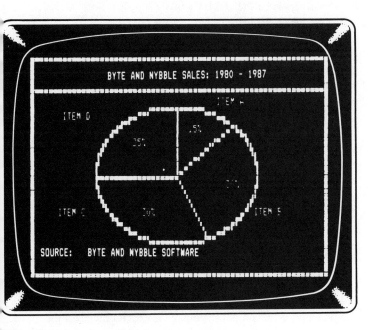

Figure 11.6   A pie chart with labels.

Polygonal Chart

Most of us have seen the sales chart hanging in the manager's office:

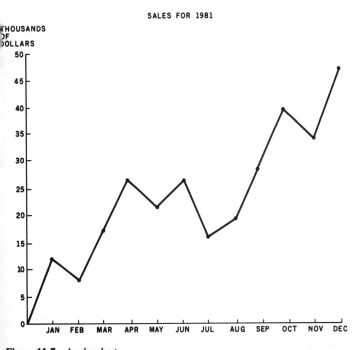

Figure 11.7   A sales chart.

This type of chart emphasizes the rate of change over a period of time. We already have the line drawing routine necessary in the current program, but we will need to add some axes. Make these changes and additions

```
*50  PRINT@ 960, CHR$(191);
 90  PRINT@ 962, "SOURCE:     BYTE AND NYBBLE
     SOFTWARE"
100  READ M1, N: L=M1: N1=INT(100/N+.5)
110  FOR I=1 TO 10: PRINT@ 129+64*I, ;
120  PRINT USING "####.#"; M1-M1/10*(I-1);
130  PRINT "   -"; CHR$(149);: NEXT I
140  PRINT@ 837, 0; TAB(11)CHR$(141);
150  PRINT@ 844, STRING$(50,140);
160  FOR I=26 TO 126 STEP N1: SET(I,41): NEXT I
170  FOR I=0 TO 7: PRINT@ 906+I*N1/2, 1980+I;:
     NEXT I
440  DATA 50, 8
RUN
```

Lines 110 through 150 come with a few modifications from the bar graph program in Chapter 9. M1 is the maximum value for the vertical axis, and N is number of endpoints to be plotted. Line 440 supplies the data for M1 and N.

Scaling

At this point, we should mention that proper scaling of the axes is crucial for the accurate representation of the data. Changes in the number scales can be misleading if they are not handled carefully. For example, eliminating a section of an axis can drastically alter the overall impression of a graph.

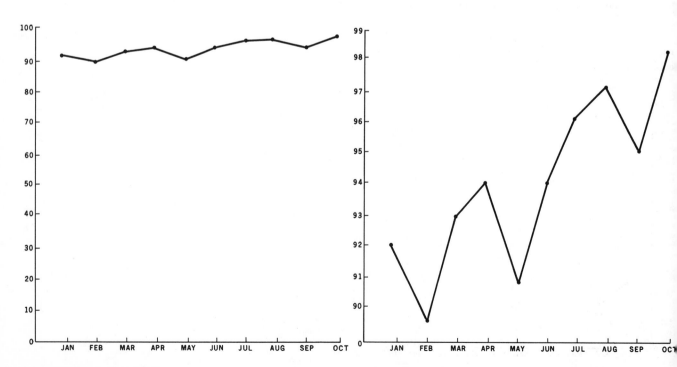

Figure 11.8   a) Easy Rider stock.   b) Rough 'n Ready stock.

Notice how volatile the Rough 'n Ready stock is compared to the Easy Rider stock? Same data, same axes, just a slight change in the scaling. The viewer should be warned of this kind of alteration by a break in the axis.

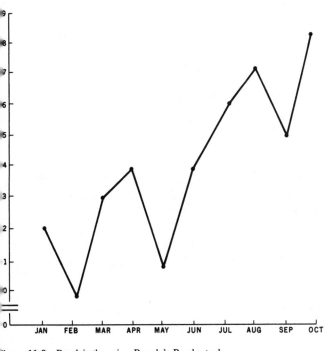

Figure 11.9   Break in the axis—Rough 'n Ready stock.

Another problem is that changes in the scaling of the axes can drastically change the appearance of the graph.

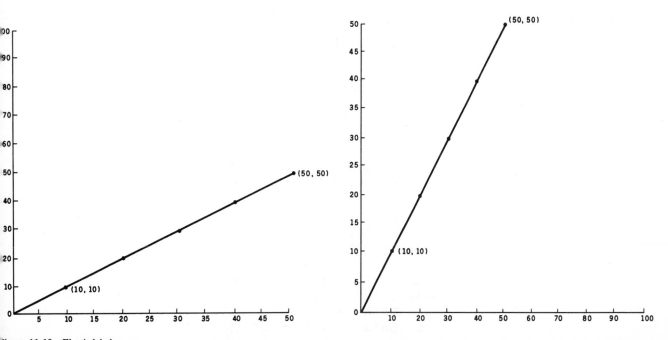

Figure 11.10   Elastic labels.

When you are constructing a graph, these factors should be given careful consideration. We will use a vertical scale ranging from zero to M1 in order to minimize this kind of distortion.

Back To The Polygon

To add the polygon, we need to feed the heights of each vertex to the line drawing routine. Add

```
400 READ Y0
410 FOR X2=26+N1 TO 126 STEP N1
420 X1=X2-N1: Y=Y0: READ Y0
430 GOSUB 500: NEXT X2
450 DATA 8,3,17,12,33,25,37,48
```

Lines 400 through 430 read the heights of each point from line 450. The X coordinate is determined by line 410. The subroutine at 500 will plot our polygon once it is modified to work with our new axes. Change 500 to

```
500 Y1=39-INT(Y/M1*30): Y2=39-INT(Y0/M1*30):
    IF X1<>X2 THEN 530
RUN
```

The data are in lines 440 and 450. If you wish to enter your own data, use up to 50 numbers in line 450, and adjust line 440 accordingly.

You might want to save this program now. The listing should be as follows:

```
*10 CLS: CLEAR 100
 20 FOR I=1 TO 15: PRINT
    CHR$(191)CHR$(254)CHR$(191);: NEXT
 30 PRINT@ 1, STRING$(62,131);
 40 PRINT@ 129, STRING$(62,140);
 50 PRINT@ 960, CHR$(191);
 60 POKE 16383, 191: PRINT@ 65,;
 70 A$="BYTE AND NYBBLE SALES: 1980 - 1987"
 80 PRINT TAB((63-LEN(A$))/2); A$;
 90 PRINT@ 962, "SOURCE:      BYTE AND NYBBLE
    SOFTWARE";
100 READ M1, N: L=M1: N1=INT(100/N+.5)
110 FOR I=1 TO 10: PRINT@ 129+64*I,;
120 PRINT USING "####.#"; M1-M1/10*(I-1);
130 PRINT "   -"; CHR$(149);: NEXT I
140 PRINT@ 837, 0; TAB(11)CHR$(141);
150 PRINT@ 844, STRING$(50,140);
160 FOR I=26 TO 126 STEP N1: SET(I,41): NEXT I
170 FOR I=0 TO 7: PRINT@ 906+I*N1/2, 1980+I;:
    NEXT I
400 READ Y0
410 FOR X2=26+N1 TO 126 STEP N1
420 X1=X2-N1: Y=Y0: READ Y0
430 GOSUB 500: NEXT X2
440 DATA 50, 8
450 DATA 8,3,17,12,33,25,37,48
```

```
499 GOTO 499
500 Y1=39-INT(Y/M1*30): Y2=39-INT(Y0/M1*30):
    IF X1<>X2 THEN 530
510 IF Y1<Y2 THEN S=1 ELSE S=-1
520 FOR Y=Y1 TO Y2 STEP S: SET(X1,Y): NEXT Y: RETURN
530 M=(Y2-Y1)/(X2-X1)
540 IF ABS(M)>1 S=ABS(1/M) ELSE S=1
550 IF X1>X2 THEN S=-S
560 FOR X=X1 TO X2 STEP S
570 SET(X,M*(X-X1)+Y1)
580 NEXT X: RETURN
```

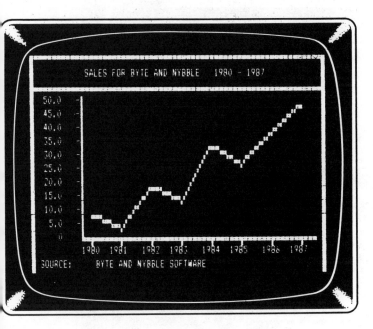

Figure 11.11   A polygonal chart of sales over time.

Time vs. Quantity Bar Graphs

Time vs. quantity bar graphs are extremely useful tools for future planning. They can show historical performance and indicate trends for the future. Either a horizontal or vertical format is possible.

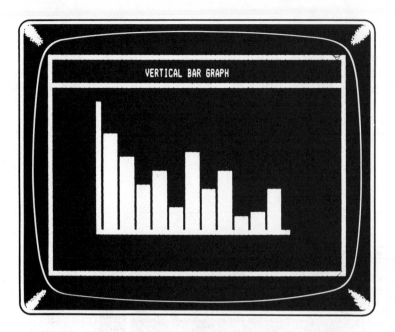

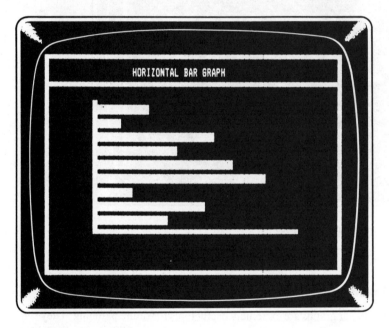

Figure 11.12   Bar graph formats.

The horizontal format is much easier both to use and to label when a printer is involved. On the other hand, most people prefer the visual impact of the vertical format. It is a little harder to work with for us programmers, but that's our job.

We can modify the current program to create a vertical time vs. quantity bar graph. Change

```
100 READ M1, N: L=M1: N1=INT(100/N)
160 FOR I=25 TO 126 STEP N1: SET(I,41): NEXT I
170 FOR I=0 TO 7: PRINT@ 909+I*N1/2, 1980+I;: NEXT I
```

These changes adjust the horizontal scale to accommodate the vertical bars. Now add

```
400 FOR D=0 TO N-1 : READ X
410 FOR Y=0 TO INT(X/M1*30+.5)
420 FOR Z=0 TO N1-2 : SET(N1*D+Z+26,40-Y)
430 NEXT Z: NEXT Y: NEXT D
RUN
```

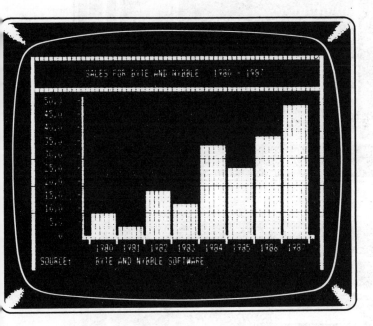

Figure 11.13   A bar graph of sales over time.

t works with the same set of data as the polygonal graph. The main difference is that he polygonal graph emphasizes the rate of change over time whereas a bar graph oints up absolute differences.

More Graphs And Charts

With a bit of perseverence and creativity, almost any kind of chart or diagram can be isplayed on the TRS-80. Here are some examples.

Multiple Graphs On One Chart

We can differentiate between two or more graphs on the same chart by using different haracters for each graph.

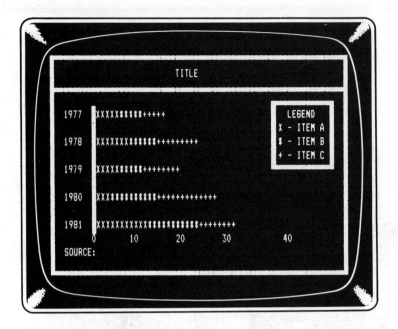

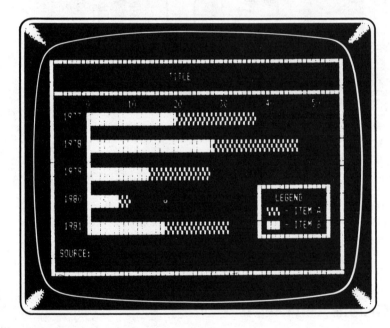

Figure 11.14   Multiple graphs.

Pictograms

An interesting variation on the bar graph can be achieved by using figures instead of bars. A legend is required to define the value associated with each figure. Properly designed, even partial figures can be used, as shown in figure 11.15

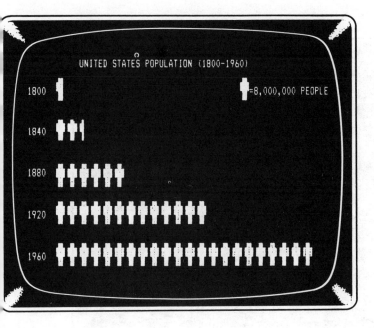

Figure 11.15   A pictogram.

The special character set of the Model III greatly extends the utility of this type of graph.

Maps

Maps can be used to describe a surprising array of information, even with the low resolution graphics of the TRS-80. A simple map showing the locations of distributorships is much more impressive than a list of words. Maps can be a rewarding way to keep track of an expanding business.

Figure 11.16   A map of the United States.

Volume

This one can be tricky, but don't let that stop you!

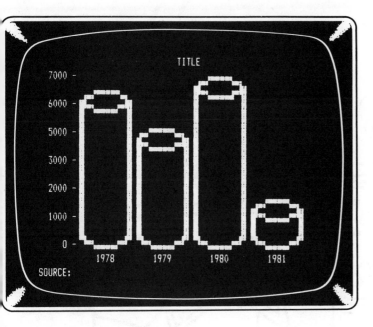

Figure 11.17   A three-dimensional graph.

Games And Animation

Games

Have you ever wondered why microcomputing is so popular? What makes people buy these overgrown calculators? Ask any microcomputer fiend, and you'll hear reasons such as word processing for business, tax preparation, payroll and accounts receivable, home budget, ... Okay, that all sounds fair enough, but what do they do on their computers at 2 A.M.? Chances are most of them would be perched, glassy-eyed and nervous on the edge of their chairs—fighting off yet another squadron of aliens.

Yes, the secret is out. One of the best things about computers is that they allow us to take a few minutes (who are we kidding—a few hours!) out of our day to become Captain of the Enterprise, climb Mount Everest, rule our own kingdom, participate in the Olympics, seek vast treasures, play pinball, or test our strategy in chess. Your TRS-80 and your imagination can lead you through an incredible variety of experiences. Don't get the wrong idea. There are people who occasionally squeeze in some work on these machines, but the fact is, computers are just plain fun!

Game programs have proliferated faster than any other kind of software. We certainly won't be able to cover the vast array of graphic applications in one chapter, but we can look at a sampling of some of the graphic techniques available to the game programmer.

Long-Lasting Flavor

Probably the most difficult challenge for a game designer is to prevent eventual user boredom. Even the best games lose their hypnotic effects after a time. Once an adventure is solved, what do we do with the darned thing? Once we have gunned down 50,000 asterisks, what do we chase next—percent signs? What is the secret to writing games with "staying power"?

Games should be challenging, for starters. Not so hard that they overwhelm the novice, but difficult enough to provide a constant challenge to players as they improve their skills. Active participation is also a key requirement. People like to interact with the computer and be a part of the scene. Finally, if a game can also simulate our imagination, it provides even more of an escape from our daily routine.

One feature that many games lack is sensory (especially audio and visual) simulation. Creative graphics and sound can charge the imagination, thereby immeasurably improving even mediocre computer games. Games that use dynamic graphic displays, animation, and sound are not likely to make an early trip to the "disk-carded" pile of programs.

2 Saving The Screen

There are nearly as many different playing surfaces as there are games—sandy sidewalks, new-mown greens, checkered tabletops. For computer games, creating a new way of looking at an old idea adds a special charm. One way to protect those displays is to store them in string arrays. If something goes wrong, you can give the player the option of redrawing the board.

Let's create a game board. Enter

```
NEW
10 CLS: CLEAR 3000: RANDOM: DIM S$(16)
20 W$=STRING$(3,191)
30 P1$="(0)": P2$="<->"
40 FOR P=276 TO 660 STEP 128
50 FOR I=0 TO 3
60 PRINT@ P+6*I, W$;: PRINT@ P+67+6*I, W$;
70 NEXT I: NEXT P
80 GOSUB 180: PRINT@ P, P1$;
90 GOSUB 180: PRINT@ P, P2$;
100 GOTO 100
180 P=209+3*RND(8)+64*RND(8): RETURN
RUN
```

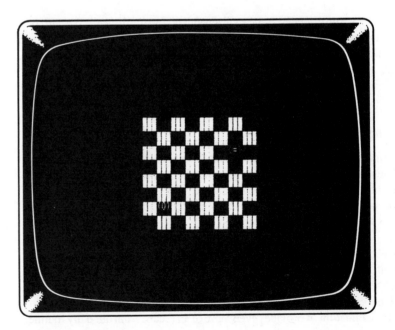

Figure 12.1 A game board.

The board is printed two rows at a time in line 60. Subroutine 180 positions the piece randomly on the board. Now we have something to save. The subroutine that will save the screen in the string array S$ is the following:

```
1000 X$="": V=VARPTR(X$): POKE V, 64
1010 FOR I=0 TO 15: J=INT(I/4)
1020 POKE V+1, 64*I-256*J: POKE V+2, 60+J
1030 S$(I+1)=X$: NEXT I
1040 RETURN
```

It works by locating the three-byte index of the dummy variable X$. The string length
of X$ is set by poking 64 into the first byte of the index. (Sneaky!) Then it pokes the
starting location of each row of the screen (15360, 15424, 15488, . . .) into bytes two
and three of the index. This forces the location of X$ to be that row of the screen,
which is then transferred to the string array (S$) in line 1030. The loop continues
until each row is stored in S$. To see the routine in action, add

```
100 PRINT@ 832,;
110 INPUT "PRESS <ENTER> TO SAVE SCREEN"; X
120 GOSUB 1000: CLS
130 INPUT "PRESS <ENTER> TO BRING IT BACK"; X
140 PRINT@ 0,;: FOR I=1 TO 15
150 PRINT S$(I);: NEXT I
160 PRINT LEFT$(S$(16),63);: POKE 16383,
     ASC(RIGHT$(S$(16),1))
170 PRINT CHR$(15);: GOTO 80
RUN
```

Press **ENTER** and the screen will be saved in S$. When the screen clears, press
ENTER again to see the screen restored. Two pieces are added each time the screen is
saved. Notice that a POKE to location 16383 is used in line 160 to stop the automatic
screen scroll. CHR$(15) is used in line 170 to turn off the cursor.

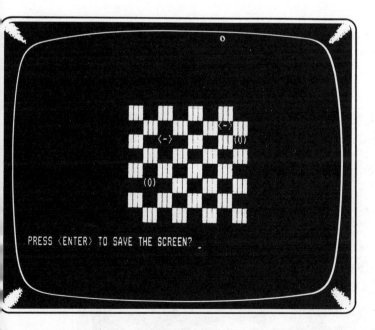

Figure 12.2   A game board with a screen-save option.

This technique of saving the screen can avoid a lot of frustration when something
unexpectedly creates chaos in the screen display. Once the screen is saved, it can be
easily recalled as needed. Save this routine now.

3 Moving Targets

Plenty of games now available on the market involve shooting at moving targets. In some of these, the projectile moves at an agonizingly slow pace, making it difficult to judge when to fire. The following program uses character strings as an alternative to SET and RESET for faster action.

Sitting Ducks

We are going to create an arcade-type game to illustrate several of the techniques shown in earlier chapters. In this program, there will be targets moving across the top of the screen and a gun at the bottom of the screen. As the program develops, be aware of the following: how the targets are moved, how the ''laser ray'' is animated, how impact is determined, how the targets are erased, and how program design affects speed.

Let's start by creating two strings S and T that will contain the targets. Enter

```
NEW
120 CLEAR 2000: DEFINT A-R: DEFSTR S-Z: CLS: A=30
140 FOR I=1 TO 20: S=S+CHR$(132)+STRING$(RND(15)
    ,32): NEXT
180 W=CHR$(166)+CHR$(179)+CHR$(153)
190 FOR I=1 TO 10: T=T+W+STRING$(6+RND(12),32):
    NEXT I
200 L=LEN(T): G=LEN(S)
230 PRINT@ 0, S: PRINT T
RUN
```

The strings S and T are composed of graphic characters separated by a random number of blank spaces. W is a temporary string variable used to build T. The lengths of strings S and T are stored in variables G and L.

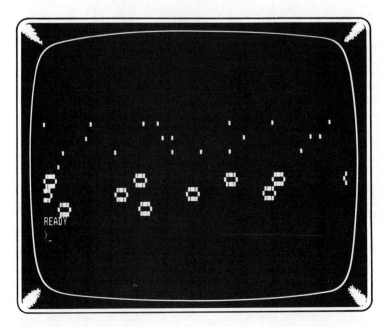

Figure 12.3   Target strings.

Let's set the targets in motion. Add

```
  GOTO 120
2 S=RIGHT$(S,G-1)+LEFT$(S,1)
3 T=RIGHT$(T,L-3)+LEFT$(T,3)
4 PRINT@ 448, LEFT$(S,64): PRINT@ 64, LEFT$(T,64)
5 RETURN
0 REM
10 GOSUB 2: GOTO 40
230 GOTO 40
RUN
```

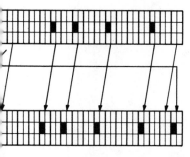

Figure 12.4   Moving targets by string manipulation.

Line 2 takes the first character in string S and moves it to the end of the string. Each time subroutine 2 is called, the targets move one place to the left. Motion for string T is similar, except that the targets are moved three spaces to the left each time the motion routine is called. This technique gives us, in effect, two endless loops. Although the strings can be as long as 255 characters, only the leftmost 64 are displayed in line 4.

The subroutine is positioned at the beginning of the program. This reduces the search time for the routine each time it is used, thus increasing the speed of the animation.

Silver Bullets

To deal with such menacing targets, we'll surely need a potent weapon. How about a laser cannon? Add

```
50 FOR I=1 TO 11: READ N: Z=Z+CHR$(N): NEXT I
60 DATA 184,135,130,27,24,24,160,180,26,173,144
70 PRINT@ 990, Z;
UN
```

We'll also need some way to fire the cannon and a flashy laser ray that will leap out and disintegrate the targets:

```
0 IF PEEK(14400)<>128 GOSUB 2: GOTO 40
0 PRINT@ 864, X;: FOR I=864 TO 32 STEP-64:
   PRINT@ I," ";: NEXT I
10 U=CHR$(149)+CHR$(27)+CHR$(24)
```

```
220 FOR I=1 TO 14: X=X+U: NEXT: GOTO 40
230 GOTO 230
RUN
```

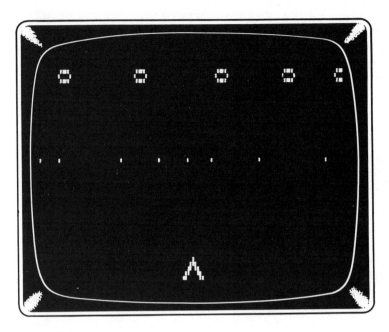

Figure 12.5   A laser cannon.

Remember PEEK input from Chapter 5? Line 50 tests location 14400 to see if the
(SPACEBAR) is depressed. If it is, location 14400 contains a 128, and control passes t•
line 90 where we get a satisfying laser blast. You can even hold down the (SPACEBA■
for fast and furious continuous firing.

The laser ray is stored in string X in line 220. A simple PRINT@ in line 90 quickly
displays the ray. The rest of line 90 erases the ray from the bottom up, producing the
illusion of motion.

As impressive as it is, the laser doesn't do much good if it has no effect on the targets
Obviously, once contact is made, something has to happen to the target. If we were
working in machine language, we could afford the luxury of exploding targets on
impact. With a slower language like BASIC, we will settle for simple erasing the
targets from the string.

Here is our plan of attack. First, we have to test for impact. Add, but don't RUN this

```
70 GOSUB 2: H=0: IF POINT(64,4) OR POINT(64,5)
   H=1: P=0
80 IF POINT(64,22) H=1: P=1
100 IF H=1 THEN 10
```

H is used to determine if a hit is made and is initialized to zero in line 70. Then sever
points along the path of the laser beam are tested to see if they are about to be zapped
If there is a target in the way, H is changed to 1. P is used to determine which target
was hit. When the hit is in the top row, P is set to 0. Otherwise, P is set to 1. If there
are two targets in the laser's path, the lower target loses.

If there is a hit, we have to test P, then erase the appropriate target. Add

```
10 IF P=1 B=B+20: S=LEFT$(S,30)+V+RIGHT$(S,G-34)
20 IF P=0 B=B+25: T=LEFT$(T,28)+Y+RIGHT$(T,L-38)
130 V=STRING$(4,32): Y=STRING$(10,32)
RUN
```

Press (SPACEBAR) to fire the laser and watch those targets disappear. Yipee! The string containing the unlucky target is modified by replacing the target with a string of spaces. B is used to keep track of the player's score.

Now for a few finishing touches. We'll print the score each time it changes, keep track of the number of shots, and stop the game after 30 shots. Add

```
30 PRINT@ 896, "SCORE:"B;: GOSUB 2
40 PRINT@ 896, "SCORE:"B;: IF A=0 PRINT@ 604,
    "GAME OVER": GOTO 230
50 A=A-1: PRINT@ 960, "SHOTS:"; A;
RUN
```

If you want to add even more frustration to this game, change line 100 to

```
100 IF H=1 THEN 10 ELSE B=B-10
RUN
```

This addition deducts 10 points for every miss. Of course, you can vary the point structure by changing the values added to B in lines 10 and 20. With the current setup, a perfect game would net 650 points. Good luck!

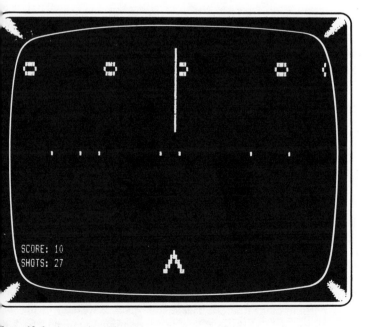

Figure 12.6   A game in motion.

If you find you just can't stop fiddling with this program, try adding USR commands to generate sound when the laser is fired and when contact is made.

Final listing:

```
*1 GOTO 120
 2 S=RIGHT$(S,G-1)+LEFT$(S,1)
 3 T=RIGHT$(T,L-3)+LEFT$(T,3)
 4 PRINT@ 448, LEFT$(S,64): PRINT@ 64, LEFT$(T,64)
 5 RETURN
10 IF P=1 B=B+20: S=LEFT$(S,30)+V+RIGHT$(S,G-34)
20 IF P=0 B=B+25: T=LEFT$(T,28)+Y+RIGHT$(T,L-38)
30 PRINT@ 896, "SCORE:"B;: GOSUB 2
40 PRINT@ 896, "SCORE:"B;: IF A=0 PRINT@ 604,
   "GAME OVER": GOTO 230
50 IF PEEK(14400)<>128 GOSUB 2: GOTO 40
60 A=A-1: PRINT@ 960, "SHOTS:"; A;
70 GOSUB 2: H=0: IF POINT(64,4) OR POINT(64,5)
   H=1: P=0
80 IF POINT(64,22) H=1: P=1
90 PRINT@ 864, X;: FOR I=864 TO 32 STEP-64:
   PRINT@ I, " ";: NEXT I
100 IF H=1 THEN 10 ELSE B=B-10
110 GOSUB 2: GOTO 40
120 CLEAR 2000: DEFINT A-R: DEFSTR S-Z: CLS: A=30
130 V=STRING$(4,32): Y=STRING$(10,32)
140 FOR I=1 TO 20: S=S+CHR$(132)+STRING$(RND(15)
    ,32): NEXT
150 FOR I=1 TO 11: READ N: Z=Z+CHR$(N): NEXT I
160 DATA 184,135,130,27,24,24,160,180,26,173,144
170 PRINT@ 990, Z;
180 W=CHR$(166)+CHR$(179)+CHR$(153)
190 FOR I=1 TO 10: T=T+W+STRING$(6+RND(12),32):
    NEXT I
200 L=LEN(T): G=LEN(S)
210 U=CHR$(149)+CHR$(27)+CHR$(24)
220 FOR I=1 TO 14: X=X+U: NEXT: GOTO 40
230 GOTO 230
```

Better save this now.

4 More On Animation

Border Crossing

We have seen several examples of string variables used to produce graphics and animation. When figures stored in strings are moved around the screen, the edge of the screen can sometimes be a problem. An error can result if we are not careful. One solution is to erase portions of the figure as it leaves the screen as we did with the sna[ ] in Chapter 4. A variation on this theme is to turn the figure around and send it back in the opposite direction. The following program demonstrates one way to do this. Ent[ ]

```
NEW
10 CLS : CLEAR 200 : DEFSTR Y, Z
20 Y=CHR$(128)+STRING$(8,172)+CHR$(143)+CHR$(143)+CHR$(128)
30 Z=CHR$(128)+CHR$(143)+CHR$(143)+STRING$(8,172)+CHR$(128)
```

These first three lines set the stage for the program. Take a look at the strings Y and Z
with

```
RUN
PRINT Y, Z
```

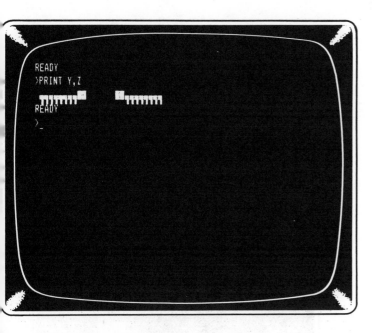

Figure 12.7   The contents of strings Y and Z.

We are going to move this creature across the screen from left to right. When it
reaches the right border, we want it to make a smooth about-face and come back from
right to left. Motion near the center of the screen is easy, but it will require some fancy
footwork at the edges. Add

```
50 L=LEN(Y): FOR P=0 TO 63
60 IF P+L>63 PRINT@ P+R*128, LEFT$(Y,64-P); :
   PRINT@ R*128+128-(L-64+P), LEFT$(Z,L-64+P);
   ELSE PRINT@ P+R*128, Y : FOR I=1 TO 2: NEXT I
70 NEXT P
RUN
```

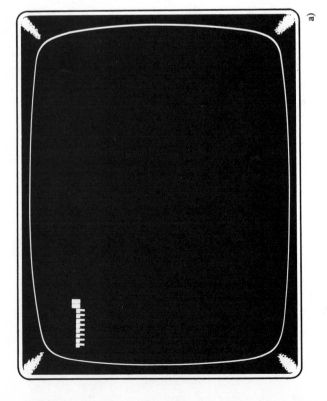

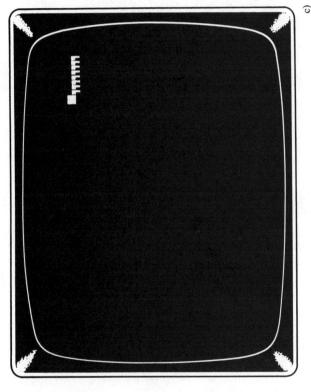

Figure 12.8   About-face sequence.

Line 60 controls the turn-around. As the creature moves across the screen, the ELSE section of line 60 prints the entire string Y. When the creature gets close to the right edge, the program displays the left portion of string Y as it goes off the screen, and the left portion of Z as it emerges onto the screen. When the turn is completed, Z is printed as it moves from right to left. The delay loop at the end of line 60 compensates for the time-consuming string manipulation as the figure is turned around.

The right-to-left motion is done in a similar fashion:

```
80 FOR P=128-L TO 64-L STEP -1
90 IF P<64 PRINT@ R*128+128, RIGHT$(Y,64-P); :
   PRINT@ R*128+64, RIGHT$(Z,L-64+P); ELSE PRINT@
   P+R*128,Z : FOR I=1 TO 2: NEXT I
100 NEXT P
RUN
```

Now we can have the little beast scurry down the entire screen by adding

```
40 FOR R=0 TO 6
110 NEXT R
RUN
```

Remember that in using this method with larger string-packed figures, the way in which the string is constructed can be very important. (See the snail program in Chapter 4.)

Figure Animation

The secret to animating larger figures lies in storing different versions of each portion of the figure in separate string variables, then displaying them in sequence to produce animation. The previous program used a single string to depict motion in a given direction. The next example shows what can be done with two strings that are alternately displayed to give the illusion of motion. Enter

```
NEW
10 CLS: CLEAR 200
20 DEFSTR A: DEFINT B-Z
30 A1=STRING$(12,128)+CHR$(26)+STRING$(12,24)
   +CHR$(143)+CHR$(173)+CHR$(156)+STRING$(7,140)
   +CHR$(172)+CHR$(156)
40 A2=STRING$(2,128)+CHR$(168)+CHR$(159)+CHR$(131)
   +CHR$(175)+CHR$(148)+CHR$(26)+STRING$(7,24)
   +CHR$(143)+CHR$(173)+CHR$(159)+CHR$(129)
   +CHR$(128)+CHR$(130)+CHR$(175)+CHR$(156)
   +STRING$(44,128)
```

To look at the strings you just created, type

```
RUN
PRINT A1, A2
```

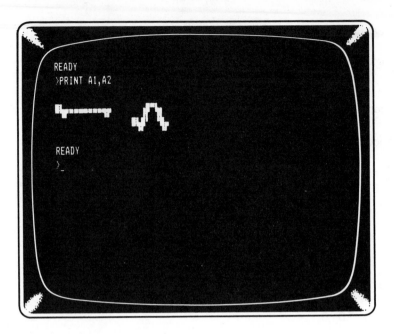

Figure 12.9   Strings A1 and A2.

Each figure is two characters high, although the top row of A1 is filled with blanks. To see the strings in action add

```
50 FOR P=115 TO 65 STEP -4
60 PRINT@ P, A1: FOR I=1 TO 200: NEXT
70 PRINT@ P, A2: FOR I=1 TO 200: NEXT
80 NEXT P
90 GOTO 90
RUN
```

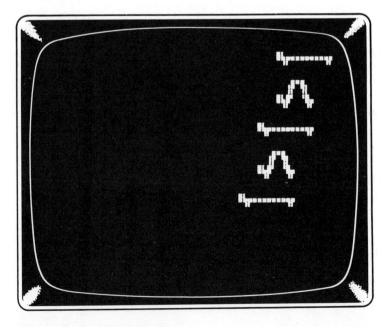

Figure 12.10   An inchworm in motion.

tring A1 is printed at P, followed by A2. This brings the back legs forward in
preparation for the next step. P is then decremented by four so that the next time A1 is
printed, the rear legs are in the same position, but the front legs have moved forward.
n short, we have simulated the motion of an inchworm. The approximation is very
ough as we used only two versions of the figure, but the eye tends to fill in the
missing steps.

n the next chapter, we will extend the notion of storing several versions of the same
igure in different strings.

Figure Animation

The market is becoming flooded with a mind-boggling array of games that have animated graphics and sound. Some of the graphics written in BASIC will make you nod off, but a few *are* quite ingenious. Leading the pack of graphic artists using BASIC is Leo Christopherson, with entries like Android Nim, Snakeggs, and Dancing Demon. These programs are written in BASIC, but pack both strings and remark lines with graphic characters and machine language routines. The result is pure delight. We can gain some insight into the magic of his creations by doing a little creating of our own.

1 Meet Critter

Shoo everyone else out of the room so that you can concentrate, and keep this book well hidden so they can't see what you're up to. In a few hours, you can surprise them with a mean and ferocious animated critter. See figure 13.1.

Figure 13.1   Critter.

Actually, it looks rather docile doesn't it? We'll leave it to you to add fangs and menacing eyes after we are all finished.

Where Do We Put Him?

Our first programming consideration should be what we want Critter to do? Do we want it to fly around the screen or just stand in one place and twitch? How about metamorphosing into a unicorn? The answer will determine our techniques for storing, displaying, and animating the figure. To keep the animation manageable, we'll have it do everyday things such as wiggle its toes and antennae, move its eyes, and maybe even grace us with a grin. No flying allowed. For the constant updating this will require, our best bet is to store each row of Critter in a separate string variable. See figure 13.2.

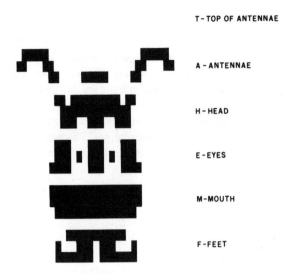

Figure 13.2   String variables used to store Critter:

There is no real advantage in storing the entire figure in one string unless it is to move around the screen. Once it is printed, we'll need to change only one or two rows at a time to simulate movement.

Let's have a look now at how the animation is to be done. We are going to store complete new versions of each section of the body, and when we want something to move, we'll print them over the current version. For starters, figure 13.3 shows several different versions of the antennae.

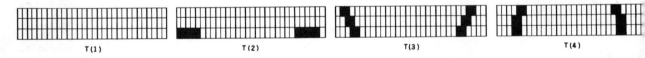

Figure 13.3   The antennae.

If the antennae tops are stored in memory as T(1), T(2), T(3), and T(4), they can easily be printed by number. For example, we could use the following to print a random sequence of antennae movements:

```
10 PRINT@ 410, T(RND(4));
20 GOTO 10
```

On To The Program!

Let's cut out this kid's stuff and get down to some serious programming. Start with some housekeeping:

```
NEW
10 '
    '  INITIALIZE VARIABLES
    '
20 CLS: CLEAR 2000
30 DEFSTR A-Z: DEFINT I, N, P
40 DIM T(5), A(2), H(2), E(7), M(5), F(2)
```

Line 10 labels this section of the program. You can use the down arrow to create the spacing shown. Lines 20 and 30 are straightforward. Line 40 reserves room for the string arrays necessary to store different versions of the figure. The variables represent the various portions of the figure:

> T—top of the antennae
> A—antennae
> H—head
> E—eyes
> M—mouth
> F—feet

Although storing the entire critter in a single two-dimension string array would require less typing, it would use more memory and be harder to follow.

2 Building The Body Parts

Read Routine

The graphic characters can be read in as data. Therefore, we'll need a READ routine. Add

```
999 STOP
1000 '
     '  SUBROUTINES
     '
1010 *** READ DATA ***
1020 X=""
1030 READ N
1040 IF N>127 X=X+CHR$(N): GOTO 1030
1050 IF N>0 READ N1: X=X+STRING$(N,N1): GOTO 1030
1060 PRINT@ 1000, X: PRINT
1070 RETURN
```

and some sample DATA such as this:

```
2000 '
     '  DATA
     '
2010 '  TOP ANTENNAE
```

```
2020 DATA 207,0
2030 DATA 2,176,144,201,2,176,144,0
2040 DATA 130,173,144,201,184,135,128,0
2050 DATA 128,168,151,200,130,189,128,128,0
2060 ' ANTENNAE
2070 DATA 142,131,139,180,194,2,176,144,128,160,
     158,131,139,132,0
2080 DATA 2,128,139,180,194,2,176,144,128,160,158,
     129,2,128,0
```

Line 999 protects the program from accidentally running into the READ routine. The
READ routine builds a figure from each data line and stores it in X. Line 1020 starts X
out as a blank string. Line 1030 reads the first number into N. If N is greater than 127,
it represents a graphic character, so it is added to the end of X, and we go back to line
1030 to read the next number. If N is greater than zero, but less than 128, the next
number is read into N1, and a string of N repeats of character N1 are added to X. This
repeat feature can significantly reduce the amount of data needed. Control is sent back
to 1030 to read the next number. The routine continues reading the data line until a
zero (or negative number) is read. Control slips through to line 1060, which prints the
figure now stored in X. This line is included so that you can visually check the figures
to make sure your data is correct. You can delete it later.

When the program returns from the READ routine, a one-line figure is stored in the
string variable X. We must transfer the figure from X to the appropriate variable. Add

```
50 FOR I=1 TO 4: GOSUB 1000: T(I)=X: NEXT I
60 FOR I=1 TO 2: GOSUB 1000: A(I)=X: NEXT I
```

Lines 50 and 60 send the program to the READ routine and store X when the
subroutine returns. At this point, you can RUN the program to check the figures
stored in T and A against figure 13.3.

Draw The Figure

We don't have the entire figure stored in memory yet, but let's print out what we do
have. Add

```
*200 '
     '    DRAWFIGURE
     '
210 CLS
220 P=600
230 GOSUB 1080
1080 ' *** DRAW ROUTINE ***
1090 PRINT@ P-131, T(1);
1100 PRINT@ P-67, A(1);
1110 PRINT@ P,H(1);
1120 PRINT@ P+64, E(1);
1130 PRINT@ P+128, M(1);
1140 PRINT@ P+192, F(1);
1150 RETURN
RUN
```

Drawing the figure is done in a subroutine to make modifications easier. Lines 210
through 230 clear the screen, choose the position for the figure, and call the

subroutine. The subroutine prints portions of the figure above and below position P.
Succeeding positions below P start in the same column (differing by 64); the antennae
are indented a bit.

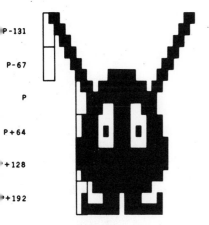

Figure 13.4   PRINT@ positions for Critter.

Twitching Antennae

Before we fill in the rest of the figure, we will look at how the animation process can
be randomized. We can move the antennae by printing a randomly chosen version of
T at position P-131, delaying briefly, then replacing it with another version. Add

```
500 '
    '    ANIMATE FIGURE
    '
510 REM
530 I=RND(4): PRINT@ P-131, T(I);
540 IF I=1 PRINT@ P-67, A(1); ELSE PRINT@
    P-67, A(2);
550 GOTO 660
660 N=60: GOSUB 1170: GOTO 510
1160 ' *** TIME DELAY ***
1170 FOR I1=1 TO N: NEXT I1: RETURN
RUN
```

Lines 500 through 999 are reserved for animation routines. Each routine will be sent
to 660 when it is finished. Line 660 controls the time delay and sends the program
back to line 510 for more animation. For the antennae, line 530 chooses a random
antennae top, and line 540 selects the appropriate bottom portion. See figure 13.5.

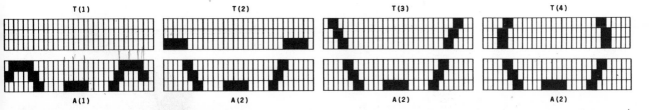

Figure 13.5   Antennae combinations.

Head

Versions of the head will be read just like the antennae. H (1) will be used most of the time:

```
70 FOR I=1 TO 2: GOSUB 1000: H(I)=X: NEXT I
2090 ' HEAD
2100 DATA 130,189,159,175,191,143,189,151,0
2110 DATA 130,189,4,191,189,151,0
RUN
```

Eyes

See figure 13.6 for the different versions of the eyes. In order to limit the amount of data necessary to implement all these versions of one body section, we will use a slightly different technique of reading in the data. We can take advantage of the similarities of all the different versions by storing these characters in temporary variables. This will be done for the left and right ends of the eye sections:

```
80 GOSUB 1000: EL=X
90 GOSUB 1000: ER=X
2130 DATA 186,191,0,191,144,0
```

Now the eyes can be created by concatenating these ends to the center portions read from the data:

```
100 FOR I=1 TO 7: GOSUB 1000: E(I)=EL+X+ER: NEXT I
2120 ' EYES
2140 DATA 136,170,191,136,170,0
2150 DATA 132,170,191,132,170,0
2160 DATA 128,174,191,128,174,0
2170 DATA 130,170,191,130,170,0
2180 DATA 160,170,191,160,170,0
2190 DATA 155,187,191,155,187,0
2200 DATA 5,191,0
RUN
```

Aren't you glad we cut down on the data? Check your figures against figure 13.6 using the **(SHIFT)** **(@)** keys to pause the display.

We are not going to use all the eye versions for random eye movement. Those that *will* be used will have to do a bit of time sharing with the antennae:

```
520 ON RND(4) GOTO 530, 560, 560, 570
560 PRINT@ P+64, E(RND(5)); : GOTO 660
570 REM
RUN
```

Line 520 choses which sections of the figure will be changed. Line 530 is the antenna and 560 the eyes; 570 will be the feet.

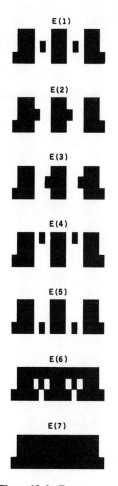

Figure 13.6   Eyes.

Mouth-To-Mouth

The mouth will be created in much the same fashion as the eyes, but we will add animation later.

```
110 GOSUB 1000: ML=X : GOSUB 1000: MR=X
120 FOR I=1 TO 5: GOSUB 1000: M(I)=ML+X+MR: NEXT I
2210 ' MOUTH
2220 DATA 175,0,133,0
2230 DATA 7,191,0
2240 DATA 3,191,175,3,191,0
2250 DATA 2,191,159,143,3,191,0
2260 DATA 191,151,139,143,131,2,191,0
2270 DATA 176,147,139,143,131,177,186,0
RUN
```

Putting Your Best Foot Forward

Last and least, we add the feet:

```
130 GOSUB 1000: FM=X
140 F(1)=CHR$(168)+FM+CHR$(184)+CHR$(128)
```

```
150 F(2)=CHR$(176)+FM+CHR$(176)+CHR$(144)
570 PRINT@ P+192, F(RND(2)); : GOTO 660
2280 ' FEET
2290 DATA 178,187,191,171,191,179,0
RUN
```

The middle portion of the feet are stored in F M, and we succumb to a brute force method of adding the toes to the two versions.

Catch Your Breath

At this point your listing should look like this:

```
*10 '
    ' *** INITIALIZE VARIABLES ***
    '
 20 CLS: CLEAR 2000
 30 DEFSTR A-Z : DEFINT I, N, P
 40 DIM T(5), A(2), H(2), E(7), M(5), F(2)
 50 FOR I=1 TO 4: GOSUB 1000: T(I)=X: NEXT I
 60 FOR I=1 TO 2: GOSUB 1000: A(I)=X: NEXT I
 70 FOR I=1 TO 2: GOSUB 1000: H(I)=X: NEXT I
 80 GOSUB 1000: EL=X
 90 GOSUB 1000: ER=X
 100 FOR I=1 TO 7: GOSUB 1000 : E(I)=EL+X+ER:
     NEXT I
 110 GOSUB 1000: ML=X : GOSUB 1000: MR=X
 120 FOR I=1 TO 5: GOSUB 1000: M(I)=ML+X+MR: NEXT I
 130 GOSUB 1000: FM=X
 140 F(1)=CHR$(168)+FM+CHR$(184)+CHR$(128)
 150 F(2)=CHR$(176)+FM+CHR$(176)+CHR$(144)
 200 '
     '   DRAW FIGURE
     '
 210 CLS
 220 P=600
 230 GOSUB 1080
 500 '
     '   ANIMATE FIGURE
     '
 510 REM
 520 ON RND(4) GOTO 530, 560, 560, 570
 530 I=RND(4): PRINT@ P-131, T(I);
 540 IF I=1 PRINT@ P-67, A(1); ELSE PRINT@ P-67,
     A(2);
 550 GOTO 660
 560 PRINT@ P+64, E(RND(5)); : GOTO 660
 570 PRINT@ P+192, F(RND(2)); : GOTO 660
 660 N=60: GOSUB 1170: GOTO 510
 999 STOP
 1000 '
      '   SUBROUTINES
      '
 1010 ' *** READ DATA ***
 1020 X=""
```

```
1030 READ N
1040 IF N>127 X=X+CHR$(N): GOTO 1030
1050 IF N>0 READ N1: X=X+STRING$(N,N1): GOTO 1030
1060 PRINT@ 1000, X: PRINT
1070 RETURN
1080 ' *** DRAW FIGURE ***
1090 PRINT@ P-131, T(1);
1100 PRINT@ P-67, A(1);
1110 PRINT@ P, H(1);
1120 PRINT@ P+64, E(1);
1130 PRINT@ P+128, M(1);
1140 PRINT@ P+192, F(1);
1150 RETURN
1160 ' *** TIME DELAY ***
1170 FOR I1=1 TO N: NEXT I1: RETURN
2000 '
     '   DATA
     '
2010 ' TOP ANTENNAE
2020 DATA 207,0
2030 DATA 2,176,144,201,2,176,144,0
2040 DATA 130,173,144,201,184,135,128,0
2050 DATA 128,168,151,200,130,189,128,128,0
2060 ' ANTENNAE
2070 DATA 142,131,139,180,194,2,176,144,128,160,158,
     131,139 132,0
2080 DATA 2,128,139,180,194,2,176,144,128,160,158,
     129,2,128,0
2090 ' HEAD
2100 DATA 130,189,159,175,191,143,189,151,0
2110 DATA 130,189,4,191,189,151,0
2120 ' EYES
2130 DATA 186,191,0,191,144,0
2140 DATA 136,170,191,136,170,0
2150 DATA 132,170,191,132,170,0
2160 DATA 128,174,191,128,174,0
2170 DATA 130,170,191,130,170,0
2180 DATA 160,170,191,160,170,0
2190 DATA 155,187,191,155,187,0
2200 DATA 5,191,0
2210 ' MOUTH
2220 DATA 175,0,133,0
2230 DATA 7,191,0
2240 DATA 3,191,175,3,191,0
2250 DATA 2,191,159,143,3,191,0
2260 DATA 191,151,139,143,131,2,191,0
2270 DATA 176,147,139,143,131,177,186,0
2280 ' FEET
2290 DATA 178,187,191,171,191,179,0
```

3 The Animation

You now have a figure that can be animated in a variety of ways. At this point in the program development, you can have great fun dreaming up new ways to amaze your friends. Most of the things we could do to Critter are more involved than simply changing one portion of the figure. Making Critter smile or blink would require a controlled sequence of events, with timing delays after each change to give the desired effect. A blink, for example, would require the sequence shown in figure 13.7.

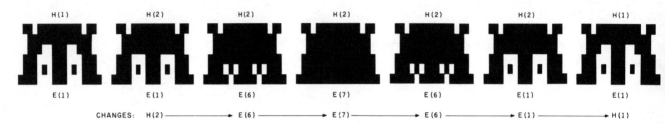

Figure 13.7   Blink sequence.

You have already typed in the data necessary to make him smile and blink, but before we add in the controlling statements, it is time to set some priorities in the animation process. The simple eye, feet, and antennae movements will occur most often, and special sequences will occur less frequently.

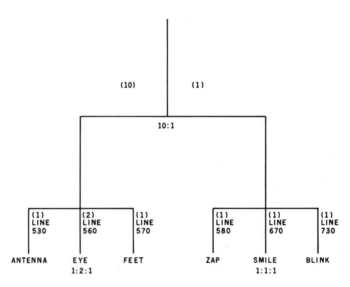

Figure 13.8   Animation priorities.

The program will be written to take the left branch shown in figure 13.8 ten times as often as the right branch. The branches can be weighted by means of the RND function. Add

```
510 IF RND(11)>1 THEN 520
515 ON RND(3) GOTO 580, 670, 730
580 ' ZAP
660 N=20: GOSUB 1170: GOTO 510
670 ' SMILE
720 GOTO 510
730 ' BLINK
830 GOTO 510
```

You could RUN this, but nothing much would happen. We have just set up the structure necessary to implement the flow illustrated in figure 13.8. You may include as many or few sequences as you desire. They may be added in any order.

Blink

We will start with this one since the sequence has been displayed in figure 13.7. Add

```
*740 N=40: GOSUB 1170
 750 I=1: GOSUB 760: GOTO 770
 760 PRINT@ P+64, E(I);: GOSUB 1170: RETURN
 770 PRINT@ P,H(2);: GOSUB 1170
 780 I=6: GOSUB 760
 790 I=7: GOSUB 760
 800 GOSUB 1170
 810 I=6: GOSUB 760
 820 I=1: GOSUB 760
 830 PRINT@ P,H(1);: GOTO 510
RUN
```

Line 740 sets the pace for the entire routine. Line 760 is a one-line subroutine that prints an eye followed by a short delay. Line 800 adds an extra pause when the eye is closed (E(7)). The rest of the lines either print the appropriate head or call subroutine 760 to print the next eye.

Say "Cheese!"

A smile is easier to implement, because there is only one row to tamper with, and the different versions of the mouth are used sequentially. Add

```
680 I2=RND(4)+1
690 FOR I=1 TO I2: PRINT@ P+128, M(I);: N=30:
    GOSUB 1170: NEXT I
700 N=60 : GOSUB 1170 : N=30
710 FOR I=I2 TO 1 STEP -1: PRINT@ P+128, M(I);:
    GOSUB 1170: NEXT I
RUN
```

Line 680 chooses how wide the smile will be: from M(2) to M(5). The sequence is printed in line 690, each version followed by a short delay, of course. Line 700 holds the smile for a bit. Line 710 prints the same sequence as 690 in reverse order.

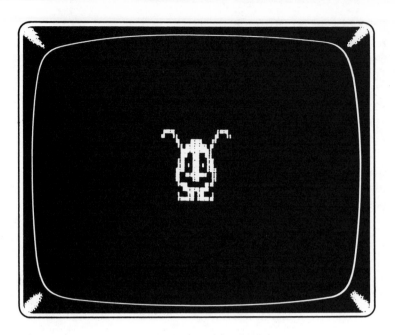

Figure 13.9   A smile.

Zap

See if you can figure out how this one works. You'll find some interesting string manipulation.

```
590 Z=STRING$(8,128+RND(3))
600 PRINT@ P-67, A(2);
610 FOR I=2 TO 4: PRINT@ P-131, T(I);: N=100:
    GOSUB 1170: NEXT I
620 FOR IJ=1 TO 2
630 FOR I=0 TO 8: PRINT@P-128, LEFT$(Z,I)STRING$
    (8-I,32);: NEXT I
640 FOR I=8 TO 0 STEP -1: PRINT@ P-128, STRING$(I,
    RIGHT$(Z,8-I);: NEXT I
650 NEXT IJ: PRINT@ P-128, STRING$(8,32);: GOTO 66
RUN
```

If You Think Rabbits Multiply...

You probably wondered why we used PRINT@P rather than PRINT@600. Because of that extra effort, we can print Critter anywhere on the screen with just a few modifications. In fact, we can print several copies of him:

```
220 P(1)=135: P(2)=600: P(3)=170
230 FOR I=1 TO 3: P=P(I): GOSUB 1080: NEXT I
510 P=P(RND(3)): IF RND(11)>1 GOTO 520
RUN
```

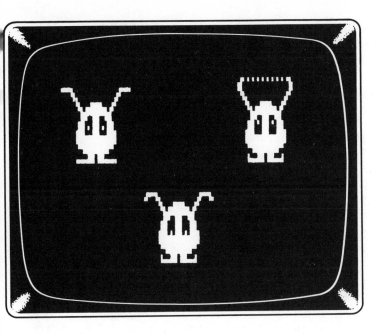

Figure 13.10   Copies of Critter.

(Good grief, they're gaining on us!) Positions are stored in the numeric array `P`. The three original figures are printed in line 230. The addition of `P=P(RND(3))` to line 510 causes a random critter to be chosen for updating.

Here is the current listing. See if by experimenting you can add your own sequences, or some sound effects. Keep Critter alive!

```
*10  '
     '  *** INITIALIZE VARIABLES ***
     '
 20 CLS: CLEAR 2000
 30 DEFSTR A-Z : DEFINT I, N, P
 40 DIM T(5), A(2), H(2), E(7), M(5), F(2)
 50 FOR I=1 TO 4: GOSUB 1000: T(I)=X: NEXT I
 60 FOR I=1 TO 2: GOSUB 1000: A(I)=X: NEXT I
 70 FOR I=1 TO 2: GOSUB 1000: H(I)=X: NEXT I
 80 GOSUB 1000: EL=X
 90 GOSUB 1000: ER=X
100 FOR I=1 TO 7: GOSUB 1000 : E(I)=EL+X+ER: NEXT I
110 GOSUB 1000: ML=X : GOSUB 1000: MR=X
120 FOR I=1 TO 5: GOSUB 1000: M(I)=ML+X+MR: NEXT I
130 GOSUB 11000: FM=X
140 F(1)=CHR$(168)+FM+CHR$(184)+CHR$(128)
150 F(2)=CHR$(176)+FM+CHR$(176)+(144)
200  '
     '   DRAW FIGURE
     '
210 CLS
220 P(1)=135: P(2)=600: P(3)=170
230 FOR I=1 TO 3: P=P(I): GOSUB 1080: NEXT I
500  '
     '   ANIMATE FIGURE
     '
```

```
510 P=P(RND(3)): IF RND(11)>1 THEN 520
515 ON RND(3) GOTO 580, 670,730
520 ON RND(4) GOTO 530, 560, 560, 570
530 I=RND(4): PRINT@ P-131, T(I);
540 IF I=1 PRINT@ P-67, A(1); ELSE PRINT@ P-67,
    A(2);
550 GOTO 660
560 PRINT@ P+64, E(RND(5)); :GOTO 660
570 PRINT@ P+192, F(RND(2)); : GOTO 660
580 ' ZAP
590 Z=STRING$(8,128+RND(3))
600 PRINT@ P-67, A(2);
610 FOR I=2 TO 4: PRINT@ P-131, T(I);: N=100:
    GOSUB 1170: NEXT I
620 FOR IJ=1 TO 2
630 FOR I=0 TO 8: PRINT@ P-128,
    LEFT$(Z,I)STRING$(8-I,32);: NEXT I
640 FOR I=8 TO 0 STEP -1:PRINT@ P-128,STRING$(I,32)
    RIGHT$(Z,8-I);: NEXT I
650 NEXT IJ: PRINT@ P-128, STRING$(8,32);: GOTO 660
660 N=20: GOSUB 1170: GOTO 510
670 ' SMILE
680 I2=RND(4)+1
690 FOR I=1 TO I2: PRINT@ P+128, M(I);: N=30:
    GOSUB 1170: NEXT I
700 N=60 : GOSUB 1170 : N=30
710 FOR I=I2 TO 1 STEP -1: PRINT@ P+128, M(I);:
    GOSUB 1170: NEXT I
720 GOTO 510
730 ' BLINK
740 N=40: GOSUB 1170
750 I=1: GOSUB 760: GOTO 770
760 PRINT@ P+64, E(I);: GOSUB 1170: RETURN
770 PRINT@ P, H(2);: GOSUB 1170
780 I=6: GOSUB 760
790 I=7: GOSUB 760
800 GOSUB 1170
810 I=6: GOSUB 760
820 I=1: GOSUB 760
830 PRINT@ P, H(1);: GOTO 510
999 STOP
1000 '
     ' SUBROUTINES
     '
1010 ' *** READ DATA ***
1020 X=""
1030 READ N
1040 IF N>127 X=X+CHR$(N): GOTO 1030
1050 IF N=0 READ N1: X=X+STRING$(N,N1): GOTO 1030
1060 PRINT@ 1000, X: PRINT
1070 RETURN
1080 ' *** DRAW FIGURE ***
1090 PRINT@ P-131, T(1);
1100 PRINT@ P-67, A(1);
1110 PRINT@ P, H(1);
1120 PRINT@ P+64, E(1);
```

```
1130 PRINT@ P+128, M(1);
1140 PRINT@ P+192, F(1);
1150 RETURN
1160 ' *** TIME DELAY ***
1170 FOR I1=1 TO N: NEXT I1: RETURN
2000 '
     ' DATA
     '
2010 ' TOP ANTENNAE
2020 DATA 207,0
2030 DATA 2,176,144,201,2,176,144,0
2040 DATA 130,173,144,201,184,135,128,0
2050 DATA 128,168,151,200,130,189,128,128,0
2060 ' ANTENNAE
2070 DATA 142,131,139,180,194,2,176,144,128,160,
     158,131,139,132,0
2080 DATA 2,128,139,180,194,2,176,144,128,160,158,
     129,2,128,0
2090 ' HEAD
2100 DATA 130,189,159,175,191,143,189,151,0
2110 DATA 130,189,4,191,189,151,0
2120 ' EYES
2130 DATA 186,191,0,191,144,0
2140 DATA 136,170,191,136,170,0
2150 DATA 132,170,191,132,170,0
2160 DATA 128,174,191,128,174,0
2170 DATA 130,170,191,130,170,0
2180 DATA 160,170,191,160,170,0
2190 DATA 155,187,191,155,187,0
2200 DATA 5,191,0
2210 ' MOUTH
2220 DATA 175,0,133,0
2230 DATA 7,191,0
2240 DATA 3,191,175,3,191,0
2250 DATA 2,191,159,143,3,191,0
2260 DATA 191,151,139,143,131,2,191,0
2270 DATA 176,147,139,143,131,177,186,0
2280 ' FEET
2290 DATA 178,187,191,171,191,179,0
```

The Art Of Graphics

The TRS-80 is subtly appealing to those with an artistic bent. With its limited resolution graphics, the TRS-80 presents an enjoyable challenge to the artist. In addition, the computer can aid artistic endeavors in at least two ways. First, it can use loops and the built-in random number function to generate an infinite variety of patterns and designs, the topic of this chapter. By manipulating variables and parameters, the programmer can control the tone of these works. Second, the computer can act as a tool to aid in sketching a picture on the screen. SKETCH programs will be discussed in Chapter 15.

Patterns And Designs

We will start off with computer-generated confusion, and work toward controlled panic. Our first program does nothing more than fill the screen with dots positioned at random. Enter

```
NEW
10 CLS: DEFINT I, J
20 FOR J=1 TO 50
30 X=RND(127): Y=RND(47)
90 SET(X,Y)
120 NEXT J
130 I$=INKEY$: IF I$="" THEN 130 ELSE 10
RUN
```

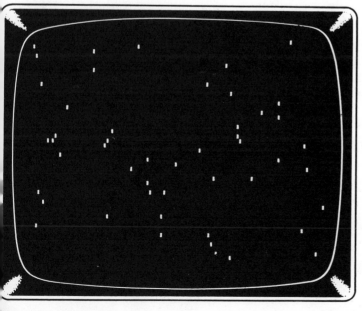

Figure 14.1   Random dots.

Big deal, you say? Okay, we understand that this wasn't the biggest thrill in your life, but be patient. We are onto something good here.

The only noteworthy item in this program is line 130. When the J loop is completed, the display freezes so that you can admire it. Then press (SPACEBAR) (or any key for that matter) to clear the screen and restart the program. Next we alter the range of X and Y by changing line 30 to

```
30 X=RND(64): Y=RND(24)
RUN
```

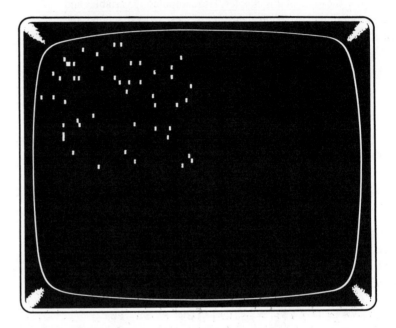

Figure 14.2   The upper-left quadrant.

This limits the printing to the upper left quarter of the screen. It still doesn't give us anything to write home about, but it does pave the way for our next move, namely replicating the upper left corner in the other three-fourths of the screen. In fact, we are going to reflect a mirror-image of this portion of the screen into the other three quadrants. Change line 90 to

```
90 SET(X,Y): SET(127-X,Y)
```

and add

```
100 SET(X,47-Y): SET(127-X,47-Y)
RUN
```

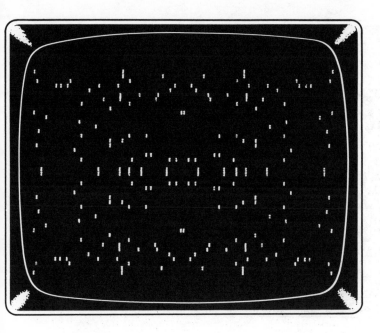

Figure 14.3   Reflections.

The entire screen is filled with dots as in the first example, but there is a much greater symmetry. Now we are making headway.

Snowflakes

At this point, we are ready to graduate from dots to lines. The lines will be drawn by starting from each randomly chosen point, choosing increments H and K in the horizontal and vertical directions, then adding these increments to X and Y in a loop 15 times. Add

```
40 H=2*RND(0)-1: K=2*RND(0)-1
50 FOR I=1 TO 15
60 X=X+H: Y=Y+K
70 IF X>64 OR Y>24 THEN 120
80 IF X<0 OR Y<0 THEN 120
110 NEXT I
RUN
```

Figure 14.4 Line segments.

H and K are set to decimal numbers between -1 and +1. If they are both close to zero, the line will be very short even though the loop is repeated 15 times. The symmetry of this design should jump out and bite you. The current listing is this:

```
10 CLS: DEFINT I,J
20 FOR J=1 TO 50
30 X=RND(64): Y=RND(24)
40 H=2*RND(0)-1: K=2*RND(0)-1
50 FOR I=1 TO 15
60 X=X+H: Y=Y+K
70 IF X>64 OR Y>24 THEN 120
80 IF X<0 OR Y<0 THEN 120
90 SET(X,Y): SET(127-X,Y)
100 SET(X,47-Y): SET(127-X,47-Y)
110 NEXT I
120 NEXT J
130 I$=INKEY$: IF I$="" THEN 130 ELSE 10
```

In this program, the starting points for each line are chosen in the upper left corner of the screen. If we change this to a toroid or doughnut-shaped region as shown in figure 14.5, our random lines will fashion a sort of four-sided snowflake.

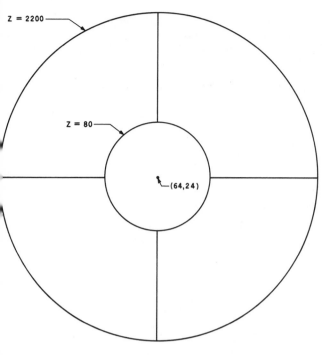

Figure 14.5 Torus.

Change lines 70 and 80 to

```
70 Z=(X-64)*(X-64)+4*(Y-24)*(Y-24)
80 IF Z<80 OR Z>2200 THEN 120
RUN
```

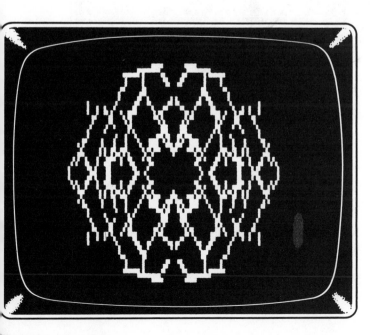

Figure 14.6 A snowflake.

Line 70 is the formula for a circle centered at (64,24). To increase the speed of the program, multiplication rather than exponentiation is used. The 4 was smuggled in to adjust for the aspect ratio of the graphic blocks. Z is the square of the radius. Line 80 provides the two circles shown in figure 14.5 by limiting the range of the radius. Go ahead and RUN it several times. This version might be a good one to save.

With two easy changes, we can give these "snowflakes" a slightly different look. Try adding

```
115 GOTO 40
RUN
```

This change causes the lines to form a long chain. Each new line starts with the end of the previous line until one of the circular borders is reached. Then a new random chain is started. Unfortunately, it gets crowded awfully fast.

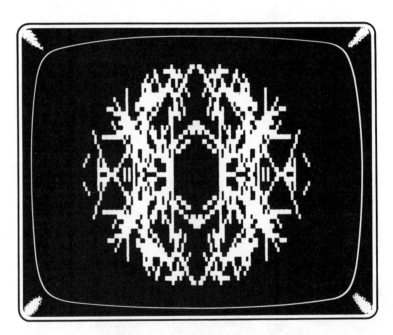

Figure 14.7   A crowded snowflake.

Change

```
20 FOR J=1 TO 20
RUN
```

That's better. In fact, we can even loosen things up a bit more by retracting the boundaries to their previous positions:

```
70 IF X>64 OR Y>24 THEN 120
80 IF X<0 OR Y<0 THEN 120
RUN
```

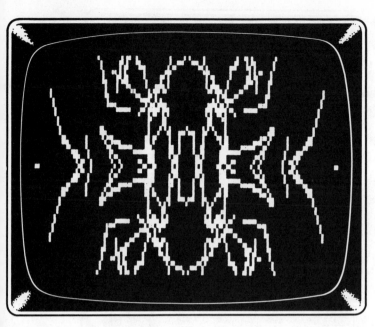

Figure 14.8   Retracted boundaries.

Inkblot

Now, for a real humdinger! Delete lines 20, 70, 110, and 115 and make these changes:

```
*10 CLS: DEFINT A-Z: K=1
 30 X=0: Y=RND(24)
 40 IF RND(2)=1 K=-K
 50 IF RND(4)=1 X=X+1
 60 Y=Y+K
 80 IF Y<0 OR Y>47 Y=Y-K
120 IF X<127 THEN 40
RUN
```

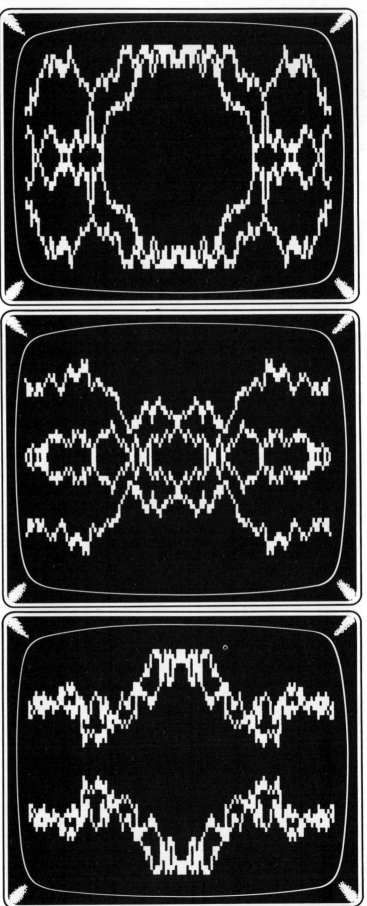

Figure 14.9   Inkblots.

Isn't that delightful? We'll wait while you RUN this several times. Notice that some of the patterns share a vague resemblance to the famous Rorschach inkblot designs.

The IF in line 120 creates a loop from 40 to 120. X starts at zero and saunters toward 127, occasionally being incremented in line 50. In the meantime, K is used to randomly add or subtract 1 from Y, so that the light blocks wander up and down the screen as they move from left to right. Here is the listing:

```
10 CLS: DEFINT A-Z: K=1
30 X=0: Y=RND(24)
40 IF RND(2)=1 K=-K
50 IF RND(4)=1 X=X+1
60 Y=Y+K
80 IF Y<0 OR Y>47 Y=Y-K
90 SET(X,Y): SET(127-X,Y)
100 SET(X,47-Y): SET(127-X,47-Y)
120 IF X<127 THEN 40
130 I$=INKEY$: IF I$="" THEN 130 ELSE 10
```

Save this one before things get more complicated.

The Humans Take Over

So far, the sequence of programs has progressed from totally random dots to a very structured movement. It's high time that the operator gained a little control over the action. Change the following lines:

```
10 CLS: DEFINT A-Z
30 P=PEEK(14400)
40 I=P AND 96: J=P AND 24
50 H=SGN((I-63)*I): K=SGN((J-15)*J)
60 IF X+H<0 OR X+H>127 THEN 30
80 SET(X,Y): X=X+H: Y=Y+K
120 GOTO 30
```

And add

```
*20 X=0: Y=0
 70 IF Y+K<0 OR Y+K>47 THEN 30
 105 IF P=1 I$=INKEY$: GOTO 130
 110 RESET(X,Y)
 RUN
```

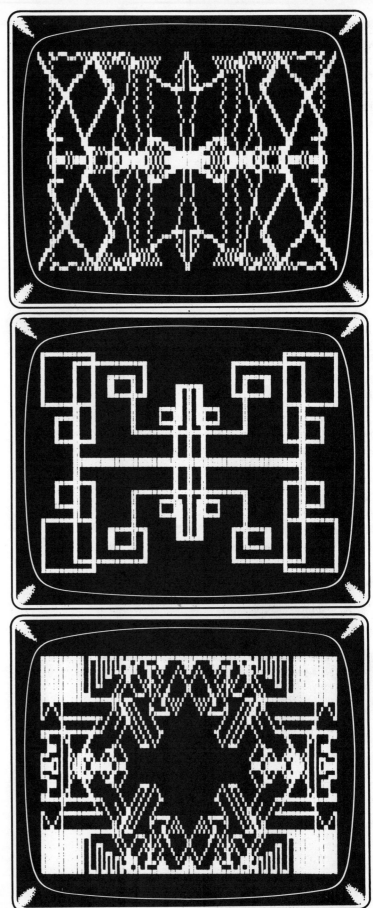

Figure 14.10   Operator control.

To operate this program, use the arrow keys to effect horizontal, vertical, and diagonal movement. Keep your eye on the flashing cursor. It starts in the upper left corner, but it may travel anywhere on the screen. When you are done with your creation, press (ENTER). The cursor will stop flashing so that you can admire your work. Then, any key will clear the screen and start the program again. Voila! *You* are in the driver's seat.

This program uses PEEK input in line 30. Lines 40 and 50 show a compact way to determine which of the arrow keys has been pressed. The SGN function is used in line 50 to determine an increment of $-1, 0,$ or $+1$ for X and Y. P AND 96 is stored in I in line 40. The AND is used to mask out everything except 32 and 64 which represent the (←) and (→) respectively. If I is zero, neither the left nor the right arrow keys were pressed, so H becomes zero. If I is 64, H will be $+1$, and if I is 32, H will be -1. K is calculated similarly. P AND 24 is stored in J. The AND tests for 8 and 16, which are returned by the (↑) and (↓). Then K is determined to be $-1, 0,$ or $+1$.

Here is the final listing:

```
10 CLS: DEFINT A-Z
20 X=0: Y=0
30 P=PEEK(14400)
40 I=P AND 96: J=P AND 24
50 H=SGN((I-63)*I): K=SGN((J-15)*J)
60 IF X+H<0 OR X+H>127 THEN 30
70 IF Y+K<0 OR Y+K>47 THEN 30
80 SET(X,Y): X=X+H: Y=Y+K
90 SET(X,Y): SET(127-X,Y)
100 SET(X,47-Y): SET(127-X,47-Y)
105 IF P=1 I$=INKEY$: GOTO 130
110 RESET(X,Y)
120 GOTO 30
130 I$=INKEY$: IF I$="" THEN 130 ELSE 10
```

You may wish to save the program now.

2 One-Liner : A New Art Form

The personal computer phenomenon has bred a new form of graphic art, the so called "one-liner." The idea is to write a self-contained program that creates a continuously changing graphics display using only one program line. Surprising things can be done in one line of computer code.

The one-liners are listed with spaces only for readability. Do *not* type any blank spaces when entering these programs.

Old Paint

Type

```
NEW
*0 DEFINTA-Z: CLS: FOR I=0TO14: X=127+RND(64):
M=X-128: Q=INT(M/16): B=-15*Q: A=INT(X/4): A=X-4*A:
Y=15*A+X+B: FOR J=1 TO 62: P=64*I+J: PRINT@ P,
```

```
CHR$(X);: PRINT@ 1023-P, CHR$(Y);: NEXT: NEXT: RUN
RUN
```

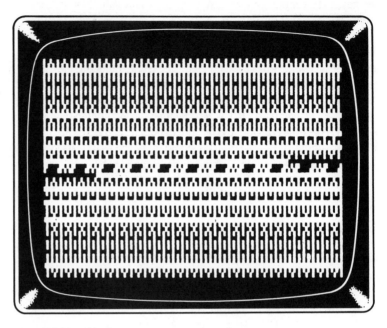

Figure 14.11   Old paint.

This one ingeniously paints the screen with graphics blocks moving from top and bottom toward the middle. The top-to-bottom symmetry is obtained by flipping the random graphics character stored in X upside-down and storing it in Y.

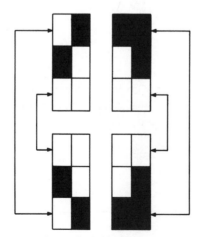

Figure 14.12   Graphics character flip.

Flashy

The next one-liner includes a machine language program. It generates rapidly changing screens full of graphic blocks. You may have to edit the line in order to squeeze the whole thing into memory. It was written for a 16 K Level II system by Patrick Boyle, and was published in the December, 1980 issue of *Softside Magazine**:

```
0 CLEAR 22: A$=STRING$(22,32): J=VARPTR(A$):
I=PEEK(J+1)+256* PEEK(J+2): FOR K=I TO I+21: READ
Z: POKE K, Z: NEXT: POKE 16526, PEEK(J+1): POKE
16527, PEEK(J+2): FOR X=1 TO 2: POKE I+10, RND
(63)+128: L=USR(0): X=1: NEXT: DATA 33,0,60,17,1,
60,1,255,3,54,0,237,176,6,5,33,0,0,43,124,181,201
```

For 48 K disk systems, subtract 65536 from I, and use DEFUSR as shown below:

```
0 CLEAR 22: A$=STRING$(22,32): J=VARPTR(A$):
I=PEEK(J+1)+256* PEEK(J+2)-65536: FOR K=I TO
I+21: READ Z:POKE K, Z: NEXT: DEFUSR=I: FOR X=1 TO
2: POKEI+10, RND(63)+128: L=USR(0): X=1: NEXT: DATA
33,0,60,17,1,60,1,255,3,54,0,237,176,6,5,33,0,0,
43,124,181,201
```

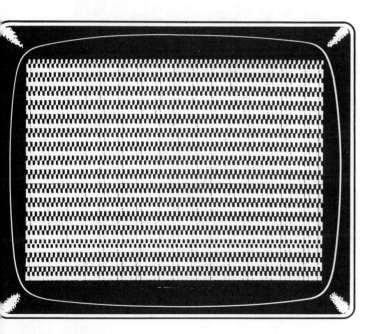

Figure 14.13   Flashy.

Spokes

In the following one-liner, we use a good portion of the line to define the strings necessary for cursor movement. This program chooses a random character, then prints strings of this character radiating from a central point like spokes of a wheel:

*Reprinted by permission of Softside Publications.

```
NEW
*0 DEFSTRP-Z: R=CHR$(24): S=CHR$(25): T=CHR$(26):
U=CHR$(27): P(1)=T: P(2)=T+R: P(3)=T+R+R:
P(4)=R+R+R: P(5)=U+R+R: P(6)=U+R: P(7)=U: P(8)=S:
CLS: FOR I=0 TO 10: N=RND(160)+31: Z=CHR$(N):
L=4*N: A=RND(3)+1: FOR J=1 TO 8: PRINT@ L, ;: FOR
K=1 TO A: PRINT Z+P(J);: NEXT: NEXT: NEXT: RUN
RUN
```

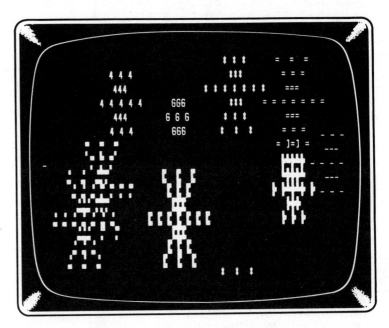

Figure 14.14   Spokes.

More Inkblots

This one-liner gives results similar to the earlier inkblot program, but it uses PRINT
instead of SET. As each random character is printed, its mirror-image is printed
using the same flip technique as in the first one-liner we saw. In addition, if the string
of characters is able to make one complete pass without going off the screen, the last
loop of the program does a top-to-bottom flip of each graphic character just for fun.

```
*0 CLS: P=448: FOR I=1 TO 60: P=P+1+(RND(3)-2)
*64: IF P<1 OR P>1022 RUN ELSE X=127+RND(64):
M=X-128: Q=INT(M/16): B=-15*Q: A=INT(X/4): A=X-4
*A: Y=15*A+X+B: PRINT@ P, CHR$(X);: PRINT@ 1023-
P, CHR$(Y);: NEXT I: FOR P=15360 TO 16383: IF PEE
(P)>128POKE P, 319-PEEK(P): NEXT: RUN ELSE NEXT:
RUN
RUN
```

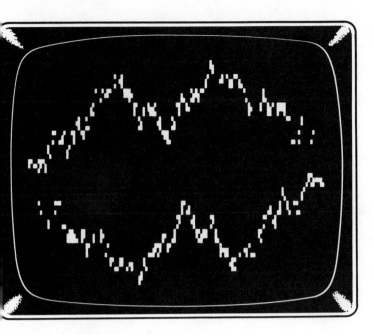

Figure 14.15 More inkblots.

3 Circular Graphics

In Chapter 8, we looked at various polar functions. We will now take a closer look at rose-leaved curves and spirals.

A Rose By Any Other Name

Rose-leaved curves can be generated by varying the radius of our figure with the sine (SIN) or cosine (COS) of the angle. Specifically, we will use the statement

```
50 R=6*SIN(C*A)
```

where R is the radius and A is the angle. The 6 is tossed in to make the figure larger on the screen, and C is a constant that determines the number of petals on the rose. Enter this program:

```
NEW
10 C=5
30 CLS
40 FOR A = 0 TO 6.28 STEP .03
50 R=6*SIN(C*A)
60 X=R*7*COS(A)+64.5
70 Y=R*3*SIN(A)+24.5
80 SET(X,Y): NEXT
100 GOTO 100
RUN
```

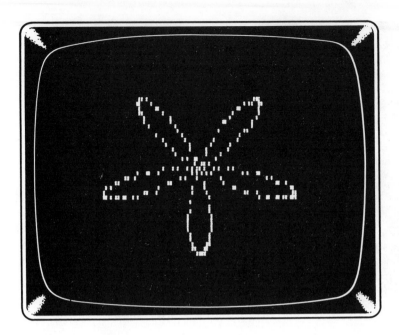

Figure 14.16 A five-petal rose.

Considering the current value of C, it's not surprising that we ended up with five petals. Change line 10 to

```
10 C=6
RUN
```

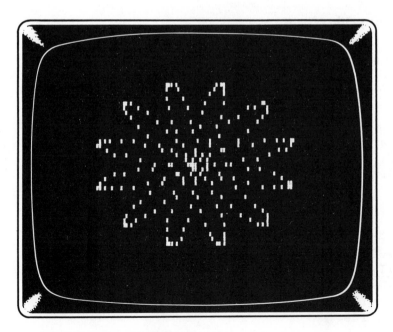

Figure 14.17 A twelve-petal rose (C = 6).

It turns out that with even numbers, we get twice as many petals as the value of C.
Test different values of C by adding

```
10 DEFINT C, X, Y
20 INPUT "ENTER CONSTANT"; C
30 CLS: PRINT@ 0, C;
100 GOTO 20
RUN
```

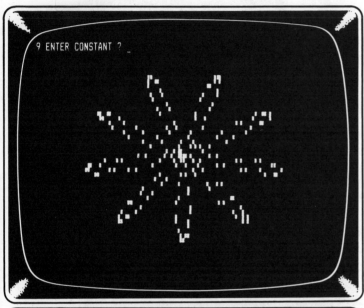

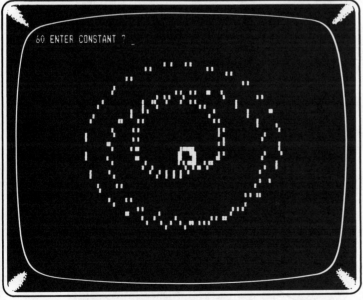

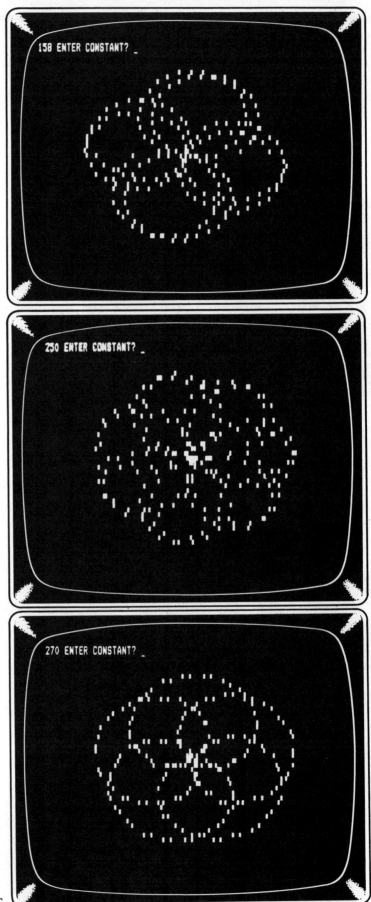

Figure 14.18   Sample values of C.

Notice that as the values become greater, the petals become less distinguishable, but several interesting patterns emerge for larger numbers. To simplify our examination of the different patterns, let's add

```
90 FOR I=1 TO 3000: NEXT: C=C+1
```

and change line 100 to

```
100 IF INKEY$=" " GOTO 20 ELSE 30
RUN
```

Figure 14.19   Automatic transmission.

Input any value for C. At the completion of each figure, line 90 causes a short pause and adds 1 to C. Then line 100 sends control back to 30 where the next figure is automatically drawn. If you wish to change the constant C, press (SPACEBAR). Upon completion of the current figure, you will be prompted for the next value of C. Here is the final listing of this program:

```
10 DEFINT C, X, Y
20 INPUT "ENTER CONSTANT"; C
30 CLS: PRINT@ 0, C;
40 FOR A = 0 TO 6.28 STEP .03
50 R=6*SIN(C*A)
60 X=R*7*COS(A)+64.5
70 Y=R*3*SIN(A)+24.5
80 SET(X,Y): NEXT: C=C+1
90 FOR I=1 TO 3000: NEXT
100 IF INKEY$=" " GOTO 20 ELSE 30
```

You may wish to tinker with various functions in line 50. Some suggestions:

```
50 R=1+6*SIN(C*A)
```

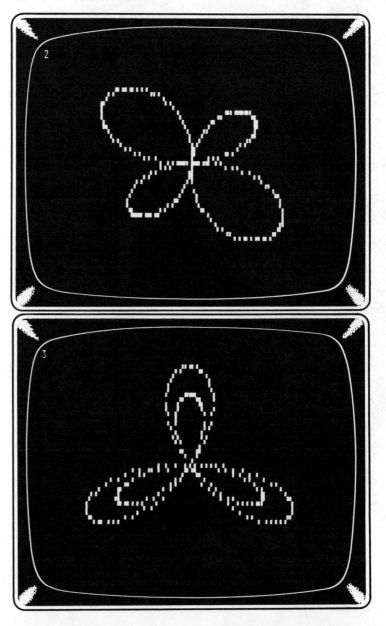

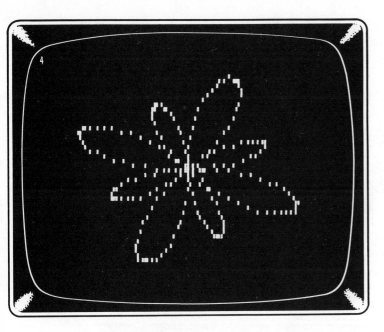

Figure 14.20   R = 1 + 6*SIN(C*A).

50 R=3-3*SIN(C*A)

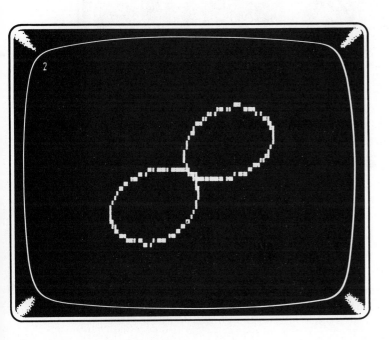

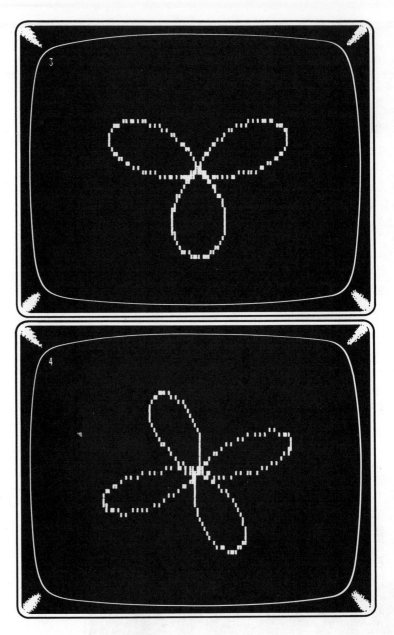

Figure 14.21   R = 3-3*SIN(C*A).

Spirals

We now turn our attention to spirals. Spirals are generated when the radius is a constant times the angle.

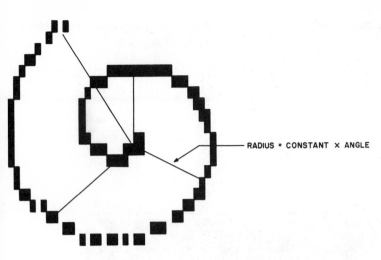

Figure 14.22   Spiral.

Enter this new program:

```
NEW
10 D=6
30 CLS: X1=64: Y1=24
40 PRINT D "DEGREES": E=D/57.296: SET(64,24)
60 FOR A=0 TO 200 STEP E
70 X=A*COS(A)+64.5: Y=A*SIN(A)*.43+24.5
80 IF X<0 OR X>127 OR Y<0 OR Y>47 THEN 210
90 SET(X,Y): GOTO 200
200 NEXT A
210 FOR I=1 TO 3000: NEXT
220 GOTO 220
RUN
```

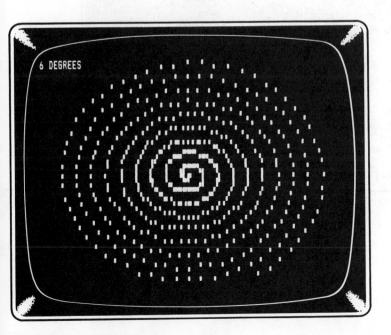

Figure 14.23   A spiral with D = 6.

Line 10 sets the angle of rotation between points to six degrees. Changing this angle can make a big difference in the shape of the spiral. Change

```
10 CLS: INPUT "ANGLE BETWEEN POINTS IN DEGREES"; D
220 IF INKEY$=" " THEN 10 ELSE D=D+1: GOTO 30
RUN
```

Try different values for D. As in the rose program, press **SPACEBAR** when you wish to change the next value of D. Save the program.

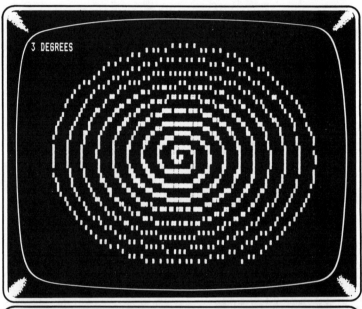

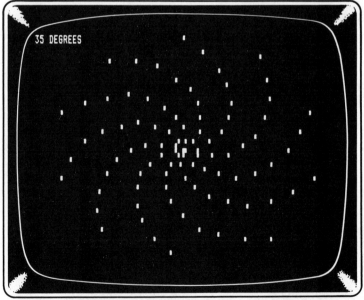

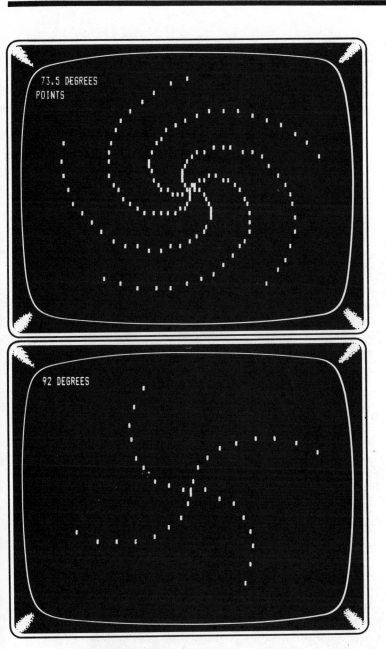

Figure 14.24 More spirals.

Linear Spirals?

Once you have exhausted the possibilities with the current program, we'll add a
surprising twist. Change

```
90 IF S$="P" SET(X,Y): GOTO 200
```

and add

```
*20 INPUT "POINTS (P) OR LINES (L)"; S$
 50 IF S$="P" THEN PRINT "POINTS" ELSE PRINT "LINES"
100 IF X1<>X THEN 130
110 IF Y1<Y THEN S=1 ELSE S=-1
120 FOR Z=Y1 TO Y STEP S: SET(X1,Z): NEXT Z: GOTO 200
```

```
130 M=(Y-Y1)/(X-X1)
140 IF ABS(M)>1 S=ABS(1/M) ELSE S=1
150 IF X1>X THEN S=-S
160 FOR Z=X1 TO X STEP S
170 SET(Z,M*(Z-X1)+Y1)
180 NEXT Z
190 X1=X: Y1=Y
RUN
```

This is another version of our often used routine. Now, lucky you, you have the option of drawing lines or points. The lines give some very interesting designs.

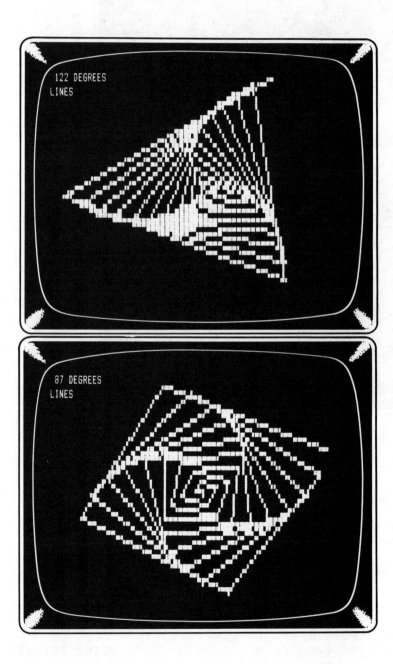

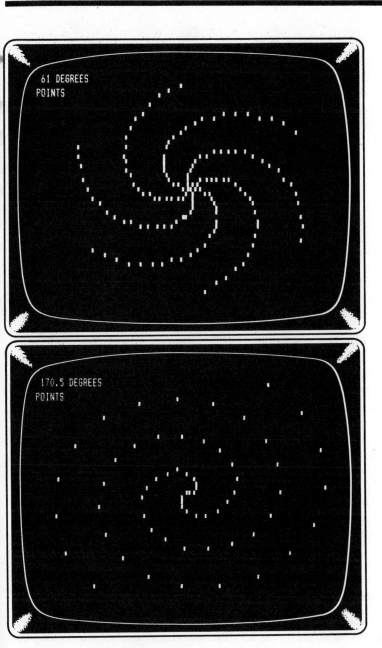

Figure 14.25   Spirals with points and lines.

Once you have responded to line 20, there is no need to use P or L unless you wish to change modes. Pressing (**ENTER**) at that point of the program will leave you in the previous mode. Here is the final listing:

```
10 CLS: INPUT "ANGLE BETWEEN POINTS IN DEGREES"; D
20 INPUT "POINTS (P) OR LINES (L)"; S$
30 CLS: X1=64: Y1=24
40 PRINT D "DEGREES": E=D/57.29578: SET(64,24)
50 IF S$="P" THEN PRINT "POINTS" ELSE PRINT "LINES"
60 FOR A=0 TO 200 STEP E
70 X=A*COS(A)+64.5: Y=A*.43+24.5
80 IF X<0 OR X>127 OR Y<0 OR Y>47 THEN 210
90 IF S$="P" SET(X,Y): GOTO 200
```

```
100 IF X1<>X THEN 130.
110 IF Y1<Y THEN S=1 ELSE S=-1
120 FOR Z=Y1 TO Y STEP S: SET(X1,Z): NEXT Z:
    GOTO 200
130 M=(Y-Y1)/(X-X1)
140 IF ABS(M)>1 S=ABS(1/M) ELSE S=1
150 IF X1>X THEN S=-S
160 FOR Z=X1 TO X STEP S
170 SET(Z,M*(Z-X1)+Y1)
180 NEXT Z
190 X1=X: Y1=Y
200 NEXT A
210 FOR I=1 TO 3000: NEXT
220 IF INKEY$=" " THEN 10 ELSE D=D+1: GOTO 30
```

4 Pictures

We now turn to the challenge of using graphic characters to paint a picture on the TRS-80 video display. The first step is usually to design a picture on a video display sheet. Then there are basically two ways to transfer it to the screen. One: write a BASIC program to print characters; or two: use a graphics sketch program. A sketch program is developed in Chapter 15, so we will concentrate on a do-it-yourself approach here.

There are many ways to attack this problem in BASIC, depending on the features of the particular picture. We could use SET statements if the picture can be described by a mathematical function. We could build strings of multi-line characters if there were enough duplication to warrant it. If speed were important, we could pack strings. We could even adopt the use of the mirror-image principles used in the first part of this chapter if the picture had enough symmetry.

The Blindfolded Approach

Let's make no assumptions about the picture as we approach this program. Because we can't count on the picture for any help, the most logical approach is simply to print characters one at a time from PRINT position 0 to position 1023; however, there are a few refinements we can make to this basic idea. The CHR$ function takes up too much room to use lines such as

```
PRINT CHR$( )CHR$( )CHR$( )CHR$( )CHR$( )...
```

Can you imagine typing 1024 CHR$s? Clearly a better way is to store the numbers in DATA statements and read them in a loop. Start the program with

```
NEW
70 CLS : ON ERROR GOTO 110 : PRINT
80 READ A : IF A>127 PRINT CHR$(A); : GOTO 80
110 X$=INKEY$: IFX$=""110
```

Well, that stroke of genius just saved us 1023 CHR$s. Line 80 reads a number, then prints it if it represents a graphic character or space compression code. (Model III users may wish to use a special character set.) The ON ERROR GOTO in line 70 will give the program a smooth exit when there is no more data to read.

Certainly we will also want to take advantage of any strings of identical consecutive characters such as

```
DATA 128,128,128,128,128,128,128,128,128,128
```

No problem. We just code them as

```
DATA 10, 128
```

and add

```
90 IF A>0 READ B: PRINT STRING$(A,B); : GOTO 80
```

Line 90 will use any value of A between 1 and 127 as a repetition factor to be used with the next character read.

Also, we could use a way to sneak in a fast carriage return if the line we are currently printing doesn't reach all the way to the right edge of the screen. No need to print those blank spaces. We will use a code of zero in the DATA lines for that purpose. Add

```
100 IF A=0 PRINT : PRINT TAB(9); : GOTO 80
```

We now have a program that eliminates any unnecessary repetition without making too many assumptions about the specific picture. That is, except for the TAB(9) in line 100. (We were hoping you wouldn't notice it!) The picture we are about to construct doesn't use the first nine columns of the screen. Speaking of the picture, let's add some data and see if this program really does what it is supposed to do. Remember our coding scheme:

128 - 191 are graphic character codes
  1 - 127 are repetition factors followed by a graphic code
    0   is used to add a carriage return

So add

```
130 ' LINE 1
140 DATA 21,128,136,172,188,2,144,2,128,160,176,
        188,132,4,128,3,176,144,0
150 ' LINE 2
160 DATA 3,128,176,4,188,180,130,175,188,146,190,
        191,189,191
170 DATA 160,190,2,191,188,190,2,191,185,2,191,3,
        143,175,183
180 DATA 131,177,3,176,144,0
190 ' LINE 3
200 DATA 2,128,190,191,139,3,191,132,131,140,187,
        191,2,143,135
210 DATA 2,131,163,129,176,184,2,188,190,143,131,
        128,176,184
220 DATA 132,2,128,131,175,191,189,2,188,2,176,0
RUN
```

Figure 14.26   The first three DATA lines.

Hold everything! Jumpin' junipers—that's a lot of data for only three lines of the screen. Looks like it's a good thing we used those shortcuts before. Remember, it takes 1024 characters to fill the screen. Add a few more lines, then we will try something fancy.

```
*230  ' LINE 4
 240  DATA 2,128,175,181,128,135,139,175,183,152,
           129,4,128,176
 250  DATA 140,131,129,146,140,145,172,191,151,184,
           190,191,135
 260  DATA 177,188,191,129,128,186,5,191,2,143,191,
           180,176,144,0
 270  ' LINE 5
 280  DATA 3,128,130,137,176,152,134,129,5,128,134,
           3,128,130,136
 290  DATA 131,128,178,5,191,190,2,191,135,160,188,
           2,191,2,143,2
 300  DATA 140,2,188,158,143,3,188,143,2,131,0
 310  ' LINE 6
 320  DATA 3,128,176,190,129,160,3,176,132,128,154,
           3,128,168,3
 330  DATA 176,144,128,136,190,3,191,188,190,183,
           188,2,191,5,143
 340  DATA 2,191,188,187,191,141,143,191,2,188,156,0
 350  ' LINE 7
 360  DATA 128,156,143,153,191,144,128,130,163,135,
           128,130,3
 370  DATA 128,160,143,2,131,177,176,188
 380  DATA 191,183,179,2,188,140,188,187,191,3,140,
           131,4,179,187
 390  DATA 191,188,178,131,140,176,187,191,188,180,
           176,0
 RUN
```

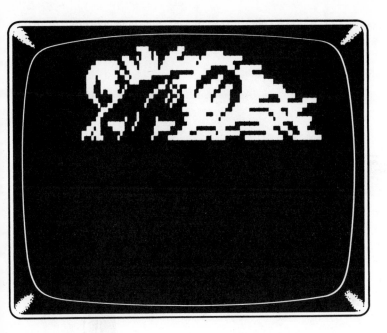

Figure 14.27   Beady eyes.

There are more data lines, but you probably get the general idea. We will list the rest later if you really want to enter them. (Of course, you will find the complete program recorded on the optional cassette/diskette made for this book.)

Screen Reverse

For now, let's turn our attention to a concern brought about by the translation of our picture from the video display sheet to the screen. Any original sketch on the display sheet will be a dark color against a light background, but the screen is just the opposite. Therefore, a picture that looks like a winner on paper may look all too much like a photographic negative on the screen. This is in fact what happened to our current picture.

Ah, but we just happen to have a cure handy. We are going to use a machine language routine for an instant screen reverse. Hang on to your chair. Add

```
10 CLEAR 300: M$=STRING$(25,32)
20 V=VARPTR(M$): LS=PEEK(V+1): MS=PEEK(V+2):
     D=LS+256*MS: IF D>32767 THEN D=D-65536
30 IF PEEK(16396)=201 POKE 16526, LS: POKE 16527, MS
     ELSE DEFUSR0=D
40 FOR I=0 TO 24: READ A: POKE D+I, A: NEXT I
50 DATA 33,0,60,126,254,32,32,4,62,191,24,5,47,246,
        128,203,183
60 DATA 119,35,62,64,188,32,235,201
```

CHECK THE DATA CAREFULLY BEFORE YOU GO ON!

Good job. Lines 50 and 60 contain the codes for the machine language program that is poked into M$ in high memory. Now add

```
120 X=USR(0): GOTO 110
RUN
```

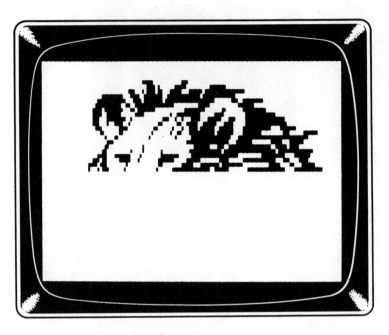

Figure 14.28 Beady eyes reversed.

After the picture is complete, press any key (except BREAK, silly!) to reverse the screen. Press it again, and the screen reverts to its original form. Isn't that fun!

Figure 14.29 shows the completed figure in both normal and reverse modes.

Figure 14.29 Lions. a) reversed. b) normal.

Here is the final listing with the rest of the DATA lines:

```
*10  CLEAR 300: M$=STRING$(25,32)
 20  V=VARPTR(M$): LS=PEEK(V+1): MS=PEEK(V+2):
     D=LS+256*MS: IF D>32767 THEN D=D-65536
 30  IF PEEK(16396)=201 POKE 16526, LS: POKE 16527,
     MS ELSE DEFUSR0=D
 40  FOR I=0 TO 24: READ A: POKE D+I, A: NEXT I
 50  DATA 33,0,60,126,254,32,32,4,62,191,24,5,47,
     246,128,203,183
 60  DATA 119,35,62,64,188,32,235,201
 70  CLS : ON ERROR GOTO 110 : PRINT
 80  READ A : IF A>127 PRINT CHR$(A); : GOTO 80
```

```
90 IF A>0 READ B: PRINT STRING$(A,B); : GOTO 80
100 IF A=0 PRINT : PRINT TAB(9); : GOTO 80
110 X$=INKEY$: IF X$=""110
120 X=USR(0): GOTO 110
130 ' LINE 1
140 DATA 21,128,136,172,188,2,144,2,128,160,176,
    188,132,4,128,3,176,144,0
150 ' LINE 2
160 DATA 3,128,176,4,188,180,130,175,188,146,190,
    191,189,191
170 DATA 160,190,2,191,188,190,2,191,185,2,191,3,
    143,175,183
180 DATA 131,177,3,176,144,0
190 ' LINE 3
200 DATA 2,128,190,191,139,3,191,132,131,140,187,
    191,2,143,135
210 DATA 2,131,163,129,176,184,2,188,190,143,131,
    128,176,184
220 DATA 132,2,128,131,175,191,189,2,188,2,176,0
230 ' LINE 4
240 DATA 2,128,175,181,128,135,139,175,183,152,
    129,4,128,176
250 DATA 140,131,129,146,140,145,172,191,151,184,
    190,191,135
260 DATA 177,188,191,129,128,186,5,191,2,143,191,
    180,176,144,0
270 ' LINE 5
280 DATA 3,128,130,137,176,152,134,129,5,128,134,
    3,128,130,136
290 DATA 131,128,178,5,191,190,2,191,135,160,188,
    2,191,2,143,2
300 DATA 140,2,188,158,143,3,188,143,2,131,0
310 ' LINE 6
320 DATA 3,128,176,190,129,160,3,176,132,128,154,
    3,128,168,3
330 DATA 176,144,128,136,190,3,191,188,190,183,
    188,2,191,5,143
340 DATA 2,191,188,187,191,141,143,191,2,188,156,0
350 ' LINE 7
360 DATA 128,156,143,153,191,144,128,130,163,135,
    128,130,3
370 DATA 128,160,143,2,131,177,176,188
380 DATA 191,183,179,2,188,140,188,187,191,3,140,
    131,4,179,187
390 DATA 191,188,178,131,140,176,187,191,188,180,
    176,0
400 ' LINE 8
410 DATA 160,158,151,190,191,189,144,140,141,131,
    4,128,136,177
420 DATA 128,188,2,191,143,2,179,159,3,143,3,191,
    2,143,131,3
430 DATA 179,184,4,188,179,159,191,144,136,3,140,
    172,2,179,191
440 DATA 0
450 ' LINE 9
```

```
460 DATA 162,158,154,183,191,135,10,128,131,175,3,
    191,143
470 DATA 172,191,2,143,191,182,191,3,179,147,2,
    140,172,176,6
480 DATA 179,141,4,179,159,3,188,191,0
490 ' LINE 10
500 DATA 191,139,184,163,149,132,147,143,3,191,
    159,143,129,144
510 DATA 136,128,186,191,2,179,175,191,143,191,
    188,142,175
520 DATA 2,191,140,176,179,2,131,163,3,179,175,
    140,172,176,131
530 DATA 140,178,131,163,179,188,179,131,191,0
540 ' LINE 11
550 DATA 133,184,161,190,189,161,176,177,176,154,
    2,176,178
560 DATA 176,178,152,172,147,2,143,191,2,179,140,
    178,131,189
570 DATA 172,128,165,136,140,180,2,179,137,180,
    130,139,175,188
580 DATA 176,130,143,188,176,137,140,166,175,191,
    2,188,0
590 ' LINE 12
600 DATA 128,3,149,154,171,180,8,128,130,190,155,
    143,175,188
610 DATA 147,159,189,146,140,174,130,189,180,130,
    140,188,180
620 DATA 128,141,178,139,189,180,146,139,175,144,
    130,191,175
630 DATA 130,180,137,155,2,191,0
640 ' LINE 13
650 DATA 2,128,175,142,176,133,191,143,191,143,
    191,135,175,2,159
660 DATA 191,129,182,171,130,191,149,191,130,175,
    138,148,175
670 DATA 182,175,189,168,144,191,128,180,138,189,
    146,139,191
680 DATA 188,144,131,189,135,170,176,139,176,179,
    147,191,0
690 ' LINE 14
700 DATA 4,128,151,190,148,168,175,128,157,144,
    138,146,149,191
710 DATA 138,163,154,176,143,154,191,149,128,149,
    189,128,171
720 DATA 189,155,191,169,183,136,191,128,191,149,
    128,175,2,191
730 DATA 144,139,188,128,170,181,164,139,2,191,0
740 ' LINE 15
750 DATA 4,128,130,139,189,2,170,184,137,146,140,
    154,191,138
760 DATA 181,149,190,168,183,182,166,165,168,169,
    191,149,170,2,191,186,173,191,189,135,176,2,
    191,128
770 DATA 170,2,191,189,144,149,170,190,191,189,
    187,186,191
```

The Data Deluge

It just doesn't seem fair that we proud TRS-80 owners should have to endure such a tedious process to create our phenomenal works of art. After all, the computer is very good at repetitive procedures. Can't it do some of the dirty work? There should be another way, and sure enough, there is.

You may have seen advertisements for sketch programs. These programs work somewhat like the Etch-a-Sketch toy you may have played with as a youngster. Also, many magazine articles list sketch programs. The various sketch programs differ considerably in the way pictures are drawn as well as in what one can do with the finished display. (More on that in the next chapter.) The point is, these programs can considerably reduce the amount of work necessary to design and implement graphic screen displays. Figure 14.30 shows a picture done on a sketch program. It was completed in much less time than it took to create the lion, character-by-character.

Figure 14.30   Albert.

You will find Chapter 15 chock-full of time-saving devices.

OTHER VISTAS

Turbo-Charged Graphics

Many people have the notion that computers ought to do as much as possible for us so that our time will be freed up to play a lot of tennis. There's no doubt that computers have greatly extended our capabilities, but it often requires more effort to use the computer than to do the same task manually. We all look forward to the day when applications software and languages reach the point where simple English commands will replace programming as we know it. Some day, we may be able to say to our household computer ''Teresa, draw me an animated picture of a dragon flying over a castle,'' and she will create a unique masterpiece. Well, software has not yet developed to that point. But Teresa can, if properly fed, take the drudgery out of some of the more monotonous chores such as creating graphic strings that can be included in programs.

This chapter gives examples of software and hardware that can simplify our programming efforts as well as alter the graphic capabilities of the computer. Keep in mind that we have a fast-moving industry, and that there are more and more enhancements appearing each day. Your favorite program or attachment may not be covered here; perhaps the examples shown, however, will stimulate you to look for something that will appeal to you.

1 Graphics Software — Commercial

Our first stop will be commercially available programs, designed to make the existing graphics of the TRS-80 easier to use. Some of them give us greater speed. The wide variety of sketch programs available now allows us to create graphics on the screen that can be dumped to a printer, saved on disk for later recall, stored in memory for animation, or poked into strings for use in other programs. Other programs give us more powerful graphics statements to eliminate some of the tedium. Here are some examples.

Level III BASIC

Level III BASIC is written by Microsoft for the purpose of extending the capabilities of Level II BASIC. It is not the BASIC that comes with a Model III computer; that is Model III BASIC. Level III does things like eliminate keyboard bounce, furnish user definable abbreviations for BASIC key words or useful strings, provide additional graphic commands, and add many Disk BASIC features to a Level II machine.

Of particular interest to readers of this book are the statements that simplify the use of graphics. A LINE statement lets you draw either a line or a rectangle between any two points on the screen. Both can be drawn with either characters or graphics blocks. Rectangles can be drawn filled or empty. All in all, LINE is quite a useful statement. And, it is fast! For example,

```
LINE (0,0)-(127,47), SET, BF
```

will white out the screen in a flash. (Ø , Ø) and (127 , 47) represent two corner points on the screen. SET indicates the use of graphics blocks to draw the line. B tells the computer to draw a box, not a line. F commands it to fill in the box with graphics blocks.

The GET@ and PUT@ statements move any rectangular portion of the screen to and from memory. The information is stored in an array. Both commands can be used with either PRINT or PLOT coordinates. GET@ transfers graphics from the screen to memory, whereas PUT@ returns the graphics to the screen with several options including reversed format, AND, OR, or XOR with the current screen.

Speed Up Programs

Several programs that can increase the speed of BASIC programs are worth looking into. Some work by reorganizing the code: deleting remarks, concatenating lines, using integer variables, etc. Some are compilers able to convert a BASIC program to machine language. By executing the machine language version of the program, the repetitive interpretation of each line is eliminated and execution speed is tremendously increased.

Once you start to rely on a compiler, be aware that you will have to learn a slightly different dialect of BASIC to use most of the compiler programs. Some compilers do not recognize all the statements found in Radio Shack BASIC. On the other hand, they may recognize additional statements not found in Radio Shack BASIC.

Speed up programs can be a tremendous boon to those who prefer to program strictly in BASIC. One can take advantage of the convenience of SET and RESET statements without a significant loss of speed. For animation fans, the increase in speed can greatly improve the efficacy of animation in BASIC.

Micro Movie

Micro Movie, a sketch program with an eye toward animation, is one of the early pieces of software designed to utilize TRS-80 graphics. Considering its early entry into the market, it is quite good. It is very easy to use, and allows both graphics and text on the screen. Animation is done by modifying the current frame. Press (ENTER) to save the current screen as a frame in memory. The program is designed so that only the changes are saved from frame to frame, making the most of available memory. The commands are simple and the short instruction manual is sufficient to get you started.

Micro Movie's fatal flaw is that the only way to save its graphic creations is on cassette. Because Micro Movie is written in machine language, it would take a bit of work to modify it so that graphics could be saved on disk. That leads us to our next example of graphics software . . .

Electra Sketch

This one is disk-based, and is quite a humdinger! Electra Sketch is written in BASIC with machine language routines embedded in the code, making it modifiable to an extent. Frames are saved on disk and can be recalled by number for viewing and editing. Creating and editing frames is relatively easy with the arrow keys. Several command keys allow the user to clear the screen, white out the screen, enter text, draw lines between two points, fill in portions of the screen with any background character, and print a frame on a line printer.

Graphics are printed as periods on the printer, but there is a way to patch it. For the early Epson MX-80s, make the following changes:

1) In the program ESK, line 100, about 40 numbers into the DATA line change 127,62,42,79 to 127,198,32,79. This adds 32 to all graphic codes so that they will reproduce accurately on the MX-80.

2) In the program ESKM, add CHR$(15) to line 280. This will print graphics in condensed mode thus reproducing the graphics on the screen more accurately.

Animation is achieved with a separate program that compiles frames into a continuous movie. The program compiles only the changes from one frame to another in order to conserve memory. There is even a provision for adding animation sequences to BASIC programs. Although it is a bit involved, it *can* be done.

2 Graphics Software — Do-It-Yourself

Of course, there are always those who would prefer to write their own sketch programs and modify them as their needs change. For you talented folks, we have created ULTRASKETCH, a combination sketcher and graphics coder that will store your creations in a string array. It is written in BASIC so that you can modify it to your heart's content.

Graphics Sketch And Coder

ULTRASKETCH features both a draw and a text mode so that graphics and text can be mixed on the same screen. Both modes support wraparound (when the cursor goes off the edge of the screen, it wraps around to the opposite edge), thus making it easier to move the cursor quickly around the screen. Each mode has a different cursor positioned independently. The program starts out in graphics mode with the menu of available commands displayed at the bottom of the screen. To sketch, use the arrow keys to leave a trail of lit graphic blocks. To erase, use (SHIFT) with any of the arrow keys. The arrow keys may be used in combination for diagonal movement; they automatically repeat as long as they are held down.

Here is the core of the program, without TEXT mode at this point:

```
*10  ' ULTRASKETCH
 20 CLEAR 1000: DEFINT A-Y: DEFSTR R, Z: P=15360:
    L=P: U=16255: C=191 : CLS
 30 MV=0: ZS=STRING$(64,32): DIM R(14): 'GOSUB 1001
 40 GOSUB 390
 50 D=PEEK(P)
 60 N=PEEK(14400): M=PEEK(14464): S=PEEK(14340)
 70 H=X: K=Y: F=POINT(H,K): IF N AND 128 MV=1-MV
 80 'IF S=4 GOSUB 510: GOSUB 390: GOTO 60
```

```
90 IF S=128 CLS: FOR I=1 TO 4: PRINT
      STRING$(224,191);: NEXT: GOSUB 390: GOTO 60
100 'IF S=16 GOTO 260
110 'IF S=1 GOSUB 420: GOSUB 390: GOTO 60
120 IF N=2 CLS: X=0: Y=0: GOSUB 390: GOTO 60
130 IF N AND 8 Y=Y-1: IF Y=-1 Y=41
140 IF N AND 16 Y=Y+1: IFY=42 Y=0
150 IF N AND 32 X=X-1: IF X=-1 X=127
160 IF N AND 64 X=X+1: IF X=128 X=0
170 RESET(H,K): FOR I=1 TO 4: NEXT I: SET(H,K)
180 IF M=1 SET(H,K): FOR I=1 TO 2: NEXT I:
      RESET(H,K): GOTO 230
190 IF MV=1 THEN 210
200 IF N=0 OR N=128 THEN 220 ELSE 230
210 PRINT@ 1016, "    ";: FOR I=1 TO 12: NEXTI:
      PRINT@ 1016, "MOVE";
220 IF F=-1 SET(H,K) ELSE RESET(H,K)
230 PRINT@ 960, STRING$(8,32);
240 PRINT@ 960, H; K;
250 GOTO 60
380 ' INSTRUCTIONS
390 PRINT@ 896, "<W> WHITE       <CLEAR> CLS
      <T>TEXT       <ENTER> DRAW    <R> RESTORE";
400 PRINT@ 969, "<P> PACK      (ARROWS: ALONE=SET
      SHIFT=RESET  SPACE=MOVE)";
410 RETURN
RUN
```

As you move the graphics cursor around the screen, the coordinates are displayed in the lower left corner to aid in transferring pictures from video display sheets to the screen.

There is also a MOVE mode so you can move the cursor around the screen without disturbing your creations. Press the (SPACEBAR) to enter this mode. The word MOVE will flash in the lower right corner as long as you are in this mode. The arrow keys will now shuttle the cursor around without affecting graphics, although it *will* destroy text, so be careful. You can erase while in MOVE mode using the (SHIFT) key, but you cannot SET any light blocks. To exit MOVE mode, press (SPACEBAR) again and verify that the word MOVE stops flashing.

You can doodle on either a white or a black background. Use the (CLEAR) key to clear the screen, and (W) to white out the screen. The instructions will remain intact at the bottom of the screen.

Let's add the TEXT mode. Change line 100 to

```
100 IF S=16 GOTO 260
```

and add

```
260 ' TEXT
270 Z=INKEY$
280 D=PEEK(P): POKE P, C:FOR I=1 TO 10: NEXT I
290 Z=INKEY$: IF Z=""POKE P, 32: FOR I=1 TO 10:
      NEXT: POKE P, D: GOTO 280
300 B=ASC(Z)
```

```
310 POKE P, D: IF B=13 THEN 50
320 IF B=8 P=P-1: IF P<L THEN P=L+63
330 IF B=9 P=P+1: IF P>U THEN P=U-63
340 IF B=10 P=P+64: IF P>U THEN P=P-896
350 IF B=91 P=P-64: IF P<L THEN P=P+896
360 IF B>31 AND B<91 POKE P, B: P=P+1: IF P>U THEN
    P=U-63
370 GOTO 280
RUN
```

Press (T) to enter the TEXT mode. The text cursor is the size of a full text character. Move it with the arrow keys. You'll notice that it doesn't have automatic repeat, but it can pass right through both text and graphics without affecting either. Position the cursor, then type in the desired text. Press (ENTER) to return to the DRAW mode. The text cursor will remain where you leave it until you reenter TEXT mode.

Detailed editing can be a chore with any sketch program, and this one is no exception. You may find it easiest to make all deletions from the MOVE mode in order to eliminate any stray graphics blocks. Then go back to normal draw mode. Note that the SET and RESET functions affect the *current* location as you move away from it. To make changes, position the cursor on the desired point, then use an arrow key to deposit a lit block, or use (SHIFT) (↓) to erase.

Once the picture is completed, what can we do with it? The program has no provision to dump the screen to a printer, but it can be done with JKL (NEWDOS) or (SHIFT) (↓) (*) on the Model III. Use (SHIFT) (@) to pause the screen. Some programs like Electra Sketch allow the screen to be saved to disk; ULTRASKETCH opts for poking it into a string array—one variable for each row. This array can then be saved and used in other programs. First we need to enter the strings. Change line 30 (i.e., delete the ' toward the end of the line) to

```
30 MV=0: ZS=STRING$(64,32): DIM R(14): GOSUB 1001
```

and add

```
*1000 ' 64 ASTERISKS PER STRING
 1001 R(1)="****************************************
      ************************"
 1002 R(2)="****************************************
      ************************"
 1003 R(3)="****************************************
      ************************"
 1004 R(4)="****************************************
      ************************"
 1005 R(5)="****************************************
      ************************"
 1006 R(6)="****************************************
      ************************"
 1007 R(7)="****************************************
      ************************"
 1008 R(8)="****************************************
      ************************"
 1009 R(9)="****************************************
      ************************"
 1010 R(10)="****************************************
      ************************"
```

```
1011  R(11.)="****************************************
      ************************"
1012  R(12)="****************************************
      ************************"
1013  R(13)="****************************************
      ************************"
1014  R(14)="****************************************
      ************************"
1015  RETURN
```

The graphics displayed on the screen can be poked into the string array R after you enter the following string = packing routine. Change line 110 to

```
110 IF S=1 GOSUB 420: GOSUB 390: GOTO 60
```

and add

```
420 ' PACK STRING ARRAY R
430 FOR I=1 TO 14: PRINT@ 960, STRING$(63,32);
440 PRINT@ 984, "PACKING LINE"I;
450 V=PEEK(VARPTR(R(I))+1)+256*PEEK(VARPTR(R(I))+2)
460 FOR J=1 TO 64
470 POKE V+J-1, PEEK(15295+J+64*I)
480 NEXT J: PRINT@ 896, ZS;: PRINT@ 896, R(I);
490 NEXT I: PRINT@ 896, ZS;
500 RETURN
```

And while we are at it, it would be nice to be able to retrieve the graphics from the string back to the screen so that it can be edited. So change line 80 to

```
80 IF S=4 GOSUB 510: GOSUB 390: GOTO 60
```

and add

```
510 ' RESTORE SCREEN
520 PRINT@ 896, ZS;
530 FOR I=1 TO 14
540 PRINT@ 918, "RESTORING LINE"I;
550 PRINT@ 64*(I-1), R(I);
560 NEXT I
570 RETURN
RUN
```

Draw something, then press (P). The first 14 lines of the screen will be poked into the string array R. As each line is packed, it will be displayed at the bottom of the screen. To verify that it worked, press (CLEAR) to clear the screen, then press (R) to restore the graphics to the screen. Once the strings have been packed, they can be printed as shown in line 550. The packed strings can be saved on disk or left in memory to be used in another program. Just delete lines 10 through 570 and 1015 (save the program first!), then use them as you see fit.

Suggested Mods

It seems that all computerists have their own ideas about what a program should be able to do for them. Here are several modifications you may wish to consider:

- Use the full screen for graphics. Delete the instructions or display them first, then erase them.

- Insert an L PR I NT option if you have a suitable graphics printer.

- Save the graphics as a disk file from the program for recall by name or number.

- Modify string pack routine to store only portions of the screen so that shorter strings could be used.

Final Listing

```
*10 ' ULTRASKETCH
 20 CLEAR 1000: DEFINT A-Y: DEFSTR R, Z: P=15360:
    L=P: U=16255: C=191: CLS
 30 MV=0: ZS=STRING$(64,32): DIM R(14): GOSUB 1001
 40 GOSUB 390
 50 D=PEEK(P)
 60 N=PEEK(14400): M=PEEK(14464): S=PEEK(14340)
 70 H=X: K=Y: F=POINT(H,K): IF N AND 128 MV=1-MV
 80 IF S=4 GOSUB 510: GOSUB 390: GOTO 60
 90 IF S=128 CLS: FOR I=1 TO 4: PRINT STRING$(224,191);:
    NEXT: GOSUB 390: GOTO 60
100 IF S=16 GOTO 260
110 IF S=1 GOSUB 420: GOSUB 390: GOTO 60
120 IF N=2 CLS: X=0:Y=0: GOSUB 390: GOTO 60
130 IF N AND 8 Y=Y-1: IF Y=-1 Y=41
140 IF N AND 16 Y=Y+1: IF Y=42 Y=0
150 IF N AND 32 X=X-1: IF X=-1: IF X=-1 X=127
160 IF N AND 64 X=X+1: IF X=128 X=0
170 RESET(H,K): FOR I=1 TO 4: NEXT I: SET(H,K)
180 IF M=1 SET(H,K): FOR I=1 TO 2: NEXT I: RESET(H,K):
    GOTO 230
190 IF MV=1 THEN 210
200 IF N=0 OR N=128 THEN 220 ELSE 230
210 PRINT@ 1016, "    ";: FOR I=1 TO 12: NEXT I: PRINT@ 1016,
    "MOVE";
220 IF F=-1 SET(H,K) ELSE RESET(H,K)
230 PRINT@ 960, STRING$(8,32);
240 PRINT@ 960, H; K;
250 GOTO 60
260 ' TEXT
270 Z=INKEY$
280 D=PEEK(P): POKE P, C: FOR I=1 TO 10: NEXT I
290 Z=INKEY$: IFZ=""POKE P, 32: FOR I=1 TO 10: NEXT: POKE P,
    D: GOTO 280
300 B=ASC(Z)
310 POKE P, D: IF B=13 THEN 50
320 IF B=8 P=P-1: IF P<L THEN P=L+63
330 IF B=9 P=P+1: IF P>U THEN P=U-63
340 IF B=10 P=P+64: IF P>U THEN P=P-896
```

```
350 IF B=91 P=P-64: IF P<L THEN P=P+896
360 IF B>31 AND B<91 POKE P, B: P=P+1: IF P>U THEN
    P=U-63
370 GOTO 280
380 ' INSTRUCTIONS
390 PRINT@ 896, "<W> WHITE      <CLEAR> CLS
    <T> TEXT      <ENTER> DRAW  <R> RESTORE";
400 PRINT@ 969, "<P> PACK      (ARROWS: ALONE=SET
    SHIFT=RESET SPACE=MOVE)";
410 RETURN
420 ' PACK STRING ARRAY R
430 FOR I=1 TO 14: PRINT@ 960, STRING$(63,32);
440 PRINT@ 984, "PACKING LINE"I;
450 V=PEEK(VARPTR(R(I))+1)+256*PEEK(VARPTR(R(I))+2)
460 FOR J=1 TO 64
470 POKE V+J-1, PEEK(15295+J+64*I)
480 NEXT J: PRINT@ 896, ZS;: PRINT@896, R(I);
490 NEXT I: PRINT@ 896, ZS;
500 RETURN
510 ' RESTORE SCREEN
520 PRINT@ 896, ZS;
530 FOR I=1 TO 14
540 PRINT@ 918, "RESTORING LINE"I;
550 PRINT@ 64*(I-1),R(I);
560 NEXT I
570 RETURN
1000 ' 64 ASTERISKS PER STRING
1001 R(1)=" **********************************
     ************************"
1002 R(2)=" **********************************
     ************************"
1003 R(3)=" **********************************
     ************************"
1004 R(4)=" **********************************
     ************************"
1005 R(5)=" **********************************
     ************************"
1006 R(6)=" **********************************
     ************************"
1007 R(7)=" **********************************
     ************************"
1008 R(8)=" **********************************
     ************************"
1009 R(9)=" **********************************
     ************************"
1010 R(10)=" **********************************
     ************************"
1011 R(11)=" **********************************
     ************************"
1012 R(12)=" **********************************
     ************************"
1013 R(13)=" **********************************
     ************************"
1014 R(14)=" **********************************
     ************************"
1015 RETURN
```

3 Graphics Hardware

Printer

Printer technology is going places—in leaps and bounds. It is an exciting area to watch. The cost of letter quality print and high resolution graphics capability has dropped steadily in this highly competitive market.

This book has emphasized graphics for the TRS-80 screen, but showing off a picture or printout of your work to the others at the office is a lot easier than lugging the computer around. First the good news: There are several printers around that support the TRS-80 graphics character set. This means we can use statements like `LPRINT CHR$(175)` to produce our graphic images on paper instead of the screen. Now the bad news: Most screen dump capabilities of the operating systems available for the Model I and III do not support graphics*. Maybe with a little friendly persuasion?

Figure 15.1   A printer photograph.

*NEWDOS users should refer to Appendix E for MX-80 patch.

Before dot matrix printers made high resolution graphics readily available, people and computers alike went to incredible lengths to use the variable densities of standard text characters to recreate drawings and photographs. Figure 15.1 is an example of a photograph reproduced by an analog-to-digital scanner, special software, and a letter quality printer.*

Amazing! Without all this special equipment and software, character graphics are quite limiting. For that matter, TRS-80 graphics are limiting when compared to high resolution dot graphics. Let's take a comparative look at three different versions of your ordinary garden variety of mushroom recreated with character graphics, block graphics, and then dot graphics.

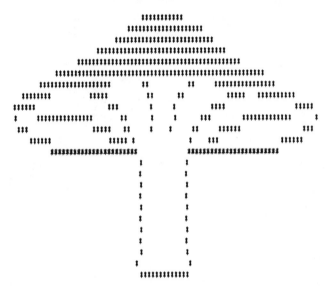

Figure 15.2   Printer character graphics.

Figure 15.2 illustrates an attempt using a single character throughout the entire figure. Barely recognizable.

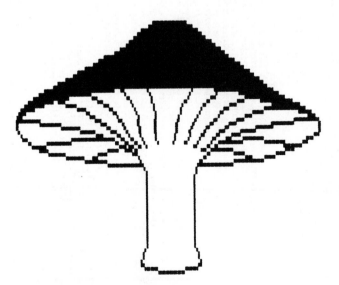

Figure 15.3   Printer block graphics.

*Reprinted by permission of BYTE Publications.

Figure 15.3 is done with TRS-80 block graphics. A BASIC program was used to read character codes from D A T A statements and transfer them to the printer. An alternative method is to use both a sketch program to create the image on the screen (if it fits) and a screen dump to send it to the printer.

Then there are those printers that allow the user to control the firing of each pin.

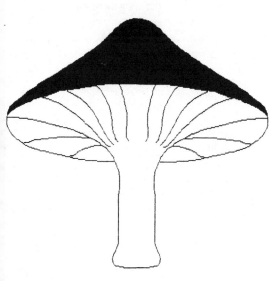

Figure 15.4   High resolution mushroom.

Wow! High resolution sure can make a difference. Here is another example:

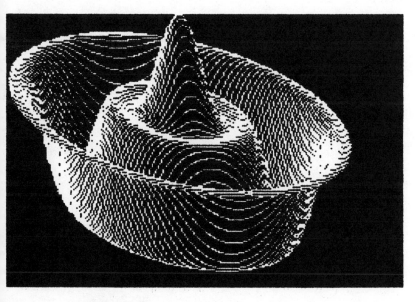

Figure 15.5   High resolution printer graphics.

Before you get too excited over these last two pictures, keep in mind that there is a heavy price to pay for the privilege of ''hi res.'' No, it is not expensive—just very time-consuming to position each dot. The volume of data required to produce a high resolution image is considerable, not to mention the time required to assemble the data. It took easily ten times as long to create the high resolution version of the mushroom as the TRS-80 graphics block version, even with the aid of a specialized graphics program.

These problems aside, printers are indeed one way of extending the graphics capability of your TRS-80. There are also plotters that can do amazing things with colors. Radio Shack offers a line of plotters (some with color) and a digitizer to take full advantage of their graphic capability.

Light Pen

The light pen is a fairly inexpensive device that may be of some use in creating graphic displays. The pen is equipped with a light-sensing device at its tip. When pointed at the screen, it can determine whether a particular location is lit or not. Unfortunately, the pen can't tell which location it is pointing at; it is up to the software to determine this. The program must examine each screen location by flashing a light block on and off until the pen registers a change in reading. Checking the entire screen is too time-consuming for BASIC; the number of points to check must be somehow limited or machine language software should be used.

One advantage of light pens is that young children may find it easier to use than a keyboard. You may decide that it is too cumbersome and inaccurate to be used in sketch programs. Test-ride one before you plunk down your money.

Look Before You Leap

Again, the programs and peripherals mentioned in this chapter are only samples of what is available. Read the ads in your favorite magazines. Examine the reviews. Become well-educated before you select your hardware and software.

APPENDICES

Appendix A
Radio Shack Video Display Worksheet

Radio Shack

TITLE _____ PROGRAMMER _____ PAGE ___ OF ___

Appendix B
Graphic Characters

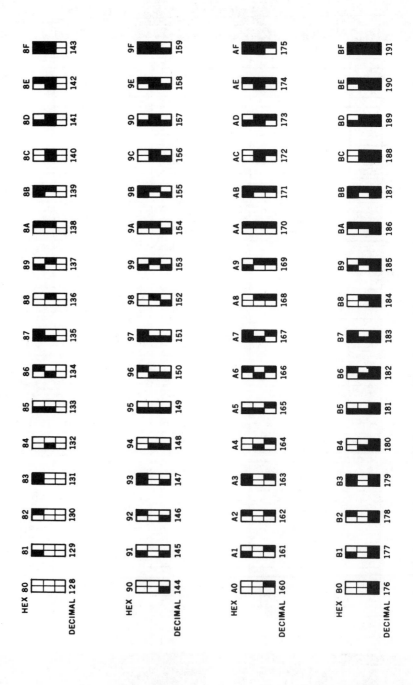

Appendix C
Special Characters

Special Characters (0-31, 192-255)

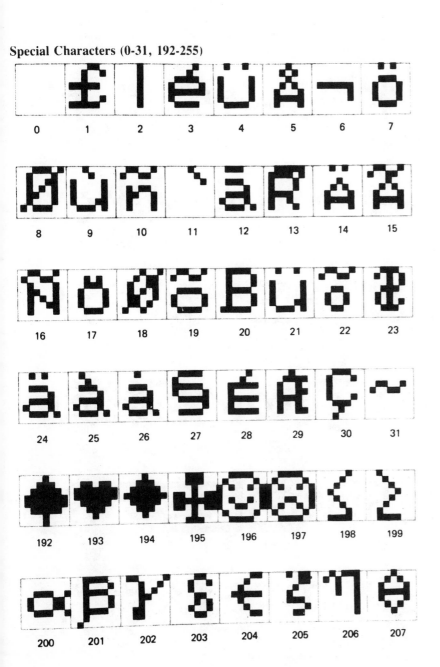

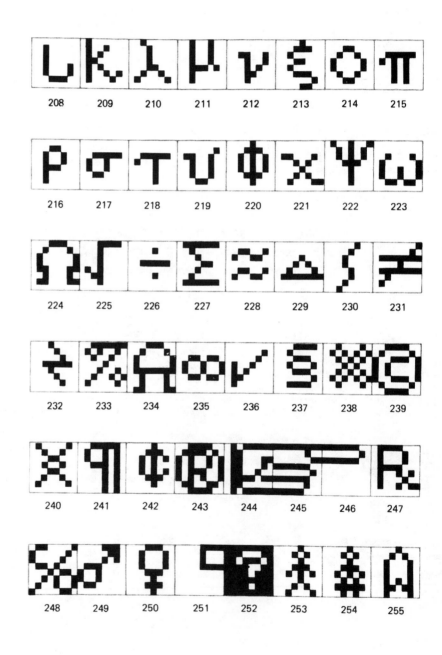

Appendix D
Useful Memory Locations

Model I

DEC	HEX	
51	0033	Call address of display character routine
96	0060	Call address of time delay routine
293	0125	Model I / Model III PEEK location Equals 73 if Model III Does not equal 73 if Model I
859	035B	Call address of INKEY$ routine
2687	0A7F	Call location to receive number from BASIC routine
2714	0A9A	Jump location to pass value back to BASIC program
5324	14CC	Call address of random routine
14336	3800	Start of keyboard memory locations
15359	3BFF	End of keyboard memory locations
15360	3C00	Start of video screen memory locations
16383	3FFF	End of video screen memory.
16396	400C	Disk status location equals 201 if no disk available
16416	4020	Two byte-cursor address
16417	4021	
16445	403D	Screen width status
16526	408E	Two byte address of USR routine
16527	408F	
16537	4099	INKEY$ buffer location
16548	40A4	Two byte index to first line of BASIC program.
16549	40A5	
16561	40B1	MEM SIZE (Top of protected RAM)
16562	40B2	

[handwritten note: 1023]

Model III

	51	0033	Call address of display character routine
	293	0125	Model I / Model III PEEK location Equals 73 if Model III Does not equal 73 if Model I
	859	035B	Call address of INKEY$ routine
	2687	0A7F	Call location to receive number from BASIC routine
	2714	0A9A	Jump location to pass value back to BASIC program
	5324	14CC	Call address of random routine
	14312	37E8	Printer status Bit 7 = 0 means "not busy"
	14336	3800	Start of keyboard memory locations
1023	15359	3BFF	End of keyboard memory locations
	15360	3C00	Start of video screen memory locations
1023	16383	3FFF	End of video screen memory
	16396	400C	Disk status location equals 201 if no disk available
	16416	4020	Two byte cursor address
	16417	4021	
	16526	408E	Two byte address of USR routine
	16527	408F	
	16537	4099	INKEY$ buffer location
	16548	40A4	Two byte index to first line of BASIC program.
	16549	40A5	
	16912	4210	Status indicator for many functions including special character sets and clock.
	16916	4214	Video display screen scroll protection. Protect up to top 8 lines from scrolling with codes 0 - 7.

Appendix E
Screen Dump Patch

At this writing, few of the standard operating systems for the Model I and Model III computers allow an exact duplication of the screen if it includes graphics. The Newdos (version 1.0 and earlier) JKL sequence and Model III (SHIFT) (⬇) (＊) screen dumps replace any ASCII codes greater than 127 with a single character like an "*" or ".". No one seems to have anticipated the widespread availability of printers with built-in TRS-80 graphics. Well, these printers are here, and where does that leave us graphics buffs?

To further complicate the issue, some of these printers may require the addition of 32 to each of the graphics codes (unless you want to sacrifice the other features of the printer). What to do?

Below is a sample patch for Model I Newdos, assuming the printer requires 32 added to the graphics code. First make a backup of the Newdos operating system. Never modify the master! Boot the backup disk in drive 0 (without a write protect tab) and use SUPERZAP to examine:

NEWDOS 80, version 1.0   NEWDOS +

Track 0, sector 7   Track 0, sector 6

Starting at byte B8 (7F for Newdos +), find

02 3E 2E CD

Change this using the MOD function to

02 C6 20 CD

Press (ENTER) when you are done. Now, reboot the system. Enter BASIC and type

`LPRINT CHR$(15)`

This puts the printer in condensed character mode so that the graphics characters will have nearly the same aspect ratio as those on the screen. Create some graphics on the screen, then press (J)(K)(L). Voila! You now have an extremely potent screen dump.

Test out this new diskette before implementing the change elsewhere.

What About Me?

Users with different operating systems may be able to make similar changes. A key sequence of codes to search for would be the following:

FE 80	Compare byte in A register to 128 decimal
38 02	Jump relative on a carry + 2
3E 2E	Load register A with the code for a period (.)

Change 3E 2E to

C6 20	Add + 32 to the contents of register A

Happy screen dumps!

Appendix F

Chapter Checkpoints

Chapter 1

1. AUTO
   - A. Generates line numbers AUTOmatically.
   - B. Is used by Machine language drivers.
   - C. Restarts the computer.
   - D. Causes AUTOmatic screen scrolling.

2. Editing a program line is
   - A. A waste of time.
   - B. Done with the arrow keys.
   - C. Done by entering the EDIT mode.
   - D. Done by retyping the program line.

3. Press the _____ key to stop a program.

4. Which of the following editing sequences changes OCCURANCE to OCCURRENCE?
   - A. sR iR (SHIFT) (⬆) cE
   - B. sA cR cE
   - C. sR iR (SHIFT) (⬆) dA iE
   - D. sA d iRE (ENTER)

5. True or False: The contents of a variable can be printed in immediate mode after a program has been run.

Chapter 2

1. True or False: We can simulate a ''not equal'' symbol (≠) on the TRS-80 screen by printing " = " and " / " in the same print position.

2. TAB
   - A. Can be set so you can indent parts of your program while typing it in.
   - B. Is used to total a column of numbers.
   - C. Has more calories than Coke.
   - D. Can be used to position characters on a print line.

3. Use the _____ statement to print information directly to any of the 1024 screen locations.

4. Print position 1023 (bottom right) of the screen
   - A. Is reserved for graphics.
   - B. Causes an automatic screen scroll when printed.
   - C. Cannot contain any character.

5. Graphic block (120,4) is near the _____ corner of the video screen.
   - A. Upper left.
   - B. Upper right.
   - C. Lower left.
   - D. Lower right.

6. A single graphic block is lit with
   - A. `POINT`.
   - B. `SET`.
   - C. `CLS`.

Chapter 3

1. Infinite loops
   - A. Can ruin a computer.
   - B. Are created only by amateurs.
   - C. Can protect graphic displays from the READY prompt.
   - D. Should not be used in BASIC programs.

2. `RND(6)`
   - A. Renumbers the program starting at line six.
   - B. Creates six random numbers.
   - C. Creates a single random integer from one to six.
   - D. Stands for "Really Nice Display" to the sixth degree.

3. A TRS-80 graphics block is unlit with the _____ statement.

4. A subroutine is
   - A. An underwater adventure game.
   - B. A *very* short program.
   - C. A useless programming technique.
   - D. A program segment called by a main program.

5. Use _____ for real-time keyboard input.

Chapter 4

1. Match each character type with the appropriate code range:
1. CONTROL CODES	A.	128-191
2. KEYBOARD CHARACTERS	B.	32-127
3. GRAPHIC CHARACTERS	C.	0-31

4. SPACE COMPRESSION CODES   D. 192-255

2. How many characters can be stored in a string variable?

3. The line `PRINT MID$("PROGRAM",5,3)` will display
    A. `OGRAM`
    B. `RAM`
    C. `?SN ERROR`

4. The purpose of the `CLEAR` statement is to
    A. Clear the screen.
    B. Delete the program.
    C. Reserve memory for string handling.

5. The process of joining strings is called _____.

6. True or False: ASCII code numbers 24-27 can be used to build a multi-line figure into a single string.

Chapter 5

1. `POKE 16383,32` will
    A. Cause an automatic screenscroll.
    B. Aggravate any self-respecting computer.
    C. Display a blank space in print position 1023.
    D. Move the cursor to print position 1023.

2. True or False: `POKE` is ideal for animating large figures.

3. _____ can be used as an alternate form of input to `INPUT` and `INKEY$`.

4. What function is used to locate the index of a string variable?

5. Dummy strings are
    A. Used by beginning programmers only.
    B. Used for string packing.
    C. Not recommended; a bad programming technique.

Chapter 6

1. Machine language routines can be stored in
    A. High user memory.
    B. Low user memory.
    C. In a BASIC program.
    D. All of the above.
    E. A standard-sized Samsonite carry-all suitcase.

2. Disk users must inform the BASIC program of the location of a machine language routine with the _____ statement.

3. Machine language programs are executed from a BASIC program via the _____ statement.

4. What string function can be used as an alternate way to create dummy strings?

Chapter 7

1. To increase execution speed use
   A. INTEGER variables.
   B. SINGLE precision variables.
   C. DOUBLE precision variables.
   D. The accelerator pedal.

2. Automatic string pool reorganization can be a nuisance unless we
   A. CLEAR lots of string space.
   B. Concatenate wherever possible.
   C. Use FRE during graphics animation.
   D. Reorganize our car pool as well.

3. Holes in the string area are
   A. Caused by a magnetic field in part of memory.
   B. Consolidated during string reorganization.
   C. Easily mended with a thread and needle.
   D. Created by space compression codes.

4. INKEY$ is best suited for
   A. Real-time input.
   B. Easy simulation of repeat key.
   C. Easy location of the cursor.

Chapter 8

1. A diagonal line can be drawn with SET(X,Y) statement by varying
   A. X only.
   B. Y only.
   C. Neither X nor Y.
   D. X and Y simultaneously.

2. Translation equations enable us to
   A. Read machine language programs.
   B. Translate from Cartesian coordinates to TRS-80 coordinates.
   C. Move string variables.
   D. Control the weather.

3. Graphing functions is most easily done with
   A. PLOT.
   B. PRINT@.
   C. SET

4. Polar coordinates are most useful
   A. For plotting circular figures.
   B. In the Arctic and Antarctic regions.
   C. For graphic animation.
   D. In high resolution graphics.

Chapter 9

1. Bar graphs are used to plot _____ data items.

2. STRING$(50,140) is used to print the _____ axis of
   the bar graph.

3. True or False: Correlation is a statistic designed to increase banana production in Brazil.

4. The normal curve program generates a bell-shaped curve because the probability of getting a high or low sum is
   A. Less than getting a sum near the middle.
   B. Equal to getting a sum near the middle.
   C. Greater than getting a sum near the middle.

5. The _____ function allows us to generate a normal curve by experiment.

Chapter 10

1. One benefit of animated graphics in education is increased student _____.

2. A program _____ is often used in educational software.

3. Which is the least effective attention getter?
   A. Sound.
   B. Time Delay.
   C. Flashing words.
   D. A Darth Vader costume and mask.

Chapter 11

1. Elements of a typical graph include the source, legend, border, and _____.

2. Pie charts are generally used to express
   A. Changes over time.
   B. Relationships at a fixed point in time.
   C. Circular functions.
   D. Projections.

3. Eliminating a portion of the vertical scale
   A. Will have little effect on the graph.
   B. Is recommended for polygonal graphs.
   C. Should be indicated by a break in the axis.
   D. Causes more problems than program bugs.

4. Time vs. quantity graphs show _____ performance and indicate trends for the future.

5. Pictograms
   A. Are a new service offered by the Post Office.
   B. Are bar graphs done with miniature figures.
   C. Eliminate the need for a legend.

Chapter 12

1. Saving the screen to a string array
   A. Is done by poking a screen location to bytes two and three of a string variable index.
   B. Requires the SAVE instruction.

   C. Improves player concentration.

2. The target moving routine in the sitting duck program is placed at the
    beginning of the program
       A. So that we won't forget where it is.
       B. To reduce search time and therefore speed up the action.
       C. To improve program readability.

3. The laser ray is "erased"
       A. By a deflector shield.
       B. By clearing the screen.
       C. From the top down.
       D. By printing blank spaces.

4. The target program tests for impact by
       A. Using POINT.
       B. Peeking at the screen memory.
       C. Testing the target strings.

5. Storing different versions of a figure in separate string variables
       A. Is a hard habit to break.
       B. Can't be done effectively with block graphics.
       C. Is almost as fast as using SET and RESET.
       D. Is a useful technique for animating large figures.

Chapter 13

1. Critter was stored in several string variables
       A. For easy access to specific body sections.
       B. So that arrays wouldn't be neglected.
       C. Because the figure wouldn't fit in a single string variable.

2. The smile sequence is a good example of
       A. The importance of proper oral hygiene.
       B. User interaction.
       C. Menu-driven program design.
       D. The advantage of using string arrays for each portion of the body.

Chapter 14

1. The purpose of the line
```
    130 I$=INKEY$:IF I$="" THEN 130 ELSE 10
```
    in the pattern and design program is
       A. To input the direction of motion.
       B. A timing delay.
       C. To freeze the screen until a key is pressed.

2. In the inkblot program, SET(X,Y) and SET(127-X,Y) light up two
    points in the same _____.

3. One liners
       A. Illustrate the ultimate in proper program design and documentation.
       B. Are very popular in singles bars.
       C. Are not useful learning tools by their very nature.

4. Which is not a useful technique in painting pictures with BASIC?

A. Reading graphic codes from DATA lines.

B. Using repetition factors to reduce the amount of data.

C. Using a carriage return code for short lines.

D. Using the POINT function to prevent overlaying graphics characters.

5. A_____ _____ routine is useful to correct the "photographic negative" effect of transferring a figure from video display sheet to the screen.

Chapter 15

1. Graphics utility programs
   A. Are used only by lazy programmers.
   B. Can greatly enhance our programming effectiveness.
   C. All do pretty much the same thing.
   D. Have been shown to cause cancer in laboratory animals.

2. ULTRASKETCH allows us to mix graphics and _____ on the screen.

3. Printers
   A. Are a good way of expanding our graphics capability.
   B. Are getting to be too expensive.
   C. Can not reproduce TRS-80 block graphics.

Answers To Chapter Checkpoints

Chapter 1: 1) A   2) C   3) BREAK   4) D   5) True
Chapter 2: 1) False   2) D   3) PRINT@   4) B   5) B   6) B
Chapter 3: 1) C   2) C   3) RESET   4) D   5) INKEY$
Chapter 4: 1) 1-C, 2-B, 3-A, 4-D   2) 225   3) B   4) C
         5) CONCATENATION   6) True
Chapter 5: 1) C   2) False   3) PEEK   4) VARPTR   5) B
Chapter 6: 1) D   2) DEFUSR   3) USR   4) STRING$
Chapter 7: 1) A   2) A   3) B   4) A
Chapter 8: 1) D   2) B   3) C   4) A
Chapter 9: 1) discrete   2) horizontal   3) False   4) A   5) RND
Chapter 10: 1) motivation   2) MENU   3) B
Chapter 11: 1) title   2) B   3) C   4) historical   5) B
Chapter 12: 1) A   2) B   3) D   4) A   5) D
Chapter 13: 1) A   2) D
Chapter 14: 1) C   2) row   3) B   4) D   5) screen reverse
Chapter 15: 1) B   2) text   3) A

INDEX

SPECIAL PROGRAM OFFER

The authors have made 35 of the major programs in this book available on cassette/diskette. All programs marked with asterisks are included, along with a few surprises.

The programs have been thoroughly tested to run the FIRST TIME, without a hitch. Completed instructions for loading and running the programs are included.

Make check or money order for $14.95 (California residents add 6% sales tax) payable to David A. Kater and Susan J. Thomas.

Please indicate cassette or diskette, and mail to:

MICROCOMPUTER AUTHOR/CONSULTANT

P.O. Box 1868
La Mesa, CA 92041

Your fingers will thank you for it!

Money orders and cashier's checks shipped next day. Allow two to three weeks for personal checks.

TRS-80 GRAPHICS

For the Model I and Model III

From basic displays and business charts to animated
figures and high-resolution printer graphics, this com-
prehensive new guide explains how to put your design
onto the video display screen of a Radio Shack TRS-80
microcomputer.

The authors begin by introducing you to the basic tools
of computer graphics, including the capabilities of the
video screen, keyboard and character control, graphics
programming techniques, machine language, and more.
Then the real fun begins as the authors consider the
myriad applications of graphics techniques. You'll learn
how to create displays ranging from business charts,
statistical graphs, and mathematical function plots to
dragons and lions, animated inchworms and snails, laser
cannons, intriguingly beautiful artistic designs, and a
unique animated figure called Critter. Complete program
listings and suggestions for modifications accompany
each of the more than one hundred graphic displays.

Besides providing guidance to those interested in
specific graphic applications, this book is also an
excellent introduction to programming in general. With it,
the novice programmer can gain valuable experience in
developing BASIC and machine language programs.

TRS-80 Graphics for the Model I and Model III is
written in a witty, readable style and complemented by
helpful reference appendices and an abundance of
detailed illustrations. Authors David Kater and Susan
Thomas have produced a book that is both a thorough
guide and an invaluable reference for anyone interested in
the graphic capabilities of computers.

ISBN 0-07-033303-3